Study Guide

for use with

SECOND CANADIAN EDITION

Psychology
A Journey

Dennis Coon   Patrick Brown   Rajesh Malik   Susanne McKenzie

Prepared by **DENNIS COON**

and **SUSANNE McKENZIE**
DAWSON COLLEGE

THOMSON

NELSON

Australia   Canada   Mexico   Singapore   Spain   United Kingdom   United States

THOMSON

NELSON

Study Guide for use with *Psychology: A Journey*
Second Canadian Edition

by Dennis Coon, Patrick Brown, Rajesh Malik, and Susanne McKenzie

Prepared by Dennis Coon and Susanne McKenzie

Associate Vice-President, Editorial Director:
Evelyn Veitch

Editor-in-Chief:
Anne Williams

Senior Marketing Manager:
Lenore Taylor

Senior Developmental Editor:
Alwynn Pinard

Content Production Manager:
Tammy Scherer

Proofreader:
Karen Rolfe

Senior Production Coordinator:
Hedy Sellers

Design Director:
Ken Phipps

Cover Design:
Maria Castelli

Project Lead, Content Management Systems:
Daryn Dewalt

Printer:
Webcom

Library and Archives Canada Cataloguing in Publication

McKenzie, Susanne Wicks, 1945-
Study guide for Psychology : a journey, second Canadian edition / Susanne McKenzie.

ISBN 0-17-610290-6

1. Psychology—Problems, exercises, etc. I. Title.

BF121.P8323 2006 Suppl. 1   150
C2006-902697-1

CONTENTS

How to Use this Study Guide

This *Study Guide* for the second Canadian edition of *Psychology: A Journey* is designed to help you learn more, study efficiently, and get better grades. The exercises in this guide are closely coordinated with text chapters so that you can practise and review what you have read.

Each *Study Guide* chapter contains the following sections:

- Chapter Overview
- Learning Objectives
- Recite and Review
- Connections
- Short-Answer Questions
- Final Survey and Review
- Mastery Test
- Solutions

A brief description of each section follows, along with suggestions for using them.

Chapter Overview

The Chapter Overview is a brief summary of the major ideas in the textbook. By summarizing the chapters, the Chapter Overview will give you a framework to build on as you learn additional ideas, concepts, and facts. Before you work on any other sections of this guide, read the Chapter Overview. In fact, it would be a good idea to reread the Chapter Overview each time you use the *Study Guide*.

Learning Objectives

This section provides you with a list of concrete topics to master. Each item in the list of Learning Objectives is necessary to your understanding and mastery of the chapter. To use them effectively, ensure that you can explain, describe, or otherwise respond to each objective.

Recite and Review

This section will give you a chance to review major terms and concepts. Recite and Review is organized with the same Survey Questions found in the textbook chapters. This exercise will help you actively process information, so that it becomes more meaningful. Recite and Review also gives you a chance to practise recalling ideas from your reading.

As you work through Recite and Review, don't worry if you can't fill in all of the blanks. Go search for the answer in your textbook. The searching will help you review the information and increase the chances that the new knowledge will be memorized. All of the solutions are listed at the end of each *Study Guide* chapter. Page numbers are provided for each section of Recite and Review so you can return to the text to clarify any points that you missed.

Connections

This section contains matching-type items. It will help you build associations between related terms, facts, concepts, and ideas. Where appropriate, art is reproduced from the text so that you can match to images, rather than words. This is a good way to add links to your memory networks. Again, solutions are listed at the end of the chapter.

Short-Answer Questions

Short-answer questions give you practice in recalling and interpreting the material, and putting it into context, and prepare you for essay questions you might find on an exam. These questions will also prepare you to participate effectively in class or other discussions about the material in each chapter.

Final Survey and Review

This exercise might seem like a repeat of the Recite and Review section, but it's not. This time, you must supply a different set of more difficult terms and concepts to complete the review. The Final Survey and Review challenges you to consolidate your earlier learning and to master key concepts from the textbook. It is not a test; don't be upset if you can't fill in some of the blanks. But do give missing ideas extra attention when you check your solutions. Indeed, try to learn more each time you complete a *Study Guide* exercise, by checking your solutions, and returning to the textbook for review and clarification.

Mastery Test

The multiple-choice items of the Mastery Test are at least as difficult as those found on typical in-class tests. If you do well on the Mastery Test, you can be confident that you are prepared for in-class tests. On the other hand, a low score is a *clear signal* that further study and review are needed. Don't expect to always get perfect scores on the Mastery Tests. In some cases, the questions cover information that was not reviewed in any of the preceding *Study Guide* sections. The Mastery Tests are designed to continue the learning process, as well as to give you feedback about your progress.

Solutions

Solutions for all of the preceding exercises are listed at the end of each *Study Guide* chapter. Solutions for the Mastery Test include page numbers so you can locate the answer in the textbook.

A Five-Day Study Plan

There is no single "best" way to use this guide. Getting the most out of the *Study Guide* depends greatly on your personal learning style and study habits. Nevertheless, as a starting point, you might want to give the following plan a try.

Days 1 and 2

Read the assigned chapter in the textbook. As you do, be sure to make use of the Knowledge Builders and all the steps of the SQ4R method described in the textbook.

Day 3

Review the textbook chapter and any notes you made as you read it. Read the Chapter Overview in the *Study Guide* and read the Learning Objectives. Now do the Recite and Review section.

Day 4

Read the margin definitions in the textbook and the Chapter Overview in the *Study Guide*. Do the Connections and Short-Answer Questions sections of the *Study Guide*. Return to the textbook and ensure you understand why any items you missed were wrong.

Day 5

Review the textbook chapter and any notes you made as you read it. Read the Chapter Overview in the *Study Guide*. Then do the Final Survey and Review section, and check your solutions. Return to the textbook and clarify any items you missed. Now take the Mastery Test. If you miss any questions, review appropriate sections of the textbook again. To really consolidate your learning, say or write responses to all of the Learning Objectives.

Summary

The close ties between *Psychology: A Journey* and the *Study Guide* make it possible for the *Study Guide* to be used in a variety of ways. You may prefer to turn to the *Study Guide* for practice and review after you have completed a reading assignment, as suggested in the Five-Day Plan. Or, you might find it more helpful to treat the *Study Guide* as a reading companion. In that case, you would complete appropriate *Study Guide* sections from each type of exercise as you progress through the textbook. In any event, it is nearly certain that if you use the *Study Guide* conscientiously, you will retain more, learn more efficiently, and perform better on tests. I hope you enjoy your journey into the fascinating realm of human behaviour.

Introducing Psychology and Research Methods

Chapter Overview

Psychology is the scientific study of behaviour and mental processes. Psychology's goals are to describe, understand, predict, and control behaviour. Psychologists answer questions about behaviour by applying the scientific method and gathering empirical evidence.

Psychology grew out of philosophy. The first psychological laboratory was established by Wilhelm Wundt, who studied conscious experience. The first school of thought in psychology was structuralism, a kind of "mental chemistry." Structuralism was followed by the rise of functionalism, behaviourism, Gestalt psychology, psychoanalytic psychology, and humanistic psychology. Five main streams of thought in modern psychology are behaviourism, humanism, the psychodynamic approach, biopsychology, and cognitive psychology.

The training of psychologists differs from that of psychiatrists, psychoanalysts, counsellors, and social workers. Clinical and counselling psychologists specialize in doing psychotherapy. Other specialties are industrial-organizational, educational, consumer, school, developmental, engineering, medical, environmental, forensic, psychometric, and experimental psychology.

Scientific investigation involves observing, defining a problem, proposing a hypothesis, gathering evidence/testing the hypothesis, publishing results, and forming a theory.

Many psychological investigations begin with naturalistic observation, which is informative despite its limitations. In the correlational method, the strength of the relationship between two measures is investigated. Correlations allow predictions, but they do not demonstrate cause-and-effect connections.

Experiments show whether an independent variable has an effect on a dependent variable. This allows cause-and-effect connections to be identified.

The clinical method employs detailed case studies of single individuals. In the survey method, people in a representative sample are asked a series of questions. This provides information on the behaviour of large groups of people.

A key element of critical thinking is an ability to weigh the evidence bearing on a claim and to evaluate the quality of that evidence.

Belief in various pseudo-psychologies is based in part on uncritical acceptance, the fallacy of positive instances, and the Barnum effect.

Information in the popular media varies greatly in quality and accuracy. It is wise to approach such information with skepticism regarding the source of information, uncontrolled observation, correlation and causation, inferences, oversimplification, single examples, and unrepeatable results.

Learning Objectives

After reading this chapter, students should be able to:

1. Define psychology.

2. Explain the four goals of psychology.

3. Trace the development of modern psychology from structuralism and functionalism through behaviourism, Gestalt psychology, psychoanalytic psychology, and humanistic psychology.

4. Compare and contrast the psychodynamic, behaviouristic, humanistic, biopsychological, and cognitive views of behaviour.

5. Describe the six basic steps of the scientific method.

6. Define the term *hypothesis*. Give examples of hypotheses that a psychologist might investigate.

7. Define the term *operational definition*. Give examples of operational definitions used by psychologists.

8. Distinguish between the five basic research methods psychologists use to answer questions about behaviour. Identify the advantages and disadvantages of each method.

9. Explain why psychologists use experiments to study behaviour.

10. Define the terms *independent variable, dependent variable*, and *extraneous variable.*

11. Discuss the issue of ethics and psychological research with both human and animal subjects.

12. Define critical thinking and explain why it is important to think critically about research on human behaviour.

13. Explain how psychological explanations of behaviour differ from other, unscientific explanations.

Practice Quizzes

Recite and Review

What is psychology? What are its goals?

Recite and Review: Pages 1–6

1. Psychology is both a science and a _____ .

2. Psychology is defined as the scientific study of behaviour and _____ processes.

3. Psychologists study overt and covert _____ .

4. Psychologists seek empirical _____ based on scientific observation.

5. Scientific observation is _____ _____ _____ so that it answers questions about the world.

6. Answering psychological questions requires a valid _____ _____ .

7. Developmental psychologists study the course of human _____ .

8. Learning theorists study how and why _____ occurs.

9. Personality _____ study personality traits and dynamics.

10. Sensation and perception psychologists study the _____ (or _____) organs and perception.
11. Comparative psychologists study different species, especially _____ .
12. Biopsychologists study the connection between biological processes and _____ .
13. Social psychologists study _____ behaviour.
14. Cultural psychologists study the ways that culture affects _____ .
15. Other species are used as _____ models in psychological research to discover principles that apply to human behaviour.
16. Psychology's goals are to describe, _____ , predict, and control behaviour.

What are the historical roots of modern psychology?
Recite and Review: Pages 6–10

17. Historically, psychology is an outgrowth of philosophy, the study of _____ , reality, and human nature.
18. The first psychological _____ was established in Germany by Wilhelm Wundt.
19. Wundt tried to apply scientific methods to the study of conscious _____ .
20. Functionalism was concerned with how the mind helps us _____ to our environments.
21. Behaviourism was launched by John B. _____ .
22. Behaviourists objectively study the relationship between stimuli and _____ .
23. The modern behaviourist B.F. Skinner believed that most behaviour is controlled by _____ reinforcers.
24. Cognitive behaviourism combines _____ , reinforcement, and environmental influences to explain behaviour.
25. Gestalt psychology emphasizes the study of _____ units, not pieces.
26. According to the Gestalt view, in psychology the whole is often _____ than the sum of its parts.
27. The psychoanalytic approach emphasized the _____ origins of behaviour.
28. Psychoanalytic psychology, developed by Austrian physician Sigmund _____ , is an early psychodynamic approach.
29. Humanistic psychology emphasizes free will, subjective experience, human potentials, and personal _____ .
30. Psychologically, humanists believe that self- _____ and self-evaluation are important elements of personal adjustment.
31. Humanists also emphasize a capacity for self-actualization—the full development of personal _____ .

What are the major trends and specialties in psychology today?
Recite and Review: Pages 11–15

32. Five main streams of thought in modern psychology are behaviourism, _____ , the psychodynamic approach, biopsychology, and cognitive psychology.
33. Much of contemporary psychology is an eclectic _____ of the best features of various viewpoints.

34. To fully understand behaviour, psychologists must be aware of human _____ (or _____) as well as human universals.

35. Psychologists who treat emotional problems specialize in _____ or counselling psychology.

36. Psychiatrists typically use both _____ and psychotherapy to treat emotional problems.

37. Freudian psychoanalysis is a specific type of _____ .

38. Counsellors have either a _____ degree or a doctoral degree. Many psychiatric social workers hold a _____ degree.

39. Some major _____ in psychology are clinical, counselling, industrial-organizational, developmental, environmental, military, family, health, and criminal justice.

40. Scientific research in psychology may be either _____ or applied.

What is the scientific method? Why is the scientific method important to psychologists?

Recite and Review: Pages 15–17

41. Scientific investigation in psychology is based on reliable evidence, accurate description and _____ , precise definition, controlled observation, and repeatable results.

42. The scientific method involves observing, defining a _____ , proposing a hypothesis, gathering evidence/testing the hypothesis, publishing _____ , and forming a theory.

43. To be scientifically _____ (or _____) a hypothesis must be testable.

44. Psychological concepts are given operational _____ so that they can be observed.

45. A _____ is a system of ideas that interrelates facts and concepts.

46. Published research reports usually include the following sections: an _____ , an introduction, a methods section, a _____ section, and a final discussion.

How do psychologists collect information?

Recite and Review: Pages 17–20

47. The tools of psychological research include naturalistic observation, the correlation method, the experimental method, the _____ method, and the survey method.

48. Naturalistic observation refers to actively observing behaviour in _____ settings.

49. Two problems with naturalistic studies are the effects of the observer on the observed (the observer _____) and _____ bias.

50. The anthropomorphic fallacy is the error of attributing human qualities to _____ .

51. Problems with naturalistic studies can be minimized by keeping careful observational _____ .

52. In the correlation method, the _____ (or _____) between two traits, responses, or events is measured.

53. Correlation coefficients range from +1.00 to −1.00. A correlation of _____ indicates that there is no relationship between two measures.

54. Correlations of +1.00 and −1.00 reveal that _____ relationships exist between two measures.

55. The closer a correlation coefficient is to +1.00 or −1.00, the _____ the measured relationship is.

56. A positive correlation shows that _____ in one measure correspond to decreases in a second measure.

57. In a negative correlation, _____ in one measure correspond to decreases in a second measure.

58. Correlations allow us to make _____ , but correlation does not demonstrate causation.

59. _____ -and-effect relationships in psychology are best identified by doing a controlled experiment.

What is an experiment? Why do psychologists use experiments to answer questions about behaviour and mental processes?

Recite and Review: Pages 20–23

60. In an experiment, conditions that might affect behaviour are intentionally _____ . Then, changes in behaviour are observed and recorded.

61. In an experiment, a variable is any condition that can _____ , and that might affect the outcome of the experiment (the behaviour of subjects).

62. Experimental conditions that are intentionally varied are called _____ variables.

63. _____ variables measure the results of the experiment.

64. Extraneous variables are conditions that a researcher wishes to _____ from affecting the outcome of the experiment.

65. Subjects exposed to the independent variable are in the experimental _____ . Those not exposed to the independent variable form the control _____ .

66. Extraneous variables that involve personal _____ , such as age or intelligence, can be controlled by randomly assigning subjects to the experimental and control groups.

67. If all extraneous variables are _____ for the experimental group and the control group, any differences in behaviour must be caused by differences in the independent variable.

68. Experiments involving drugs must control for the placebo _____ .

69. In a single- _____ study, subjects don't know if they are getting a drug or a placebo. In a double- _____ study, neither experimenters nor subjects know who is receiving a real drug.

70. Researchers must minimize the experimenter effect (the tendency for people to do what is _____ of them).

What other research methods do psychologists use?

Recite and Review: Pages 23–25

71. Clinical psychologists frequently gain information from _____ studies.

72. Case studies may be thought of as _____ clinical tests.

73. In the survey method, information about large populations is gained by asking people in a representative _____ a series of carefully worded questions.

74. The value of surveys is lowered when the sample is _____ .

75. Internet surveys have been used to study topics such as anger, decision making, religion, and _____ _____ .

Why is it important for psychologists to consider ethical issues when doing research?

Recite and Review: Pages 25–26

76. The Tri-Council guidelines for research with humans requires that all potential subjects give
_____ _____ before they participate.

77. In general, the Tri-Council considers _____ to be unethical.

What is critical thinking? Why is it important?

Recite and Review: Pages 26–28

78. Critical thinking is the ability to _____ , compare, analyze, critique, and synthesize information.

79. In psychology, _____ thinking skills help evaluate claims about human behaviour.

80. Critical thinking involves a willingness to _____ evaluate _____ .

81. Scientific observations usually provide the highest quality _____ about various claims.

How do psychological explanations differ from other (unscientific) explanations of behaviour?

Recite and Review: Pages 28–30

82. Palmistry, phrenology, graphology, and astrology are _____ systems or pseudo-psychologies.

83. Belief in pseudo-psychologies is encouraged by uncritical acceptance, the fallacy of positive instances, and the _____ effect, named after a famous showman who had "something for everyone."

Can you trust the psychological information you find on the Internet and in popular media?

Recite and Review: Psychology in Action, Pages 31–33

84. _____ and critical thinking are called for when evaluating claims in the popular media.

85. You should be on guard for _____ (or _____) or biased sources of information in the media.

86. Many claims in the media are based on unscientific observations that lack control _____ .

87. In the popular media, a failure to distinguish between correlation and _____ is common.

88. Inferences and opinions may be reported as if they were _____ (or _____) observations.

89. Single cases, unusual _____ , and testimonials are frequently reported as if they were valid generalizations.

Connections

1. _____ covert behaviour
2. _____ EEG
3. _____ scientific observation
4. _____ comparative psychology
5. _____ description
6. _____ psychology
7. _____ understanding
8. _____ biopsychology
9. _____ empirical evidence
10. _____ personality theorist

a. hidden from view
b. brain waves
c. systematic observation
d. animal behaviour
e. detailed record
f. human and animal behaviour
g. "why" questions
h. brain and behaviour
i. direct observation
j. traits, dynamics, individual differences

11. _____ psychometrics
12. _____ control
13. _____ Wundt
14. _____ Titchener
15. _____ James
16. _____ Darwin
17. _____ Skinner
18. _____ Pavlov
19. _____ Wertheimer
20. _____ Ladd-Franklin

a. father of psychology
b. natural selection
c. behaviourism
d. mental measurement
e. functionalism
f. conditioned responses
g. Gestalt
h. colour vision
i. introspection
j. influencing behaviour

21. _____ Freud
22. _____ Maslow
23. _____ psychodynamic view
24. _____ behaviouristic view
25. _____ humanistic view
26. _____ biopsychology
27. _____ cognitive view
28. _____ psychologist
29. _____ psychiatrist
30. _____ scientific method

a. self-actualization
b. self-image
c. psychoanalysis
d. information processing
e. Ph.D., Psy.D., Ed.D.
f. M.D.
g. internal forces
h. physiological process
i. controlled observation
j. environmental forces

31. _____ common sense
32. _____ hypothesis
33. _____ operational definition
34. _____ Clever Hans
35. _____ observational record
36. _____ correlational study
37. _____ correlation of +3.5
38. _____ identify causes of behaviour
39. _____ independent variable
40. _____ dependent variable

a. tentative explanation
b. formal log
c. measure of variables
d. related traits, behaviours
e. math errors
f. head signals
g. effect on behaviour
h. experimental method
i. unscientific information
j. varied by experimenter

41. _____ extraneous variables		a.	Phineas Gage
42. _____ control group		b.	done by using chance
43. _____ random assignment to groups		c.	participation is voluntary
44. _____ lobotomy		d.	excluded by experimenter
45. _____ placebos		e.	clinical method
46. _____ endorphins		f.	representative of population
47. _____ case studies		g.	inaccurate answers
48. _____ valid sample		h.	chemical
49. _____ courtesy bias		i.	reference for comparison
50. _____ ethical research		j.	sugar pills

Short-Answer Questions

1. Describe the four goals of psychology.

2. Briefly describe structuralism, including its focus of study, research methods, and limitations.

3. Briefly describe functionalism, including its focus of study.

4. Briefly describe behaviourism, including its focus of study, its emphasis, and its current influence on psychology.

5. Compare and contrast the psychodynamic and humanistic schools of psychology.

6. Define and give an example of a hypothesis.

7. Define and give an example of an operational definition.

8. Describe the technique of naturalistic observation. What are the advantages and limitations of this method?

9. Describe a correlational study. What are the advantages and limitations of this method?

10. Define and give an example for each of the following: independent variable, dependent variable, and extraneous variable.

11. Identify the advantages and disadvantages of the experimental method.

12. Briefly describe the clinical method of research. What are the advantages and disadvantages of this method?

13. Briefly describe the survey method of research. What are the advantages and disadvantages of this method?

14. List the suggestions given in the textbook to help people become more critically aware of the psychological information found in the popular media and on the Internet.

Final Survey and Review

What is psychology? What are its goals?

1. Psychology is both a _____ and a _____ .

2. Psychology is defined as the scientific study of _____ and _____ _____ .

3. Psychologists study both overt and _____ behaviour.

4. Psychologists seek _____ evidence based on scientific observation. They settle disputes by collecting _____ .

5. _____ observation is structured and systematic.

6. Answering psychological questions requires a valid _____ _____ .

7. _____ psychologists study the course of human development.

8. Learning _____ study how and why learning occurs.

9. _____ theorists study personality traits and dynamics.

10. _____ and perception psychologists study the sense organs and perception.

11. _____ psychologists study different species, especially animals.

12. _____ study biological processes and behaviour.

13. Social psychologists study _____ _____ .

14. _____ psychologists study the ways that culture affects behaviour.

15. Other species are used as _____ _____ in psychological research to discover principles that apply to human behaviour.

16. Psychology's goals are to describe, understand, _____ , and _____ behaviour.

What are the historical roots of modern psychology?

17. Historically, psychology is an outgrowth of _____ .

18. The first psychological laboratory was established in Germany by _____ _____ .

19. His goal was to apply scientific methods to the study of _____ _____ .

20. The first school of thought in psychology was _____ , a kind of "mental chemistry."

21. _____ was concerned with how the mind helps us adapt to our environments. William _____ was one of its proponents.

22. _____ was launched by John B. Watson, who wanted to study the relationship between _____ and responses.

23. The modern behaviourist B.F. _____ believed that most behaviour is controlled by positive _____ .

24. _____ behaviourism combines thinking and environmental influences to explain behaviour.

25. _____ psychology emphasizes the study of whole experiences, not elements or pieces.

26. According to Max _____ and other _____ psychologists, the whole is often greater than the _____ of its parts.

27. The _____ (or _____) approach emphasizes the unconscious origins of behaviour.

28. Austrian physician Sigmund _____ developed a psychodynamic system called _____ .

29. _____ psychology emphasizes free will, subjective experience, human _____ , and personal growth.

30. Psychologically, humanists believe that _____ , self-evaluation, and one's _____ of reference are important elements of personal adjustment.

31. Humanists also emphasize a capacity for _____ —the full development of personal potential.

What are the major trends and specialties in psychology today?

32. Five main streams of thought in modern psychology are _____ , _____ , the psychodynamic approach, _____ , and cognitive psychology.

33. Much of contemporary psychology is an _____ blend of the best features of various viewpoints.

34. To fully understand behaviour, psychologists must be aware of human _____ , as reflected in personal and _____ differences.

35. Psychologists who treat emotional problems specialize in _____ or _____ psychology.

36. _____ are medical doctors who typically use both drugs and _____ to treat emotional problems.

37. Freudian _____ is a specific type of psychotherapy.

38. _____ can have either a masters or doctoral degree while _____ _____ workers could hold a masters degree.

39. _____ psychologists specialize in the growth of children; _____ psychologists help design machines; psychologists in _____ study classroom dynamics.

40. Scientific research in psychology may be either basic or _____ .

What is the scientific method? Why is the scientific method important to psychologists?

41. Scientific investigation in psychology is based on reliable _____ , accurate description and _____ , precise definition, controlled observation, and repeatable results.

42. The scientific method involves observing, defining a problem, proposing a hypothesis, gathering evidence/testing the _____ , publishing results, and forming a _____ .

43. To be _____ valid a hypothesis must be _____ .

44. Psychological concepts are given _____ definitions so that they can be observed. Such definitions state the exact _____ used to represent a concept.

45. A _____ is a system of ideas that interrelates facts and concepts. In general, good _____ summarize existing _____ , explain them, and guide further research.

46. The results of scientific studies are _____ in professional _____ so they will be publicly available.

How do psychologists collect information?

47. The tools of psychological research include naturalistic observation, the correlational method, the _____ method, the clinical method, and the _____ method.

48. Naturalistic observation refers to actively observing behaviour in _____ _____ , which are the typical _____ in which people and animals live.

49. Two problems with naturalistic observation are the effects of the observer on the _____ and observer _____ .

50. The _____ fallacy is the error of attributing human qualities to animals.

51. Problems with naturalistic observation can be minimized by keeping careful _____ _____ .

52. The _____ method finds the strength of the relationship between two measures.

53. A correlation of _____ indicates that there is no relationship between two measures. Correlations of +1.00 and −1.00 reveal that _____ relationships exist between two measures.

54. The _____ a correlation coefficient is to +1.00 and −1.00, the stronger the measured relationship is.

55. A _____ correlation or relationship shows that increases in one measure correspond to increases in a second measure.

56. In a negative correlation, _____ in one measure correspond to _____ in a second measure.

57. Correlations allow prediction, but correlation does not demonstrate _____ .

58. Cause-and-effect relationships in psychology are best identified by doing a _____ _____ .

59. In an experiment, conditions that might affect behaviour are intentionally varied. Then, changes in behaviour are _____ and _____ .

What is an experiment? Why do psychologists use experiments to answer questions about behaviour and mental processes?

60. In an experiment a _____ is any condition that can change, and that might affect the outcome of the experiment.

61. Experimental conditions that are intentionally varied are called _____ variables; they are potential _____ of changes in behaviour.

62. _____ variables measure the results of the experiment; they reveal any _____ on behaviour.

63. _____ variables are conditions that a researcher wishes to prevent from affecting the _____ of the experiment.

64. Extraneous variables are _____ by making sure that they are the same for all subjects in an experiment.

65. Subjects exposed to the independent variable are in the _____ group. Those not exposed to the independent variable form the _____ group.

66. Extraneous variables that involve _____ characteristics, such as age or intelligence, can be controlled by _____ assigning subjects to the experimental and control groups.

67. If all extraneous variables are identical for the experimental group and the control group, any differences in behaviour must be caused by differences in the _____ variable.

68. Experiments involving drugs must control the _____ effect.

69. In a _____ - _____ study, subjects don't know if they are getting a drug or a placebo. In a _____ - _____ study, neither experimenters nor subjects know who is receiving a real drug.

70. Researchers must also minimize the _____ _____ (the tendency for people to do what is expected of them).

What other research methods do psychologists use?

71. Clinical psychologists frequently gain information from _____ _____ , which focus on all aspects of a single _____ .

72. Case studies may be thought of as natural _____ _____ of the effects of brain tumours, accidental poisonings, and other unusual conditions.

73. In the survey method, information about large _____ is gained by asking people in a _____ sample a series of carefully worded questions.

74. The value of surveys is lowered when the sample is _____ and when replies to _____ are inaccurate or untruthful.

Why is it important for psychologists to consider ethical issues when doing research?

75. Research on humans must respect the _____ and _____ of the participants.

76. Participation is _____ and researchers keep personal information _____ .

77. Animals are used as research subjects when it is _____ to experiment on humans, when the behaviour in question is _____ or _____ by other factors, or to extend our knowledge to other _____ .

What is critical thinking? Why is it important?

78. Critical thinking is the ability to evaluate, compare, analyze, _____ , and _____ information.

79. In psychology, critical thinking skills help _____ claims about human behaviour.

80. Critical thinking involves evaluating the quality of the _____ used to support various claims.

81. _____ observations usually provide the highest quality evidence about various claims.

How do psychological explanations differ from other (unscientific) explanations of behaviour?

82. Palmistry, _____ , graphology, and astrology are _____ -psychologies.

83. Belief in false psychologies is encouraged by _____ acceptance, the fallacy of _____ instances, and the _____ effect.

Can you trust the psychological information you find on the Internet and in popular media?

84. _____ and _____ thinking are called for when evaluating claims in the popular media.

85. You should be on guard for unreliable or _____ sources of information in the media.

86. Many claims in the media are based on unscientific observations that lack _____ groups.

87. _____ does not demonstrate causation. In the popular media, a failure to distinguish between _____ and causation is common.

88. Inferences and opinions may be reported as if they were objective _____ .

89. Single _____ , unusual examples, and testimonials are frequently reported as if they were valid _____ .

Mastery Test

1. Data in psychology are typically gathered to answer questions about
   a. clinical problems
   b. human groups
   c. human cognition
   d. overt or covert behaviour

2. Who among the following would most likely study the behaviour of gorillas?
   a. developmental psychologist
   b. comparative psychologist
   c. environmental psychologist
   d. forensic psychologist

3. An engineering psychologist helps redesign an airplane to make it safer to fly. The psychologist's work reflects which of psychology's goals?
   a. understanding
   b. control
   c. prediction
   d. description

4. Who among the following placed the greatest emphasis on introspection?
   a. Watson
   b. Wertheimer
   c. Washburn
   d. Wundt

5. Which pair of persons had the most similar ideas?
   a. Titchener–Skinner
   b. James–Darwin
   c. Watson–Rogers
   d. Wertheimer–Maslow

6. The behaviourist definition of psychology clearly places great emphasis on
   a. overt behaviour
   b. conscious experience
   c. psychodynamic responses
   d. introspective analysis

7. As a profession, psychology is fully open to men and women, a fact that began with the success of
   a. O'Sullivan–Calkins
   b. Tyler–James
   c. Ladd–Franklin
   d. Neal–Collins

8. The idea that threatening thoughts are sometimes repressed would be of most interest to a
   a. structuralist
   b. psychoanalyst
   c. humanist
   d. Gestaltist

9. "A neutral, reductionistic, mechanistic view of human nature." This best describes which viewpoint?
   a. psychodynamic
   b. cognitive
   c. psychoanalytic
   d. biopsychological

10. Which of the following professional titles usually requires a doctorate degree?
    a. psychologist
    b. psychiatric social worker
    c. counsellor
    d. all of the preceding

11. The majority of all psychologists specialize in what branches of psychology?
    a. counselling and comparative
    b. applied and counselling
    c. psychodynamic and clinical
    d. counselling and clinical

12. When critically evaluating claims about behaviour it is important to also evaluate
    a. the source of anecdotal evidence
    b. the credentials of an authority
    c. the quality of the evidence
    d. the strength of one's intuition

13. Which of the following pairs is most different?
    a. pseudo-psychology–critical thinking
    b. graphology–pseudo-psychology
    c. palmistry–phrenology
    d. psychology–empirical evidence

14. A tendency to believe flattering descriptions of oneself is called
    a. the Barnum effect
    b. the astrologer's dilemma
    c. the fallacy of positive instances
    d. uncritical acceptance

15. Descriptions of personality that contain both sides of several personal dimensions tend to create
    a. an illusion of accuracy
    b. disbelief and rejection
    c. the astrologer's dilemma
    d. a system similar to graphology

16. If an entire population is surveyed, it becomes unnecessary to obtain a
    a. control group
    b. random comparison
    c. random sample
    d. control variable

17. Control groups are most often used in
    a. naturalistic observation
    b. the clinical method
    c. Para science
    d. experiments

18. Concealing the observer can be used to minimize the
    a. observer bias effect
    b. double-blind effect
    c. observer effect
    d. effects of extraneous correlations

19. A psychologist studying lowland gorillas should be careful to avoid the
    a. anthropomorphic fallacy
    b. Gestalt fallacy
    c. psychodynamic fallacy
    d. fallacy of positive instances

20. Testing the hypothesis that frustration encourages aggression would require
    a. a field study
    b. operational definitions
    c. adult subjects
    d. perfect correlations

21. In experiments involving drugs, experimenters remain unaware of who received placebos in a _____ arrangement.
    a. zero-blind
    b. single-blind
    c. double-blind
    d. control-blind

22. In psychology, the _____ variable is the suspected cause of differences in _____.
    a. independent, the control group
    b. dependent, the experimenter effect
    c. independent, behaviour
    d. dependent, correlations

23. A person who is observed crying may not be sad. This suggests that it is important to distinguish between
    a. individual cases and generalizations
    b. correlation and causation
    c. control groups and experimental groups
    d. observation and inference

24. In an experiment on the effects of hunger on the reading scores of elementary school children, reading scores are the
    a. control variable
    b. independent variable
    c. dependent variable
    d. reference variable

25. Which of the following correlation coefficients indicates a perfect relationship?
    a. +1.00
    b. 100.0
    c. −1.00
    d. both a and c

26. Jane Goodall's studies of chimpanzees in Tanzania are good examples of
    a. field experiments
    b. experimental control
    c. correlation studies
    d. naturalistic observations

27. To equalize the intelligence of members of the experimental group and the control group in an experiment, you could use
    a. extraneous control
    b. random assignment
    c. independent control
    d. subject replication

28. Which method would most likely be used to study the effects of tumors in the frontal lobes of the brain?
    a. sampling method
    b. correlation method
    c. clinical method
    d. experimental method

29. The release of endorphins by the pituitary gland helps explain the
    a. experimenter effect
    b. placebo effect
    c. multiple-personality effect
    d. gender-bias effect

30. Cause is to effect as _____ variable is to _____ variable.
    a. extraneous, dependent
    b. dependent, independent
    c. independent, extraneous
    d. independent, dependent

31. The specific procedures used to gather data are described in which section of a research report?
    a. introduction
    b. abstract
    c. method
    d. discussion

32. Which of the following correlations demonstrates a cause-effect relationship?
    a. .980
    b. 1.00
    c. .50
    d. none of the preceding

Solutions

Recite and Review

1. profession
2. mental
3. behaviour
4. evidence
5. planned or structured
6. research method
7. development
8. learning
9. theorists
10. sense; sensory
11. animals
12. behaviour
13. social
14. behaviour
15. animal
16. understand
17. knowledge
18. laboratory
19. experience
20. adapt
21. Watson
22. responses
23. positive
24. thinking
25. whole
26. greater
27. unconscious
28. Freud
29. growth
30. image
31. potentials
32. humanism
33. blend
34. diversity; differences
35. clinical
36. drugs
37. psychotherapy
38. masters; masters
39. divisions
40. basic
41. measurement
42. problem; results
43. valid; useful
44. definitions
45. theory
46. abstract; results
47. clinical
48. natural
49. effect; observer
50. animals
51. records
52. correlation; relationship
53. zero
54. perfect
55. stronger
56. increases
57. increases
58. predictions
59. Cause
60. varied
61. change
62. independent
63. Dependent
64. prevent
65. group; group
66. characteristics
67. identical
68. effect
69. blind; blind
70. expected
71. case
72. natural
73. sample
74. biased
75. sexual attitudes
76. informal consent
77. deception
78. evaluate
79. critical
80. actively; ideas
81. evidence
82. false
83. Barnum
84. Skepticism
85. unreliable; inaccurate
86. groups
87. causation
88. valid; scientific
89. examples

Connections

1. A
2. B
3. C
4. D
5. E
6. F
7. G
8. H
9. I
10. J
11. D
12. J
13. A
14. I
15. E
16. B
17. C
18. F
19. G
20. H
21. C
22. A
23. G
24. J
25. B
26. H
27. D
28. E
29. F
30. I
31. I
32. A
33. C
34. F
35. B
36. D
37. E
38. H
39. J
40. G
41. D
42. I
43. B
44. A
45. J

46. H
47. E
48. F
49. G
50. C

Short-Answer Questions

1. The four goals of psychology are (1) description: to describe behaviour carefully and objectively; (2) understanding: to explain the behaviour or identify the causes of a behaviour; (3) prediction: to accurately forecast future behaviour; and (4) control: to alter the circumstances that affect behaviour in predictable ways.

2. Structuralism was founded by Wundt and brought to North America by Titchener. Called structuralism because it attempts to describe the structure of mental life, it uses introspection to measure reactions to various physical stimuli. It is limited because it provides no way to resolve disagreements as to the structure of mental life.

3. William James broadened the focus of psychology to include animal behaviour, religious experience, and abnormal behaviour, among other topics. Functionalism comes from an interest in how the mind functions to help an individual adapt to changes in the environment. Functionalists describe consciousness as an ever-changing stream or flow of images rather than a set of building blocks. Functionalism was influenced by Darwin and the principle of natural selection.

4. Watson objected to the study of the mind as unscientific and shifted the emphasis from philosophy to science as well as to observable behaviours and the relationship between stimuli and responses. Its current emphasis is on cognitive behaviourism (using both cognition and learning) to explain behaviour.

5. The psychodynamic approach states that behaviour is directed by internal conflicts between hidden or unconscious forces within one's personality. Developed by Freud, it presents a negative and pessimistic view. The humanistic approach states that behaviour is guided by a person's self-image, subjective perceptions of the world, and need for personal growth. Developed by Maslow, it is a positive view of human nature.

6. A hypothesis is a testable explanation of an event or the relationship between events. Example: frustration leads to aggression.

7. An operational definition states the procedure used to measure a concept. For example, intelligence may be operationally defined as a score on an IQ test.

8. Naturalistic observation involves observing behaviour in its natural setting. Careful and complete observations are important, and observations must be objective descriptions of the actual behaviours observed. One advantage includes the possibility of observing interesting and unusual events, such as chimpanzees using twigs as tools to extract termites from a nest. Limitations include the fact that the presence of an observer may alter the behaviours being observed (observer effect); the observers may see what they expect to see (observer bias); and the observer may attribute human thoughts, feelings, or emotions to animals (anthromorphic fallacy).

9. A correlational study looks for a statistical relationship (correlation) between two behaviours, traits, or events. These behaviours or events can move in the same direction (increasing or decreasing), different directions (one increasing, the other decreasing) or in a way in which a change in one is not related to a change in the other. One advantage of correlational studies is if two traits or events are correlated, knowing the level of one will allow us to predict the level of the other. This method also allows researchers to study the connection between behaviours and various diseases, such as smoking and lung cancer. Disadvantages include the fact that two behaviours, traits, or events are correlated does not necessarily mean that one causes the other.

10. Independent variable: in an experiment, the conditions of interest that are changed, or varied by the experimenter; for example, type of test (multiple choice, fill in the blank, essay). Dependent variable: the results of the experiment (usually some measure of behaviour); for example, test scores. Extraneous variable(s): other variables that might affect the outcome of the experiment; for example, number of hours of sleep, intelligence.

11. Advantages: the experimental method allows the researcher

to determine whether the relationship between two variables involves cause and effect; that is, if changes in one variable directly cause changes in another. Disadvantages: behaviour may be altered because a person is expecting an effect (placebo effect); the experimenter may unintentionally affect the outcome (experimenter effect) and get the results they were expecting (self-fulfilling prophecy); it may not always be feasible or ethical to conduct a particular experiment.

12. The clinical method involves studying individual cases of the behaviour or trait in question. A case study is an in-depth study that focuses on all aspects of a single individual. Its advantages include providing insights into unusual or rare events (such as rampage violence or the consequences of traumatic brain injury); it may be the only way to study some psychological problems. Its limitations include the lack of a control group, which limits the conclusions that can be drawn.

13. Surveys use polling techniques to ask people about the issue in question. Because it is not practical to question all members of a population, samples are used instead. A representative sample is a smaller group that accurately represents the population in question. Surveys are carried out by newspapers and magazines, governments, and web sites. Advantages of surveys include their low cost, especially for Internet surveys, to reach large numbers of people. The results are valid if the

sampling technique is unbiased. However, a biased sample will yield inaccurate results, and people may respond untruthfully to avoid embarrassment or because they have a tendency to give socially desirable answers (courtesy bias).

14. Be skeptical, consider the source of the information, look for the presence of a control group, note errors in distinguishing between correlation and causation, distinguish between observation and inference, be aware of oversimplification, and remember that examples are not proof.

Final Survey and Review

1. science; profession
2. behaviour; mental processes
3. covert
4. empirical; data
5. Scientific
6. research method
7. Developmental
8. theorists
9. Personality
10. Sensation
11. Comparative
12. Biopsychologists
13. social behaviour
14. Cultural
15. animal models
16. predict; control
17. philosophy
18. Wilhelm Wundt
19. conscious experience
20. structuralism
21. Functionalism; James
22. Behaviourism; stimuli
23. Skinner; reinforcers
24. Cognitive
25. Gestalt
26. Wertheimer; Gestalt; sum
27. psychoanalytic; psychodynamic
28. Freud; psychoanalysis
29. Humanistic; potentials
30. self-image; frame
31. self-actualism
32. behaviourism; humanism; biopsychology
33. eclectic
34. diversity; cultural
35. clinical; counselling
36. Psychiatrists; psychotherapy
37. psychoanalysis
38. Counsellors; psychiatric social
39. Developmental; industrial; education
40. applied
41. evidence; measurements
42. hypothesis; theory
43. scientifically; testable
44. operational; procedures
45. theory; theories; observations
46. published; journals
47. experimental; survey
48. natural settings; environments
49. observed; bias
50. anthropomorphic
51. observational records
52. correlation
53. zero; perfect
54. closer
55. positive
56. increases; decreases
57. causation
58. controlled experiment
59. observed; recorded
60. variable
61. independent; causes
62. Dependent; effects
63. Extraneous; outcome
64. controlled
65. experimental; control
66. personal; randomly
67. independent
68. placebo
69. single blind; double blind
70. experimenter effect
71. case studies; subject
72. clinical tests
73. populations; representatives

74. biased; questions
75. dignity; welfare
76. voluntary; confidential
77. unethical; complex; complicated; species
78. critique; synthesize
79. evaluate
80. evidence
81. Scientific
82. phrenology; pseudo
83. uncritical; positive; Barnum
84. Skepticism; critical
85. biased
86. control
87. Correlation; correlation
88. observations
89. cases; generalizations

Mastery Test

1. D (p. 2)
2. B (p. 4)
3. B (p. 5)
4. D (p. 6)
5. B (p. 7)
6. A (p. 7)
7. C (p. 9)
8. B (p. 9)
9. D (p. 11)
10. A (p. 13)
11. D (p. 13)
12. C (p. 27)
13. A (p. 28)
14. D (p. 28)
15. A (p. 29)
16. C (p. 24)

17. D (p. 21)
18. C (p. 18)
19. A (p. 18)
20. B (p. 16)
21. C (p. 22)
22. C (p. 20)
23. D (p. 34)
24. C (p. 21)
25. D (p. 19)
26. D (p. 17)
27. B (p. 21)
28. C (p. 23)
29. B (p. 22)
30. D (p. 21)
31. C (p. 17)
32. D (p. 19)

Brain and Behaviour

Chapter Overview

The brain and nervous system comprise networks of neurons. Nerve impulses are basically electrical. Communication between neurons is chemical in that neurons release neurotransmitters that affect other neurons. Rather than merely carrying messages, neuropeptides regulate the activity of neurons in the brain. Neurogenesis is a process that grows new cells in the nervous system both in children and adults. Using stem cells to repair brain damage is a new method.

The nervous system includes the central nervous system (CNS), consisting of the brain and spinal cord, and the peripheral nervous system (PNS). The PNS includes the somatic system and the autonomic system, with its sympathetic and parasympathetic branches.

Conventional brain research relies on dissection, staining, ablation, deep lesioning, electrical recording, electrical stimulation, micro-electrode recording, EEG recording, and clinical studies. Newer methods make use of computer-enhanced images of the brain and its activities.

The basic functions of the lobes of the brain are as follows: occipital lobes—vision; parietal lobes—bodily sensation; temporal lobes—hearing and language; frontal lobes—motor control, speech, and abstract thought. Association areas of the cortex are related to complex abilities such as language, memory, and problem solving. The left and right cerebral hemispheres have different specialized abilities.

The brain is subdivided into the forebrain, midbrain, and hindbrain. The subcortex includes important brain structures at all three levels. These are the medulla ("vegetative" functions), the cerebellum (coordination), the reticular formation (sensory and motor messages and arousal), the thalamus (sensory information), and the hypothalamus (basic motives). The limbic system is related to emotion.

The endocrine system provides chemical communication in the body through the release of hormones into the bloodstream.

Hand dominance ranges from strongly left- to strongly right-handed, with mixed handedness and ambidexterity in between. In general, the left-handed are less strongly lateralized in brain function than are right-handed persons.

Learning Objectives

After reading this chapter the student should be able to:

1. Describe the structure of the neuron. Explain how action potentials arise and trace the path of a neural impulse from one cell to another.
2. Describe how nerve cells communicate with each other. Explain the roles of the major neurotransmitters such as acetylcholine, serotonin, dopamine, and norepinephrine.
3. Describe the organization of the nervous system and explain the functions of the major parts.
4. Describe the different ways that are used to study the structure and functioning of the brain. Explain how computers have contributed to our understanding of the structure of the brain and how it works.
5. Identify the different parts of the brain. Describe the major functions of the left and right hemispheres.
6. Identify each lobe of the cerebral cortex and list the major function(s) of each.
7. Identify the association areas, describe their function, and explain what happens when they are injured.
8. List the behaviours controlled by the subcortex.
9. Describe the functions of the glandular system. Explain how hormones released from the endocrine system affect metabolism, growth, and reactions to anger.
10. Explain how hand dominance is related to brain functioning.

Practice Quizzes

Recite and Review

How do nerve cells operate and communicate?

Recite and Review: Pages 38–43

1. The _____ and nervous system are made up of linked nerve cells called _____ , which pass information from one to another through synapses.
2. The basic conducting fibres of neurons are _____ , but dendrites (a receiving area), the soma (the cell body) and also a receiving area), and _____ terminals (the branching ends of a neuron) are also involved in communication.
3. The firing of an action potential (_____ _____) is basically electrical, whereas communication between neurons is chemical.
4. An action potential occurs when the _____ potential is altered enough to reach the threshold for firing. At that point, sodium _____ flow into the axon, through _____ channels.
5. After each action potential, the neuron has a brief _____ after-potential. Next, potassium ions flow out of the _____ , restoring the resting potential.
6. The _____ potential is an all-or-nothing event.
7. Neurons release _____ substances called neurotransmitters at the synpase. These cross to _____ sites on the receiving cell, causing it to be excited or inhibited. For example, the transmitter chemical acetylcholine activates _____ .

8. Chemicals called neuropeptides do not carry messages directly. Instead, they _____ the activity of other neurons.

9. Opiate-like neural regulators called enkephalins and endorphins are released in the brain to relieve _____ and stress.

How is the nervous system organized and what are the functions of its major parts?

Recite and Review: Pages 43–47

10. Nerves are made of large bundles of _____ and dendrites. Neurons and nerves in the peripheral nervous system can often regenerate; damage in the central nervous system is usually _____ , unless a repair is attempted by grafting or implanting healthy tissue.

11. The layer of fatty tissue coating the axon is called _____ .

12. The nervous system can be divided into the _____ nervous system (the _____ and spinal cord) and the peripheral nervous system.

13. While we lose many brain cells every day, it is now believed that _____ neurons grow to replace some of them.

14. A new method to treat some types of brain damage involve _____ stem cells. These are _____ cells that will team up with existing cells in the damaged area.

15. The capacity of the brain to grow, change, and reorganize its neural pathways is known as

_____ _____ .

16. The PNS includes the somatic (_____) and autonomic (_____) nervous systems.

17. The autonomic system has two divisions: the sympathetic (emergency, activating) _____ and the parasympathetic (sustaining, conserving) _____ .

18. Thirty-one pairs of spinal _____ leave the spinal cord. Twelve pairs of cranial _____ leave the brain directly. Together, they carry sensory and motor messages between the brain and the body.

19. The simplest _____ is a reflex arc, which involves a sensory neuron, a connector neuron, and a _____ neuron.

How do we know how the brain works? What are the methods by which scientists study the brain?

Recite and Review: Pages 47–49

20. Conventional brain research relies on dissection, staining, ablation, deep lesioning, and _____ studies.

21. Computer-enhanced techniques are providing three-dimensional _____ of the living human brain and its _____ . Examples of such techniques are CT scans, MRI scans, and PET scans.

How is the brain organized and what do its higher structures do?

Recite and Review: Pages 50–56

22. The human _____ is marked by advanced corticalization, or enlargement of the cerebral _____ , which covers the outside surface of the cerebrum.

23. The _____ cerebral hemisphere contains speech or language "centres" in most people. It also specializes in _____ , calculating, judging time and rhythm, and ordering complex movements.

24. The _____ hemisphere is largely non-verbal. It excels at spatial and perceptual skills, visualization, and recognition of _____ , faces, and melodies.

25. "Split brains" have been created by _____ the corpus callosum. This type of surgery is usually performed on _____ patients. The split-brain individual shows a remarkable degree of independence between the right and left _____ .

26. Individuals born without a _____ callosum do not show as much independence between the two hemispheres probably because other brain _____ take over some of the functions of the corpus _____ .

27. Another way to summarize specialization in the brain is to say that the _____ hemisphere is good at analysis and processing information sequentially; the _____ hemisphere processes information simultaneously and holistically.

28. The most basic functions of the lobes of the cerebral cortex are as follows: occipital lobes — _____ ; parietal lobes—bodily sensation; temporal lobes— _____ and language; frontal lobes—motor control, speech, and abstract thought.

Why are the brain's association areas important? What happens when they are injured?

Recite and Review: Pages 56–57

29. Association areas receive their input from the _____ areas and are involved in transforming this information in the complex skills expressed by the brain such as perception, language, memory, and problem solving.

30. Damage to either Broca's area or Wernicke's area causes _____ and language problems known as aphasias.

31. Damage to Broca's area causes problems with _____ and pronunciation. Damage to Wernicke's area causes problems with the _____ of words.

What kinds of behaviours are controlled by the subcortex?

Recite and Review: Pages 57–60

32. All of the brain areas below the _____ are called the subcortex.

33. The medulla contains centres essential for reflex control of _____ _____ , breathing, and other "vegetative" functions.

34. The cerebellum maintains _____ , posture, and muscle tone.

35. The reticular formation directs sensory and motor messages, and part of it, known as the RAS, acts as an _____ system for the cerebral cortex.

36. The thalamus carries _____ information to the cortex. The hypothalamus exerts powerful control over eating, drinking, sleep cycles, body temperature, and other basic _____ and behaviours.

37. The limbic system is strongly related to _____ and motivated behaviour. It also contains distinct reward and punishment areas.

38. A part of the limbic system called the amygdala is related to an alert system that triggers a _____ response in a danger situation. An area known as the hippocampus is important for forming _____ .

How does the glandular system affect behaviour?

Recite and Review: Pages 60–64

39. The endocrine system provides _____ communication in the body through the release of _____ into the bloodstream. Endrocrine glands influence moods, behaviour, and even personality.

40. Many of the endocrine glands are influenced by the pituitary (the " _____ gland"), which is in turn influenced by the hypothalamus.

41. The pituitary supplies _____ hormone. Too little GH causes _____ ; too much causes giantism or acromegaly.

42. Body rhythms and _____ cycles are influenced by melatonin, secreted by the pineal gland.

43. The thyroid gland regulates _____ . Hyperthyroidism refers to an overactive thyroid gland; hypothyroidism to an underactive thyroid.

44. The adrenal glands supply _____ and norepinephrine to activate the body. They also regulate salt balance and responses to stress, and are a secondary source of _____ hormones.

45. Evidence shows that part of the gender differences in mental abilities (mathematical reasoning, verbal skills, motor skills) are due to the presence of _____ hormones in male and female _____ .

How do right- and left-handed individuals differ?

Recite and Review: Psychology in Action

46. Hand dominance ranges from strongly left- to strongly right-handed, with _____ handedness and ambidexterity in between.

47. Ninety percent of the population is basically _____ - _____ , 10 percent _____ - _____ .

48. The vast majority of people are right-handed and therefore _____ brain dominant for motor skills. Ninety-seven percent of right-handed persons and 68 percent of the left-handed also produce _____ from the left hemisphere.

49. In general, the _____ - _____ are less strongly lateralized in brain function than are _____ - _____ persons.

Connections

1. _____ soma
2. _____ neurilemma
3. _____ axon collateral
4. _____ myelin
5. _____ dendrites
6. _____ axon terminals
7. _____ axon

8. _____ spinal cord
9. _____ autonomic system
10. _____ parasympathetic
11. _____ peripheral nervous system
12. _____ sympathetic branch
13. _____ brain
14. _____ somatic system

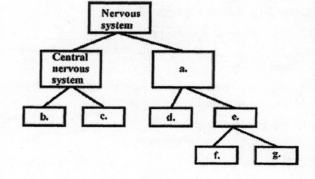

15. _____ Wernicke's area
16. _____ temporal lobe
17. _____ cerebellum
18. _____ Broca's area
19. _____ parietal lobe
20. _____ frontal lobe
21. _____ occipital lobe

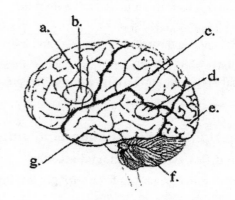

22. _____ midbrain
23. _____ reticular formation
24. _____ cerebrum
25. _____ medulla
26. _____ hypothalamus
27. _____ corpus callosum
28. _____ pituitary
29. _____ spinal cord
30. _____ thalamus

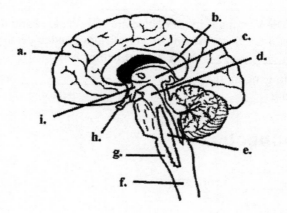

31. _____ pituitary		a.	brain waves
32. _____ pineal gland		b.	radioactive glucose
33. _____ thyroid gland		c.	testosterone
34. _____ adrenal glands		d.	surgery
35. _____ testes		e.	metabolism
36. _____ CT scan		f.	electrode
37. _____ EEG		g.	growth hormone
38. _____ ablation		h.	epinephrine
39. _____ deep lesioning		i.	computerized X-rays
40. _____ PET scan		j.	melatonin

Short-Answer Questions

1. Describe the effects of myelin on the nerve impulse.

2. Differentiate between the two branches of the autonomic nervous system.

3. Explain the reflex arc.

4. Briefly describe the techniques used to study the brain.

5. Explain the role of the corpus callosum.

6. Describe the relationship between the size of the various parts of the somatosensory and motor areas of the cortex and the degree of sensitivity or importance of the corresponding part of the body.

7. Explain the function of each of the following structures: medulla, cerebellum, and reticular formation.

8. Briefly explain the function of the thalamus and hypothalamus.

9. Discuss the relationship between hormones and gender differences in behaviour.

Final Survey and Review

How do nerve cells operate and communicate?

1. The brain and nervous system are made up of linked _____ , which pass information from one to another through _____ .

2. The basic conducting fibres of neurons are axons, but _____ (a receiving area), the _____ (the cell body and also a receiving area), and axon terminals (the branching ends of an axon) are also involved in communication.

3. The firing of an _____ _____ (nerve impulse) is basically electrical, whereas communication between neurons is chemical.

4. An action potential occurs when the resting potential is altered enough to reach the _____ for firing. At that point, _____ ions flow into the axon, through ion channels.

5. After each action potential, the neuron has a brief negative _____ - _____ . Next, _____ ions flow out of the axon, restoring the resting potential.

6. The action potential is an _____ - _____ - _____ event.

7. In chemical synapses, neurons release _____ . These cross to receptor sites on the receiving cell, causing it to be excited or inhibited. For example, the transmitter chemical _____ activates muscles.

8. Chemicals called _____ do not carry messages directly. Instead, they regulate the activity of other neurons.

9. Opiate-like neural regulators called enkephalins and _____ are released in the brain to relieve pain and stress.

How is the nervous system organized and what are the functions of its major parts?

10. _____ are made of axons and associated tissues. Neurons and nerves in the _____ nervous system can often regenerate; damage in the _____ nervous system is usually permanent.

11. The layer of fatty tissue coating the _____ is called myelin.

12. The nervous system can be divided into the _____ nervous system (the brain and _____ _____) and the peripheral nervous system.

13. While we lose many brain cells every day, it is now believed that new neurons grow to replace _____ of them.

14. A new method to treat some types of brain damage involves injecting _____ _____ . These immature cells will _____ _____ with existing cells in the damaged area.

15. The capacity of the brain to _____ , _____ , and _____ its neural pathways is known as brain plasticity.

16. The PNS includes the _____ (bodily) and _____ (involuntary) nervous systems.

17. The autonomic system has two divisions: the _____ (emergency, activating) branch and the _____ (sustaining, conserving) branch.

18. Thirty-one pairs of spinal nerves leave the _____ cord. Twelve pairs of _____ nerves leave the brain directly. Together, these nerves carry sensory and _____ messages between the brain and the body.

19. The simplest behaviour is a _____ _____ , which involves a sensory neuron, a _____ neuron, and a _____ neuron.

How do we know how the brain works? What are the methods by which scientists study the brain?

20. Conventional brain research relies on _____ (separation into parts), staining, ablation, deep lesioning, electrical recording, electrical _____ , micro-electrode recording, EEG recording, and clinical studies.

21. Computer-enhanced techniques are providing three-dimensional images of the living human brain and its activities. Examples of such techniques are CT scans, _____ scans, and _____ scans, which record brain activity.

How is the brain organized and what do its higher structures do?

22. The human brain is marked by advanced _____ , or enlargement of the cerebral cortex, which covers the outside surface of the _____ .

23. The right cerebral _____ contains speech or language "centres" in most people. It also specializes in writing, calculating, judging time and rhythm, and ordering complex _____ .

24. The left hemisphere is largely non-verbal. It excels at _____ and perceptual skills, visualization, and recognition of patterns, _____ , and melodies.

25. "Split brains" have been created by cutting the _____ _____ of adult patients. The split-brain individual shows a remarkable degree of independence between the right and left _____ .

26. Individuals born without a _____ _____ do not show as much independence between the two _____ probably because other _____ structures take over some of the functions.

27. Another way to summarize specialization in the brain is to say that the left hemisphere is good at _____ and processing information sequentially; the right hemisphere processes information _____ and holistically.

28. The most basic functions of the lobes of the cerebral _____ are as follows: occipital lobes—vision; parietal lobes—bodily _____ ; temporal lobes—hearing and language; frontal lobes—motor control, _____ , and abstract thought.

Why are the brain's association areas important? What happens when they are injured?

29. Association areas on the cortex are neither _____ nor _____ in function. They are related to more complex skills such as _____ , memory, recognition, and problem solving.

30. Damage to either Broca's area or Wernicke's area causes speech and language problems known as _____ .

31. Damage to _____ area causes problems with speech and pronunciation. Damage to _____ area causes problems with the meaning of words.

What kinds of behaviours are controlled by the subcortex?

32. All of the brain areas below the cortex are called the _____ .

33. The _____ contains centres essential for reflex control of heart rate, breathing, and other "vegetative" functions.

34. The _____ maintains coordination, posture, and muscle tone.

35. The _____ formation directs sensory and motor messages, and part of it, known as the RAS, acts as an activating system for the _____ _____ .

36. The _____ carries sensory information to the cortex. The _____ exerts powerful control over eating, drinking, sleep cycles, body temperature, and other basic motives and behaviours.

37. The _____ system is strongly related to emotion and motivation. It also contains distinct _____ and punishment areas.

38. A part of the limbic system called the _____ is related to fear. An area known as the _____ is important for forming lasting memories.

How does the glandular system affect behaviour?

39. The _____ system provides chemical communication in the body through the release of hormones into the _____ .

40. Many of the endocrine glands are influenced by the _____ (the "master gland"), which is in turn influenced by the _____ .

41. The _____ supplies growth hormone. Too little GH causes dwarfism; too much causes giantism or _____ .

42. Body rhythms and sleep cycles are influenced by _____ , secreted by the _____ gland.

43. The thyroid gland regulates metabolism. Hyperthyroidism refers to an _____ thyroid gland; hypothyroidism to an _____ thyroid.

44. The _____ glands supply epinephrine and norepinephrine to activate the body. They also regulate salt balance and responses to _____ , and are a secondary source of sex hormones.

45. Evidence shows that part of the gender differences in _____ _____ are due to the presence of different _____ in male and female fetuses.

How do right- and left-handed individuals differ?

46. _____ _____ ranges from strongly left- to strongly right-handed, with mixed handedness and _____ in between.

47. _____ percent of the population is basically right-handed, _____ percent left-handed.

48. The vast majority of people are _____ - _____ and therefore _____ brain dominant for motor skills. Ninety-seven percent of right-handed persons and sixty-eight percent of the left-handed produce speech from the _____ hemisphere.

49. In general, the left-handed are less strongly _____ in brain function than are right-handed persons.

Mastery Test

1. At times of emergency, anger, or fear, what part of the nervous system becomes more active?
   a. corpus callosum of the forebrain
   b. sympathetic branch of the ANS
   c. parasympathetic branch of the PNS
   d. Broca's area

2. The highest and largest brain area in humans is the
   a. cerebrum
   b. cerebellum
   c. frontal lobes
   d. grey matter of the callosum

3. A tumor in which brain area would most likely cause blind spots in vision?
   a. occipital lobe
   b. temporal lobe
   c. somatosensory area
   d. association cortex

4. Neurotransmitters are found primarily in
   a. the spinal cord
   b. the neurilemma
   c. axon terminals
   d. motor neurons

5. Enkephalins are an example of
   a. acetylcholine blockers
   b. neuropeptides
   c. receptor sites
   d. adrenal hormones

6. Electrically stimulating a portion of which brain area would produce movements in the body?
   a. occipital lobe
   b. frontal lobe
   c. parietal lobe
   d. temporal lobe

7. When a neuron reaches its threshold, a/an _____ occurs.
   a. volume potential
   b. ion potential
   c. action potential
   d. dendrite potential

8. A person's ability to work as a commercial artist would be most impaired by damage to the
   a. left temporal lobe
   b. right cerebral hemisphere
   c. left cerebral hemisphere
   d. frontal association cortex

9. ESB will most likely produce anger if it is applied somewhere in the
   a. association cortex
   b. limbic system
   c. parasympathetic branch
   d. reticular activating system

10. Information in neurons usually flows in what order?
    a. soma, dendrites, axon
    b. dendrites, soma, axon
    c. dendrites, myelin, axon terminals
    d. axon, soma, axon terminals

11. Regulating the activity of other neurotransmitters is most characteristic of
    a. neuropeptides
    b. acetylcholine
    c. reflex arcs
    d. resting potentials

12. Nerve impulses occur when _____ rush into the axon.
    a. sodium ions
    b. potassium ions
    c. negative charges
    d. neurotransmitters

13. Attempts to repair brain injuries by injecting immature stem cells into the damaged area make use of the recently discovered existence of
    a. myelin
    b. neurogenesis
    c. neuropeptides
    d. corticalization

14. Negative after-potentials are caused by the outward flow of _____ from the axon.
    a. negative charges
    b. potassium ions
    c. neurotransmitters
    d. sodium ions

15. A person who says "bife" for bike and "seep" for sleep probably suffers from
    a. Broca's aphasia
    b. Wernicke's aphasia
    c. spatial neglect
    d. the condition known as "mindblindness"

16. Damage to which part of the limbic system would most likely impair memory?
    a. thalamus
    b. hypothalamus
    c. amygdala
    d. hippocampus

17. Changes in heart rate, blood pressure, digestion, and sweating are controlled by the
    a. thoracic nerves
    b. parietal lobes
    c. somatic system
    d. autonomic system

18. In which of the following pairs are both structures part of the forebrain?
    a. medulla, hypothalamus
    b. cerebrum, cerebellum
    c. medulla, thalamus
    d. cerebrum, thalamus

19. Which of the following is a specialized type of X-ray?
    a. PET scan
    b. CT scan
    c. MRI scan
    d. EEG scan

20. Which two problems are associated with the pituitary gland?
    a. dwarfism, acromegaly
    b. virilism, acromegaly
    c. mental retardation, dwarfism
    d. giantism, premature puberty

21. The cerebral hemispheres are interconnected by the
    a. reticular system
    b. cerebellum
    c. cerebrum
    d. corpus callosum

22. Damage to which of the following would most likely make it difficult for a person to play catch with a ball?
    a. reticular formation
    b. limbic system
    c. cerebellum
    d. association cortex

23. Speech, language, calculation, and analysis are special skills of the
    a. right cerebral hemisphere
    b. limbic system
    c. left cerebral hemisphere
    d. right somatosensory area

24. The usual flow of information in a reflex arc is
    a. cranial nerve, connector nerve, spinal nerve
    b. sensory neuron, connector neuron, motor neuron
    c. effector cell, interneuron, connector neuron
    d. sensory neuron, connector neuron, reflex neuron

25. A person will "hear" a series of sounds when which area of the cortex is electrically stimulated?
    a. frontal lobe
    b. parietal lobe
    c. occipital lobe
    d. temporal lobe

26. Which of the following pairs contains the "master gland" and its master?
    a. pineal—thalamus
    b. thyroid—RAS
    c. pituitary—hypothalamus
    d. adrenal—cortex

27. Many basic motives and emotions are influenced by the
    a. thalamus
    b. hypothalamus
    c. corpus callosum
    d. cerebellum

28. Both surgical ablation and _____ remove brain tissue.
    a. the MEG technique
    b. tomography
    c. micro-electrode sampling
    d. deep lesioning

29. Which of the following techniques requires access to the interior of the brain?
    a. micro-electrode recording
    b. EEG recordings
    c. PET scanning
    d. functional MRI

30. Which of the following statements about handedness is FALSE?
    a. Handedness is inherited from one's parents.
    b. A majority of left-handers produce speech from the left hemisphere.
    c. The left-handed are less lateralized than the right-handed.
    d. Left-handedness is an advantage in boxing and fencing.

31. Which of the following explanations is true concerning the relationship found between hormone levels and the behavioural differences between men and women?
    a. Sex differences are due to the presence of different hormones in male and female fetuses.
    b. Finding such a relationship is a guarantee that hormone levels are the cause of gender differences.
    c. These sex differences are caused by the different upbringing boys and girls receive in our society.
    d. Both A and C are two possible causes for this relationship.

32. Which famous Canadian neurosurgeon did research in the 1960s on the specialization of the cerebral cortex using electrical stimulation?
    a. Doreen Kimura
    b. Liisa Galea
    c. Wilder Penfield
    d. Donald Hebb

Solutions

Recite and Review

1. brain; neurons
2. axons; axon
3. nerve impulse
4. resting; ions; ion
5. negative; axon
6. action
7. chemical; receptor; muscles
8. regulate
9. pain
10. axons; permanent
11. myelin
12. central; brain
13. new
14. injecting; immature
15. brain plasticity
16. bodily; involuntary
17. branch; branch
18. nerves; nerves
19. behaviour; motor
20. clinical
21. images; activity
22. brain; cortex
23. left; writing
24. right; patterns
25. cutting; adult; hemispheres
26. corpus; structures; callosum
27. left; right
28. vision; hearing
29. sensory
30. speech
31. grammar; meaning
32. cortex
33. heart rate
34. coordination
35. activating
36. sensory; motives
37. emotion
38. fear; memories
39. chemical; hormones
40. master
41. growth; dwarfism
42. sleep
43. metabolism
44. epinephrine; sex
45. different; fetuses
46. mixed
47. right handed; left handed
48. left; speech
49. left handed; right handed

Connections

1. G
2. D
3. E
4. C
5. A
6. F
7. B
8. C or B
9. E
10. F or G
11. A
12. F
13. C or B
14. D
15. D
16. G
17. F
18. B
19. C
20. A
21. E
22. D
23. E
24. A
25. G
26. I
27. B
28. H
29. F
30. C
31. G
32. J
33. E
34. H
35. C
36. I
37. A
38. D
39. F
40. B

Short-Answer Questions

1. Myelin is a layer of fatty tissue that wraps around some axons. Gaps in the myelin layer may increase the speed of nerve transmission. When this layer is damaged, a person may experience numbness, weakness, or paralysis. Multiple sclerosis occurs when the body's immune system attacks the myelin layer.

2. The sympathetic branch activates the body for action ("fight or flight"), raises blood pressure, and increases heart rate. The parasympathetic branch activates after an emotional event to return heart rate, blood pressure, etc. to normal levels. The two work together to maintain moderate levels of arousal.

3. Stimulation of a sensory neuron (for example, you step on a tack) activates a connector neuron in the spinal cord, which activates a motor neuron that stimulates effector cells in the muscles (you pick up your foot).

4. Clinical studies relate changes in behaviour or personality to known brain injury, neurosurgery, or disease. A part of the brain may be removed (ablation) or stimulated to identify the effects on behaviour. Electroencephalography (EEG) records brain activity as it happens. Computerized tomography (CT) scans are specialized X-rays that form an image of the brain. Magnetic

resonance imaging (MRI) techniques use a magnetic field to produce a 3-D image of the brain. Functional MRIs make brain activity visible. A positron emission tomography scan (PET scan) shows which areas in the brain use more energy by detecting the presence of radioactive glucose in the brain.

5. The corpus callosum is a thick band of fibres that connects the two hemispheres. It allows both hemispheres to share sensory and other information. People who have the corpus callosum divided to control epilepsy may have difficulty coordinating tasks such as dressing, and may have difficulty identifying objects that are shown to only one hemisphere. People who are born without a corpus callosum generally do not show these deficits, although they may have some difficulties in performing tasks that are learned with only one hand.

6. Generally, the size of the area on the cortex reflects the importance or sensitivity of the part of the body, rather than its size. For example, the lips, face, and hands take up more space on the cortex than the trunk, legs, or feet.

7. The medulla is important in the reflex control of vital functions (breathing, heart rate, swallowing, etc). The cerebellum regulates posture, muscle tone, and coordination, and contains memories related to skills and habits. The reticular formation influences attention, and modifies outgoing messages to the body to affect muscle tone, posture, and movement of the eyes, face head, body, and limbs. It also controls reflexes involved in breathing, sneezing, and coughing.

8. All sensory messages except smell pass through the thalamus on the way to the cortex, so damage to the thalamus can cause blindness, deafness, and loss of the sense of taste and touch. The hypothalamus is the master control for emotion and many basic motives. It is involved in sexual arousal, rage, control of body temperature, endocrine function, eating and drinking, sleep, waking, and emotion.

9. There is evidence that spatial learning in rats is affected by the presence of male hormones. Males castrated right after birth show a decline in their ability to learn a path or route, and females given androgens right after birth show improvement in performance on spatial tasks. In humans, there are sex differences in mathematical reasoning, spatial tasks, and some gross motor tasks (men do better) as well as verbal skills like word puzzles, arithmetical calculations, and fine motor tasks (women do better). Whether this is due to the effects of different amounts of androgens on the developing brain, or to differences in rearing and educational experiences, has not been determined.

Final Survey and Review

1. neurons; synpases
2. dendrites; soma
3. action potential
4. threshold; sodium
5. after potential; potassium
6. all or nothing
7. neurotransmitters; acetylcholine
8. neuropeptides
9. endorphins
10. Nerves; peripheral; central
11. axon
12. central; spinal cord
13. some
14. stem cells; team up
15. grow; change; reorganize
16. somatic; autonomic
17. sympathetic; parasympathetic
18. spinal; cranial; motor
19. reflex arc; connector; motor
20. dissection; stimulation
21. MRI; PET
22. corticalization; cerebrum
23. hemisphere; movements
24. spatial; faces
25. corpus callosum; hemispheres
26. corpus callosum; hemispheres; brain
27. analysis; simultaneously
28. cortex; sensation; speech
29. sensory; motor; language
30. aphasias
31. Broca's; Wernicke's
32. subcortex
33. medulla
34. cerebellum
35. reticular; cerebral cortex
36. thalamus; hypothalamus
37. limbic; reward
38. amygdala; hippocampus
39. endocrine; bloodstream
40. pituitary; hypothalamus
41. pituitary; acromegaly
42. melatonin; pineal
43. overactive; underactive
44. adrenal; stress
45. mental abilities; hormones
46. Hand dominance; ambidexterity
47. Ninety; ten
48. right handed; left; left
49. lateralized

Mastery Test

1. B (p. 46)
2. A (p. 50)
3. A (p. 54)
4. C (p. 41)
5. B (p. 43)
6. B (p. 56)
7. C (p. 40)
8. B (p. 54)
9. B (p. 59)
10. B (p. 38)
11. A (p. 43)

12. A (p. 40)
13. B (p. 43)
14. B (p. 40)
15. A (p. 56)
16. D (p. 59)
17. D (p. 45)
18. D (p. 58)
19. B (p. 48)
20. A (p. 60)
21. D (p. 51)
22. C (p. 58)
23. C (p. 53)

24. B (p. 46)
25. D (p. 55)
26. C (p. 60)
27. B (p. 59)
28. D (p. 47)
29. A (p. 48)
30. A (p. 66)
31. D (p. 62)
32. C (p. 47)

Human Development

Chapter Overview

Heredity affects personal characteristics, including temperament, and it organizes the human growth sequence. Environmental influences can have lasting effects, especially during critical periods in development. Prenatal development is affected by diseases, drugs, radiation, and the mother's diet, health, and emotions. Early perceptual, intellectual, and emotional deprivation seriously retards development. Deliberate enrichment of the environment has a beneficial effect on early development.

Most psychologists accept that heredity and environment are inseparable and interacting forces. A child's developmental level reflects heredity, environment, and the effects of the child's own behaviour.

Human newborns have adaptive reflexes, are capable of learning, and have visual preferences, especially for familiar faces. Maturation underlies the orderly sequence of motor, cognitive, language, and emotional development.

Emotional attachment of infants to their caregivers is a critical event in social development.

Caregiving styles affect social, emotional, and intellectual development. Optimal caregiving includes proactive involvement, a good fit between the temperaments of parent and child, and responsiveness to a child's needs and signals. Three major parenting styles are authoritarian, permissive, and authoritative (effective). Effective parental discipline tends to emphasize child management techniques, rather than power assertion or withdrawal of love.

Language development is based on a biological predisposition, which is augmented by learning. Language acquisition begins with prelanguage communication between parent and child.

Jean Piaget theorized that children go through a series of cognitive stages as they develop intellectually. Learning principles provide an alternate explanation that does not assume that cognitive development occurs in stages. Lev Vygotsky's sociocultural theory says that cognitive gains occur primarily in a child's zone of proximal development. Adults who engage in the scaffolding of a child's intellectual growth also impart cultural values and beliefs to the child.

Responsibility, mutual respect, consistency, love, encouragement, and clear communication are features of effective parenting.

Learning Objectives

After reading this chapter, the student should be able to:

1. Explain the nature-nurture controversy.

2. Describe how inherited characteristics are passed from parent to child.

3. Explain how prenatal development may be affected by environmental influences, giving examples of both beneficial and harmful effects.

4. Describe the adaptive behaviours of the neonate.

5. Define maturation. Explain the influence of maturation on motor and emotional development.

6. Explain the importance of a secure emotional bond between parent and child.

7. Show how different parenting styles can influence development.

8. Trace the development of language from infancy to age three or four.

9. Describe the four stages of Piaget's theory of cognitive development

10. Describe Vygotsky's sociocultural theory of cognitive development.

11. Identify Erikson's eight life stages. Describe the major psychosocial dilemma associated with each stage.

12. Explain the most effective methods for disciplining a child.

Practice Quizzes

Recite and Review

How do heredity and environment affect development?

Recite and Review: Pages 72–77

1. Developmental psychology is the study of progressive changes in _____ and abilities, from _____ to _____ .

2. The nature-nurture debate concerns the realtive contributions to development of heredity (_____) and environment (_____).

3. Hereditary instructions are carried by _____ in the form of chromosomes and _____ in each cell of the body.

4. Dominant genes include _____ hair, extra _____ or _____ , and type A or _____ _____ blood.

5. _____ genes include light eye colour, light _____ , and type O blood.

6. Most characteristics are polygenic (influenced by a combination of _____) and reflect the combined effects of dominant and recessive _____ .

7. Heredity organizes the general human growth sequence—the general pattern of _____ _____ from birth to death.

8. Heredity also influences differences in temperament (the physical core of _____). Most infants fall into one of three temperament categories: easy children, _____ children, and slow-to-warm-up children.

9. Environment refers to all _____ conditions that affect development.

10. A variety of sensitive periods (times of increased _____ to environmental influences) exist in development.

11. Prenatal development is subject to _____ influences in the form of diseases, drugs, radiation, and the mother's diet, health, and emotions.

12. Prenatal damage to the fetus may cause congenital problems, or _____ _____ . In contrast, genetic problems are inherited from one's parents.

13. Early perceptual, intellectual, and emotional deprivation seriously retards _____ .

14. Poverty greatly increases the likelihood that children will experience various forms of _____ .

15. Research on deprivation suggests that attachment and perceptual stimulation are essential for _____ development.

16. Deliberate enrichment of the _____ in infancy and early childhood has a beneficial effect on development.

17. Ultimately, most psychologists accept that heredity and _____ are inseparable and interacting forces.

18. A child's developmental level (current state of development) reflects _____ , environment, and the effects of the child's own behaviour.

What can newborn babies do?

Recite and Review: Pages 77–80

19. The human _____ (newborn) has a number of _____ reflexes, including the grasping, rooting, sucking, and Moro reflexes.

20. Newborns begin to _____ immediately and they imitate adults.

21. Tests in a looking chamber reveal a number of _____ preferences in the newborn. The neonate is drawn to complex, _____ , curved and brightly lit designs.

22. Infants prefer human face patterns, especially _____ _____ . In later infancy, interest in the unfamiliar emerges.

What is maturation? What influence does maturation have on a child's early development?

Recite and Review: Pages 80–82

23. Maturation of the body and nervous system underlies the orderly _____ of motor, cognitive, language, and emotional development.

24. While the rate of maturation varies from child to child, the _____ is nearly universal.

25. The development of _____ control (motor development) is cephalocaudal (from head to toe) and proximodistal (from the _____ of the body to the extremities).

26. Many early _____ are subject to the principle of readiness.

27. Emotional development begins with a capacity for _____ excitement. After that, the first pleasant and unpleasant emotions develop.

28. Some psychologists believe that basic emotional expressions are _____ and that some appear as early as 2.5 months of age.

29. By age 10 months, babies display a social smile when other _____ are nearby.

Why is the emotional bond between parent and child so important?

Recite and Review: Pages 82–85

30. _____ development refers to the emergence of self-awareness and forming relationships with parents and others.

31. Emotional attachment of human infants to their _____ is a critical early event.

32. Infant attachment is reflected by _____ anxiety (distress when infants are away from parents).

33. Mary Ainsworth was a _____ psychologist who did extensive research on _____ - _____ _____ .

34. Ainsworth classified the quality of infant-mother attachment as _____ , insecure-avoidant, or insecure-ambivalent.

35. High-quality day care does not _____ children; high-quality care can, in fact, accelerate some areas of development.

36. A child's _____ development is also affected by playing with other children. For example, cooperative _____ is a major step toward participation in social life outside the family.

37. An infant's affectional needs are every bit as important as more obvious _____ for physical care.

What are parenting styles? How important are different parenting styles to a child's development?

Recite and Review: Pages 85–88

38. Caregiving styles (patterns of parental care) have a substantial impact on emotional and intellectual _____ .

39. Maternal influences (the effects _____ have on their children) tend to centre on caregiving.

40. Optimal caregiving includes proactive maternal _____ , a good fit between the temperaments of parent and child, and responsiveness to a child's needs and _____ .

41. Paternal influences differ in their impact because _____ tend to function as a playmate for the infant.

42. Authoritarian parents enforce rigid _____ and demand strict obedience to _____ .

43. Overly permissive parents give little _____ and don't hold children accountable for their actions.

44. Authoritative (_____) parents supply firm and consistent guidance, combined with love and affection.

45. Effective child _____ is based on a consistent framework of guidelines for acceptable behaviour.

46. Good discipline tends to emphasize child management techniques (especially communication), rather than _____ assertion or withdrawal of _____ .

47. _____ techniques tend to produce the highest levels of self-esteem in children.

How do children acquire language?
Recite and Review: Pages 88–92

48. Language development proceeds from control of _____ , to cooing, then babbling, the use of single words, and then to telegraphic _____ .

49. The patterns of early speech suggest a _____ predisposition to acquire language.

50. Psycholinguists (psychologists who study _____) believe that innate language predispositions are augmented by _____ .

51. Prelanguage communication between parent and child involves shared rhythms, non-verbal _____ , and turn-taking.

52. Parents help children learn language by using distinctive caretaker _____ or parentese.

How do children learn to think?
Recite and Review: Pages 92–97

53. The intellects of children are _____ abstract than those of adults. Jean Piaget theorized that _____ growth occurs through a combination of assimilation and accommodation.

54. Piaget also held that children go through a fixed series of cognitive _____ .

55. These are sensorimotor (0–2), preoperational (2–7), _____ operational (7–11), and formal _____ (11–adult).

56. Learning theorists dispute the idea that cognitive development occurs in _____ . Recent studies suggest infants are capable of levels of thinking beyond that observed by _____ .

57. Young children don't seem to understand that the _____ of other people contain different information, beliefs, and thoughts than theirs do. In other words, they have a very simplified theory of _____ .

58. According to the sociocultural theory of Russian scholar Lev Vygotsky, a child's interactions with others are most likely to aid _____ development if they they take place within the child's _____ of proximal _____ .

59. Adults help children learn how to think by scaffolding, or _____ , their attempts to solve problems or discover principles.

60. During their collaborations with adults, children learn important cultural _____ and values.

What are the typical tasks and dilemmas that confront people through the life span?
Recite and Review: Pages 97–101

61. Psychologists are interested in _____ milestones, or prominent landmarks in personal development.

62. According to Erik Erikson, each life stage provokes a specific psychosocial _____ .

63. During childhood these are trust versus mistrust, autonomy versus _____ and doubt, initiative versus _____ , and industry versus _____ .

64. In _____ , identity versus role confusion is the principal dilemma.

65. In young adulthood we face the dilemma of intimacy versus _____ . Later, generativity versus _____ becomes prominent.

66. Old age is a time when the dilemma of integrity versus _____ must be faced.

67. In addition, each life stage requires successful mastery of certain _____ tasks (personal changes required for optimal development).

What is the most effective way to discipline a child?

Recite and Review: Psychology in Action

68. Responsibility, mutual _____ , consistency, love, encouragement, and clear _____ are features of effective parenting.

69. Much misbehaviour can be managed by use of I- _____ and by applying _____ and logical consequences to children's behaviour.

Connections

1. _____ grasping reflex
2. _____ rooting reflex
3. _____ Moro reflex
4. _____ readiness
5. _____ gene
6. _____ chromosome
7. _____ senescence
8. _____ heredity
9. _____ environment
10. _____ prenatal period

a. rapid motor learning
b. DNA area
c. old age
d. nature
e. palm grip
f. nurture
g. startled embrace
h. conception to birth
i. coloured body
j. food search

11. _____ FAS
12. _____ Vygotsky
13. _____ motor development
14. _____ super mother
15. _____ critical period
16. _____ attachment
17. _____ affectional needs
18. _____ cooing
19. _____ babbling
20. _____ parentese

a. control of muscles and movement
b. caregiving style
c. love and attention
d. vowel sounds
e. prenatal alcohol
f. sociocultural theory
g. vowels and consonants
h. emotional bond
i. caretaker speech
j. environmental sensitivity

21. _____ assimilation		a.	changing existing mental patterns
22. _____ accommodation		b.	egocentrism
23. _____ sensorimotor stage		c.	applying mental patterns
24. _____ preoperational stage		d.	abstract principles
25. _____ concrete operations		e.	social development
26. _____ formal operations		f.	stage theory of cognitive development
27. _____ psychosocial dilemmas		g.	Erikson
28. _____ cooperative play		h.	conservation
29. _____ Piaget		i.	adolescence
30. _____ role confusion		j.	object permanence

Short-Answer Questions

1. Briefly discuss the concept of sensitive periods.
2. Explain how two brown-eyed parents could have a blue-eyed child.
3. Discuss the effects of enrichment on development.
4. Discuss the effects of deprivation on development.
5. Describe Baumrind's three styles of parenting.
6. What are the effects of power assertion and withdrawal of love on children's behaviour and self-esteem?
7. Distinguish between assimilation and accommodation according to Piaget.
8. Describe the major elements of effective communication.

Final Survey and Review

How do heredity and environment affect development?

1. _____ psychology is the study of _____ changes in behaviour and abilities, from birth to death.
2. The nature-nurture debate concerns the relative contributions to development of _____ (nature) and _____ (nurture).
3. Hereditary instructions are carried by DNA (_____ acid) in the form of _____ ("coloured bodies") and genes in every cell.
4. Dominant genes include dark _____ , _____ fingers or toes, and _____ _____ or type B blood.
5. Recessive genes include _____ eye colour, _____ hair and type _____ blood.
6. Most characteristics are _____ (influenced by a combination of genes) and reflect the combined effects of dominant and _____ genes.
7. Heredity organizes the general human _____ _____ —the general pattern of physical development from birth to death.
8. Heredity also influences differences in _____ (the physical foundations of personality). Most infants fall into one of three categories: _____ children, difficult children, and _____ - _____ - _____ - _____ children.

9. _____ refers to all external conditions that affect development.

10. A variety of _____ _____ (times of increased sensitivity to environmental influences) exist in development.

11. During pregnancy, _____ development is subject to environmental influences in the form of diseases, _____ , _____ , and the mother's diet, health, and emotions.

12. Prenatal damage to the fetus may cause _____ problems, or birth defects. In contrast, _____ problems are inherited from one's parents.

13. Early perceptual and intellectual _____ seriously retards development.

14. _____ greatly increases the likelihood that children will experience various forms of deprivation.

15. Research on deprivation suggests that secure _____ and perceptual _____ are essential for normal development.

16. Deliberate _____ of the environment in infancy and early childhood has a beneficial effect on development.

17. Ultimately, most psychologists accept that heredity and environment are inseparable and _____ forces.

18. A child's _____ _____ (current state of development) reflects heredity, environment, and the effects of the child's own behaviour.

What can newborn babies do?

19. The human neonate (newborn) has a number of adaptive reflexes, including the _____ , rooting, _____ , and _____ reflexes.

20. Newborns begin to learn immediately and they _____ (mimic) adults.

21. Tests in a _____ _____ reveal a number of visual preferences in the newborn. The neonate is drawn to _____ , circular, curved, and brightly lit designs.

22. Infants prefer _____ _____ patterns, especially familiar faces. In later infancy, interest in the _____ emerges.

What is maturation? What influence does maturation have on a child's early development?

23. _____ of the body and _____ _____ underlies the orderly sequence of motor, cognitive, language, and emotional development.

24. While the _____ of maturation varies from child to child, the order is nearly _____ .

25. The development of muscular control (_____ development) is _____ (from head to toe) and _____ and from the centre of the body to the extremities.

26. Many early skills are subject to the principle of _____ .

27. Emotional development begins with a capacity for general _____ . After that, the first _____ and _____ emotions develop.

28. Some psychologists believe that basic _____ expressions are innate and that some appear as early as 2.5 _____ of age.

29. By age 10 months, babies display a _____ smile when other people are nearby.

Why is the emotional bond between parent and child so important?

30. Social development refers to the emergence of self- _____ and forming _____ with parents and others.

31. Emotional _____ of human infants to their caregivers is a critical early event.

32. Infant attachment is reflected by separation _____ (distress when infants are away from parents).

33. _____ _____ was a developmental psychologist who did extensive research on _____ - _____ attachment.

34. _____ classified the quality of infant-mother attachment as secure, insecure- _____ , or insecure- _____ .

35. _____ - _____ day care does not harm children; excellent care can, in fact, _____ some areas of development.

36. A child's social development is also affected by playing with other children. For example, _____ play is a major step toward participation in social life outside the family.

37. An infant's _____ needs are every bit as important as more obvious needs for physical care.

What are parenting styles? How important are different parenting styles to a child's development?

38. _____ _____ (patterns of parental care) have a substantial impact on emotional and intellectual development.

39. _____ influences (the effects mothers have on their children) tend to centre on _____ .

40. Optimal caregiving includes _____ maternal involvement, a good fit between the _____ of parent and child, and responsiveness to a child's needs and signals.

41. _____ influences differ in their impact because fathers tend to function as a _____ for the infant.

42. _____ parents enforce rigid rules and demand strict obedience to authority.

43. Overly _____ parents give little guidance and don't hold children accountable for their actions.

44. _____ (effective) parents supply firm and consistent guidance, combined with love and affection.

45. Effective child discipline is based on consistent parental _____ concerning acceptable behaviour.

46. Good discipline tends to emphasize child _____ techniques (especially communication), rather than power _____ or withdrawal of love.

47. Management techniques tend to produce the highest levels of _____ in children.

How do children acquire language?

48. Language development proceeds from control of crying, to _____ , then _____ , the use of single words, and then to _____ speech (two-word sentences).

49. The patterns of early speech suggest a biological _____ to acquire language.

50. _____ (psychologists who study language) believe that innate language predispositions are augmented by learning.

51. _____ communication between parent and child involves shared rhythms, non-verbal signals, and _____ -taking.

52. Parents help children learn language by using distinctive caretaker speech or _____ .

How do children learn to think?

53. The intellects of children are less _____ than those of adults. Jean Piaget theorized that cognitive growth occurs through a combination of _____ and accommodation.

54. Piaget also held that children go through a fixed series of _____ stages.

55. The stages are _____ (0–2), _____ (2–7), concrete operational (7–11), and formal operations (11–adult).

56. _____ theorists dispute the idea that cognitive development occurs in stages. Recent studies suggest infants are capable of levels of _____ beyond that observed by Piaget.

57. Young children don't seem to understand that the _____ of other people contain different information, beliefs, and thoughts than theirs do. In other words, they have a very simplified _____ of _____ .

58. According to the _____ theory of Russian scholar Lev _____ , a child's interactions with others are most likely to aid cognitive development if they they take place within the child's zone of _____ development.

59. Adults help children learn how to think by _____ , or supporting, their attempts to solve problems or discover principles.

60. During their collaborations with others, children learn important _____ beliefs and values.

What are the typical tasks and dilemmas that confront people through the life span?

61. Psychologists are interested in developmental _____ , or prominent landmarks in personal development.

62. According to Erik _____ , each life stage provokes a specific _____ dilemma.

63. During childhood these are _____ versus mistrust, _____ versus shame and doubt, initiative versus guilt, and _____ versus inferiority.

64. In adolescence, _____ versus _____ confusion is the principal dilemma.

65. In young adulthood we face the dilemma of _____ versus isolation. Later, _____ versus stagnation becomes prominent.

66. Old age is a time when the dilemma of _____ versus despair must be faced.

67. In addition, each life stage requires successful mastery of certain developmental _____ (personal changes required for optimal development).

What is the most effective way to discipline a child?

68. Responsibility, mutual respect, _____ , love, _____ , and clear communication are features of effective parenting.

69. Much misbehaviour can be managed by use of I-messages and by applying natural and _____ _____ to children's behaviour.

Mastery Test

1. The universal patterns of the human growth sequence can be attributed to
   a. recessive genes
   b. environment
   c. polygenic imprinting
   d. heredity

2. Exaggerated or musical voice inflections are characteristic of
   a. prelanguage turn-taking
   b. parentese
   c. telegraphic speech
   d. prompting and expansion

3. The emotion most clearly expressed by newborn infants is
   a. joy
   b. fear
   c. anger
   d. excitement

4. Explaining things abstractly or symbolically to a child becomes most effective during which stage of cognitive development?
   a. post-conventional
   b. formal operations
   c. preoperational
   d. post-intuitive

5. An infant startled by a loud noise will typically display
   a. a Moro reflex
   b. a rooting reflex
   c. a Meltzoff reflex
   d. an imprinting reflex

6. If one identical twin has a Y chromosome, the other must have a
   a. recessive chromosome
   b. sex-linked trait
   c. dominant chromosome
   d. Y chromosome

7. Piaget's ideas about stages and the cognitive abilities of infants are challenged by infants' reactions to
   a. hypothetical possibilities
   b. impossible events
   c. turn-taking
   d. separation anxiety

8. The type of play that is observed first in most children is called
   a. selective play
   b. secure play
   c. solitary play
   d. social play

9. The largest percentage of children display what type of temperament?
   a. easy
   b. difficult
   c. slow-to-warm-up
   d. generic

10. Which of the following is a congenital problem?
    a. FAS
    b. sickle-cell anemia
    c. hemophilia
    d. muscular dystrophy

11. A child might begin to question the idea that Santa Claus's sack could carry millions of toys when the child has grasped the concept of
    a. assimilation
    b. egocentricism
    c. conservation
    d. reversibility of permanence

12. In most areas of development, heredity and environment are
    a. independent
    b. interacting
    c. conflicting
    d. responsible for temperament

13. According to Erikson, developing a sense of integrity is a special challenge in
    a. adolescence
    b. young adulthood
    c. middle adulthood
    d. late adulthood

14. According to Erikson, the first dilemma a newborn infant must resolve is
    a. independence versus dependence
    b. initiative versus guilt
    c. trust versus mistrust
    d. attachment versus confusion

15. By definition, a trait that is controlled by a dominant gene cannot be
    a. eugenic
    b. hereditary
    c. carried by DNA
    d. polygenic

16. _____ development proceeds head-down and centre-outward.
    a. Cognitive
    b. Motor
    c. Prelanguage
    d. Preoperational

17. You could test for _____ by videotaping a child and then letting the child see the video on television.
    a. social referencing
    b. self-awareness
    c. the quality of attachment
    d. the degree of readiness

18. After age two, infants become much more interested in
    a. bonding
    b. non-verbal communication
    c. familiar voices
    d. unfamiliar faces

19. According to Piaget, one of the major developments during the sensorimotor stage is emergence of the concept of
    a. assimilation
    b. accommodation
    c. object permanence
    d. transformation

20. Poverty is to deprivation as early childhood stimulation is to
    a. imprinting
    b. enrichment
    c. responsiveness
    d. assimilation

21. Which principle is most relevant to the timing of toilet training?
    a. readiness
    b. critical periods
    c. non-verbal signals
    d. assimilation

22. High self-esteem is most often a product of what style of child discipline?
    a. power assertion
    b. child management
    c. withdrawal of love
    d. the natural consequences method

23. Consonants first enter a child's language when the child begins
    a. babbling
    b. cooing
    c. the single-word stage
    d. turn-taking

24. Physically arousing play is typically an element of
    a. the zoo-keeper mother's caregiving style
    b. paternal influences
    c. proactive maternal involvement
    d. secure attachment

25. Insecure attachment is revealed by
    a. separation anxiety
    b. seeking to be near the mother after separation
    c. turning away from the mother after separation
    d. social referencing

26. A healthy balance between the rights of parents and their children is characteristic of
    a. authoritarian parenting
    b. permissive parenting
    c. authoritative parenting
    d. consistent parenting

27. Studies of infant imitation
    a. are conducted in a looking chamber
    b. confirm that infants mimic adult facial gestures
    c. show that self-awareness precedes imitation
    d. are used to assess the quality of infant attachment

28. Threatening, accusing, bossing, and lecturing children is most characteristic of
    a. PET
    b. you-messages
    c. applying natural consequences
    d. management techniques

29. Three-year-old Sheila is unable to fully understand what other people think and feel, because at her age she has a very limited
    a. attachment to others
    b. theory of mind
    c. sensorimotor capacity
    d. zone of proximal development

30. According to Vygotsky, children learn important cultural beliefs and values when adults provide _____ to help them gain new ideas and skills.
    a. scaffolding
    b. proactive nurturance
    c. imprinting stimuli
    d. parentese

31. One thing that all forms of effective child discipline have in common is that they
    a. are consistent
    b. make use of punishment
    c. involve temporary withdrawal of love
    d. emphasizes you-messages

32. This Canadian psychologist became one of the most influential developmental psychologists due to her work on parent and child attachment.
    a. Jean Piaget
    b. Noam Chomsky
    c. Mary Ainsworth
    d. Kristin Nantais

33. You are looking for day care for your two-year-old son. What day care option should you immediately scratch off your list?
    a. A private home care where one woman takes care of four children and offers stimulating activities.
    b. An established day care centre where three trained caregivers take care of 30 children between the ages of three months and three years.
    c. A new day care centre with 6 trained caregivers and 36 children between the ages of 2 and 5 years.
    d. An established day care centre called "The Children's Stockade."

Solutions

Recite and Review

1. behaviour; birth; death
2. nature; nurture
3. DNA; genes
4. dark; fingers; toes; type B
5. Recessive; hair
6. genes; genes
7. physical development
8. personality; difficult
9. external
10. sensitivity
11. environmental
12. birth defects
13. development
14. deprivation
15. normal
16. environment
17. environment
18. heredity
19. neonate; adaptive
20. learn
21. visual; circular
22. familiar faces
23. sequence
24. order
25. muscular; centre
26. skills
27. general
28. innate
29. people
30. Social
31. caregivers
32. separation
33. developmental; infant; mother attachment
34. secure
35. harm
36. social; play
37. needs
38. development
39. mothers
40. involvement; preferences
41. fathers
42. rules; authority
43. guidance
44. effective
45. discipline
46. power; love
47. Management
48. crying; speech
49. biological
50. language; learning
51. signals
52. speech
53. less; intellectual
54. stages
55. concrete; operations
56. stages; Piaget
57. minds; mind
58. cognitive; zone; development
59. supporting
60. beliefs
61. developmental
62. dilemma
63. shame; guilt; inferiority
64. adolescence
65. isolation; stagnation
66. despair
67. developmental
68. respect; communication
69. messages; natural

Connections

1. E
2. J
3. G
4. A
5. B
6. I
7. C
8. D
9. F
10. H
11. E
12. F
13. A
14. B
15. J
16. H
17. C
18. D
19. G
20. I
21. C
22. A
23. J
24. B
25. H
26. D
27. G
28. E
29. F
30. I

Short-Answer Questions

1. Sensitive periods are times of increased sensitivity to environmental influences that occur during development. For example, certain diseases such as German measles will have serious consequences for the fetus if a woman contracts them in early pregnancy, but will have no effect in later pregnancy. Sensitive periods also refer to a period where certain events must happen for normal development to occur.
2. If both parents have a gene for dark eyes and a gene for light eyes, there is a one in four chance that any offspring will have light eyes.
3. When rats are raised in enriched environments, they have larger, heavier brains with a thicker cortex than rats raised in deprived environments. Children whose parents frequently read to them did better in kindergarten and Grade 1 than children whose parents did not read to them.

4. Children raised in complete isolation are usually mute, appear retarded, and suffer emotional damage. Poverty can also have a negative effect on intellectual and emotional development; children who grow up in poor homes are more likely to show hostile and aggressive behaviour.

5. Authoritarian parents demand strict obedience to rigid rules, and children have few rights but many adult responsibilities. Children are taught to accept what the parents say as right and true. Overly permissive parents provide little guidance and few, if any, rules or responsibilities. Children have too much freedom and are not held accountable for their actions. Authoritative parents provide firm and consistent guidance combined with love and affection. The rights of children and parents are balanced. Children are encouraged to act responsibly and to make good decisions.

6. Power assertion (use of physical punishment) is associated with fear or hatred of parents, rebellious behaviour, and low self-esteem. Withdrawing love is associated with children who are well behaved, anxious, insecure, dependent on adults for approval, and who have low self-esteem.

7. Assimilation means using existing mental patterns in new ways (e.g., using a toy car as a hammer to pound on a block) or modifying existing ideas to fit new requirements (e.g., a young child thinks that a dime is worth less than a nickel because it's smaller; older children know that the dime has more value because you can purchase more with it).

8. All feelings are appropriate and can be expressed. Parents can help a child distinguish between feelings and behaviour. Encourage children by recognizing what they've done, being supportive, etc. Using "I-messages" ("I think …," "I feel …," "I would like …") rather than "you-messages" ("You always…," "You never…," "You're such a…").

Final Survey and Review

1. Developmental; progressive
2. heredity; environment
3. deoxyribonucleic; chromosomes
4. hair; extra; type A
5. light; light; O
6. polygenic; recessive
7. growth sequence
8. temperament; easy; slow to warm up
9. Environment
10. critical periods
11. prenatal; drugs; radiation
12. congenital; genetic
13. deprivation
14. Poverty
15. attachment; stimulation
16. enrichment
17. interacting
18. developmental level
19. grasping; sucking; Moro
20. imitate
21. looking chamber; complex
22. human face; unfamiliar
23. Maturation; nervous system
24. rate; universal
25. motor; cephalocaudal; proximodistal
26. readiness
27. excitement; pleasant; unpleasant
28. emotional; months
29. social
30. awareness; relationships
31. attachment
32. anxiety
33. Mary Ainsworth; mother; infant
34. Ainsworth; avoidant; ambivalent
35. High; quality; accelerate
36. cooperative
37. affectional
38. Caregiving styles
39. Maternal; caregiving
40. proactive; temperaments
41. Paternal; playmate
42. Authoritarian
43. permissive
44. Authoritative
45. guidance
46. management; assertion
47. self-esteem
48. cooing; babbling; telegraphic
49. predisposition
50. Psycholinguists
51. Prelanguage; turn
52. parentese
53. abstract; assimilation
54. cognitive
55. sensorimotor; preoperational
56. Learning; thinking
57. minds; theory; mind
58. sociocultural; Vygotsky; proximal
59. scaffolding
60. cultural
61. milestones
62. Erikson; psychosexual
63. trust; autonomy; industry
64. identity; role
65. intimacy; generativity
66. integrity
67. tasks
68. consistency; encouragement
69. logical consequences

Mastery Test

1. D, (p. 72)
2. B, (p. 90)
3. D, (p. 81)
4. B, (p. 94)
5. A, (p. 78)
6. D, (p. 72)

7. B (p. 96)
8. C (p. 85)
9. A (p. 73)
10. A (p. 75)
11. C (p. 93)
12. B (p. 77)
13. D (p. 100)
14. C (p. 98)
15. D (p. 72)

16. B (p. 80)
17. B (p. 82)
18. D (p. 80)
19. C (p. 93)
20. B (p. 76)
21. A (p. 81)
22. B (p. 88)
23. A (p. 89)
24. B (p. 86)

25. C (p. 83)
26. C (p. 86)
27. B (p. 78)
28. B (p. 104)
29. B (p. 94)
30. A (p. 96)
31. A (p. 101)
32. D (p. 83)
33. D (p. 84)

Sensation and Perception

Chapter Overview

Sensory systems collect, select, transduce, analyze, and code information from the environment and send it to the brain.

Vision and visual problems can be partly understood by viewing the eyes as optical systems. However, the visual system also analyzes light stimuli to identify patterns and basic visual features. Colour sensations are explained by the trichromatic theory (in the retina) and the opponent-process theory (for the rest of the visual system).

The inner ear is a sensory mechanism for transducing sound waves in the air into nerve impulses. The frequency and place theories of hearing explain how sound information is coded.

Olfaction is based on receptors that respond to gaseous molecules in the air. The lock-and-key theory and the locations of olfactory receptors activated by different scents explain how various odours are coded. Taste is another chemical sense. A lock-and-key match between dissolved molecules and taste receptors also explains many taste sensations.

The somesthetic, or bodily, senses include the skin senses, the kinesthetic senses, and the vestibular senses.

Our awareness of sensory information is altered by sensory adaptation, selective attention, and sensory gating.

Perception involves organizing sensations into meaningful patterns. Visual perceptions are stabilized by size, shape, and brightness constancies. The most basic perceptual pattern (in vision) is figure-ground organization. Sensations tend to be organized on the basis of nearness, similarity, continuity, closure, contiguity, and common region.

Depth perception depends on accommodation, convergence, retinal disparity, and various pictorial cues. The pictorial cues include linear perspective, relative size, light and shadow, overlap, texture gradients, aerial haze, and relative motion.

Learning, in the form of perceptual habits, influences perceptions. Perceptions are also greatly affected by attention, motives, values, and expectations (perceptual sets).

Because perceptions are reconstructions of events, eyewitness testimony can be unreliable. Perceptual accuracy can be improved by reality testing, dishabituation, actively paying attention, breaking perceptual habits, using broad frames of reference, and being aware of perceptual sets.

Learning Objectives

After reading this chapter, students should be able to:

1. Explain the general functioning of the sensory systems.
2. Describe the structure of the eye. Trace the path of light from the time it enters the eye until it reaches the receptor cells.
3. Distinguish between rods and cones, and identify their characteristics and functions with respect to light, colour, and visual acuity.
4. Describe the trichromatic and opponent-process theories of colour vision.
5. Describe the structure of the ear. Explain how sounds are converted into nerve impulses.
6. Explain how pitch is sensed.
7. Explain smell and taste. Describe how tastes and odours are identified.
8. Describe the somesthetic senses and explain why they are important.
9. Identify the three kinds of perceptual constancy.
10. Explain the Gestalt principles of perceptual organization.
11. Explain the contributions of muscular cues, stereoscopic vision, and pictorial cues to the perception of depth and distance.
12. Show how perceptions may be altered by learning, expectations, and motives.

Practice Quizzes

Recite and Review

In general, how do sensory systems function?
Recite and Review: Pages 110–112

1. Sensory organs transduce physical energies into _____ impulses.
2. The senses act as _____ reduction systems that select, _____ , and filter sensory information.
3. A good example of sensory analysis is the identification of basic _____ features in a stimulus pattern.
4. In fact, many sensory systems act as feature _____ .
5. Phosphenes and visual pop-out are examples of feature detection and _____ coding in action.
6. Sensory response can be partially understood in terms of _____ localization in the brain. That is, the area of the brain _____ ultimately determines which type of sensory experience we have.

How is vision accomplished?
Recite and Review: Pages 116–120

7. The _____ spectrum consists of electromagnetic radiation in a narrow range.

8. The electromagnetic spectrum ranges from violet, with a _____ of 400 nanometres, to red with a _____ of 700 nanometres.

9. Hue refers to a colour's name, which corresponds to its _____ . Saturated or "pure" colours come from a _____ band of wavelengths. Brightness corresponds to the amplitude of light waves.

10. The eye is in some ways like a camera. At its back lies an array of photoreceptors, called _____ and _____ , that make up a light-sensitive layer called the retina.

11. Vision is focused by the _____ of the cornea and lens and by changes in the _____ of the lens, called accommodation.

12. Four common visual defects, correctable with glasses, are myopia (_____), hyperopia (farsightedness), presbyopia (loss of _____), and astigmatism (in which portions of vision are out of focus).

13. In the retina, the _____ specialize in night vision, black and white reception, and motion detection.

14. The _____ , found exclusively in the fovea and otherwise toward the middle of the eye, specialize in _____ vision, acuity (perception of fine detail), and daylight vision.

15. The _____ supply much of our peripheral vision. Loss of peripheral vision is called tunnel vision.

16. The hypothesis that two separate visual systems exist, one for movement (_____ - _____ - _____) and one to perceive (_____ - _____ - _____), is supported by a specific case study (the Scottish woman who suffered from carbon monoxide intoxication).

17. In the _____ , colour vision is explained by the trichromatic theory. The theory says that three types of _____ exist, each most sensitive to either red, green, or blue.

18. Three types of light-sensitive visual pigments are found in the _____ ; each pigment is most sensitive to either red, green, or blue light.

19. Beyond the retina, the visual system analyzes colours into _____ - _____ messages. According to the opponent-process theory, colour information can be coded as either red or green, yellow or blue, and _____ _____ _____ messages.

20. _____ colour blindness is rare, but 8 percent of males and 1 percent of females are red-green colour blind or colour weak.

21. The Ishihara test is used to detect _____ _____ .

22. Dark adaptation, an _____ in sensitivity to light, is caused by increased concentrations of visual pigments in the _____ and the _____ .

23. Most dark adaptation is the result of increased rhodopsin concentrations in the _____ .

What are the mechanisms of hearing?
Recite and Review: Pages 120–125

24. Sound waves are the stimulus for hearing. Sound travels as waves of compression (_____) and rarefaction (_____) in the air.

25. The _____ of a sound corresponds to the frequency of sound waves. Loudness corresponds to the amplitude (_____) of sound waves.

26. Sound waves are transduced by the _____ , auditory ossicles, oval window, cochlea, and ultimately, the _____ cells in the organ of Corti.

27. The _____ theory says that the _____ of nerve impulses in the auditory nerves matches the frequency of incoming sounds (up to 4000 hertz).

28. Place theory says that _____ tones register near the base of the cochlea and _____ tones near its tip.

29. Three basic types of deafness are _____ deafness, conduction deafness, and stimulation deafness.

30. Conduction deafness can often be overcome with a hearing aid. _____ deafness can sometimes be alleviated by cochlear implants.

31. Stimulation deafness can be prevented by avoiding excessive exposure to _____ sounds. Sounds above 120 decibels pose an immediate danger to hearing. Two warning signs of stimulation deafness are temporary threshold _____ and tinnitus.

How do the chemical senses operate?

Recite and Review: Pages 125–127

32. Olfaction (_____) and gustation (_____) are chemical senses responsive to airborne or liquefied molecules.

33. The lock-and-key theory partially explains smell. In addition, the _____ of the olfactory receptors in the nose helps identify various scents.

34. The top outside edges of the tongue are responsive to sweet, salty, sour, and _____ tastes. It is suspected that a fifth taste quality called umami also exists.

35. Taste also appears to be based in part on lock-and-key _____ of molecule shapes.

What are the somesthetic senses and why are they important?

Recite and Review: Pages 128–130

36. The somesthetic senses include the _____ senses, vestibular senses, and kinesthetic senses (receptors that detect muscle and joint positioning).

37. The skin senses include touch, _____ , pain, cold, and warmth. Sensitivity to each is related to the _____ of receptors found in an area of skin.

38. Distinctions can be made between warning system pain, and _____ system pain.

39. Pain can be reduced by _____ anxiety and redirecting attention to stimuli other than the pain stimulus.

40. Feeling that you have control over a stimulus tends to _____ the amount of pain you experience.

41. Various forms of motion sickness are related to messages received from the vestibular system, which senses gravity and _____ movement.

42. The otolith organs detect the pull of _____ and rapid head movements.

43. The movement of _____ within the semicircular canals, and the movement of the _____ within each ampulla, detects head movement and positioning.

44. According to sensory conflict theory, motion sickness is caused by a _____ of visual, kinesthetic, and vestibular sensations. Motion sickness can be avoided by minimizing sensory conflict.

Why are we more aware of some sensations than others?

Recite and Review: Pages 130–133

45. Incoming sensations are affected by sensory adaptation (a _____ in the number of nerve impulses sent).

46. Selective attention (selection and diversion of messages in the brain) and sensory _____ (blocking or alteration of messages flowing toward the brain) also alter sensations.

47. Selective gating of pain messages apparently takes place in the _____ _____ . Gate control theory proposes an explanation for many pain phenomena.

How do perceptual constancies affect our perceptions?

Recite and Review: Pages 133–135

48. In vision, the retinal _____ changes from moment to moment, but the external world appears stable and undistorted because of _____ constancies.

49. In size and shape _____ , the perceived sizes and shapes of objects remain the same even though their retinal images change size and shape. The apparent brightness of objects remains stable (a property called brightness constancy) because each reflects a _____ proportion of light.

50. Perceptual constancies are partly native (_____) and partly empirical (_____).

What basic principles do we use to group sensations into meaningful patterns?

Recite and Review: Pages 135–137

51. The most basic organization of sensations is a division into figure and ground (_____ and _____). Reversible figures, however, allow figure-ground organization to be reversed.

52. A number of factors, identified by the Gestalt psychologists, contribute to the _____ of sensations. These are nearness, similarity, continuity, closure, contiguity, _____ region, and combinations of the preceding.

53. Stimuli near one another tend to be perceptually _____ together. So, too, do stimuli that are similar in _____ . Continuity refers to the fact that perceptions tend to be organized as simple, uninterrupted patterns.

54. Closure is the tendency to _____ a broken or incomplete pattern. Contiguity refers to nearness in _____ and space. Stimuli that fall in a defined area, or common region, also tend to be grouped together.

55. A perceptual organization may be thought of as an _____ held until evidence contradicts it. Camouflage patterns disrupt perceptual _____ , especially figure-ground perceptions.

56. Perceptual organization shifts for ambiguous _____ , which may have more than one interpretation. An example is Necker's _____ . Impossible figures resist stable organization altogether.

How is it possible to see depth and judge distance?

Recite and Review: Pages 138–143

57. _____ perception is the ability to perceive three-dimensional space and judge distances.

58. Depth perception is present in basic form soon after _____ as shown by testing with the visual cliff and other methods. As soon as infants become active _____ they refuse to cross the visual cliff.

59. Depth perception depends on the muscular cues of accommodation (bending of the _____) and convergence (inward movement of the _____).

60. A number of pictorial _____ , which will work in _____ paintings, drawings, and photographs, also underlie normal depth perception.

61. Some pictorial cues are linear perspective (the apparent convergence of _____ _____), relative size (more distant objects appear _____), height in the _____ plane, light and shadow (shadings of light), and overlap or interposition (one object overlaps another).

62. Additional pictorial cues include texture gradients (textures become _____ in the distance), aerial haze (loss of colour and detail at large distances), and relative _____ or _____ parallax (differences in the apparent movement of objects when a viewer is moving).

63. All the pictorial cues are monocular depth cues (only _____ _____ is needed to make use of them).

64. The moon illusion refers to the fact that the moon appears _____ near the horizon than it does when overhead.

65. The moon illusion appears to be explained by the apparent _____ hypothesis, which emphasizes the greater number of depth cues present when the moon is on the _____ .

How is perception altered by learning, expectations, and motives?

Recite and Review: Pages 144–150

66. Perception is the process of assembling sensations into _____ that provide a usable mental _____ of the world.

67. Organizing and interpreting sensations is greatly influenced by learned perceptual _____ . An example is the Ames room, which looks rectangular but is actually distorted so that objects in the room appear to change _____ .

68. Sensitivity to perceptual _____ is also partly learned. Studies of inverted vision show that even the most basic organization is subject to a degree of change.

69. Illusions are often related to perceptual _____ . One of the most familiar of all illusions, the Müller-Lyer illusion, seems to be related to perceptual learning based on experience with box-shaped _____ and rooms.

70. Linear perspective and _____ - _____ invariance relationships contribute to the Müller-Lyer illusion.

71. Personal motives and _____ _____ stimuli often alter perceptions by changing the evaluation of what is seen or by altering attention to specific details.

72. Perceptions may be based on _____ - _____ or bottom-up processing of information.

73. In bottom-up processing, perceptions begin with the organization of low-level _____ . In top-down processing, previous knowledge is used to rapidly _____ sensory information.

74. Attention, prior experience, suggestion, and motives combine in various ways to create perceptual sets, or _____ . A perceptual set is a readiness to perceive in a particular way, induced by strong expectations.

How can I learn to perceive events more accurately?

Recite and Review: Psychology in Action

75. Perceptions are a reconstruction of events. This is one reason eyewitness testimony is surprisingly _____ .

76. In many crimes, eyewitness accuracy is further damaged by weapon _____ . Similar factors, such as observer stress, brief exposure times, cross-racial inaccuracies, and the wording of questions can _____ eyewitness accuracy.

77. An underlying difficulty of perceptual accuracy comes from the innate ability of our _____ system to habituate (_____ _____).

78. Perceptual accuracy is enhanced by reality _____ , dishabituation, and conscious efforts to pay _____ .

79. It is also valuable to break perceptual habits, to _____ frames of reference, to beware of perceptual sets, and to be aware of the ways in which motives and emotions influence perceptions.

Connections

1. _____ ciliary muscle
2. _____ iris
3. _____ cornea
4. _____ blind spot
5. _____ lens
6. _____ fovea
7. _____ retinal veins
8. _____ optic nerve
9. _____ aqueous humour
10. _____ pupil
11. _____ retina

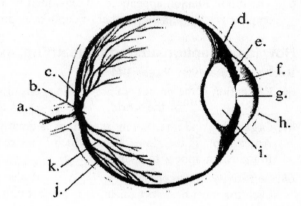

12. _____ vestibular system
13. _____ cochlea
14. _____ round window
15. _____ auditory canal
16. _____ stapes
17. _____ auditory nerve
18. _____ incus
19. _____ oval window
20. _____ tympanic membrane
21. _____ malleus

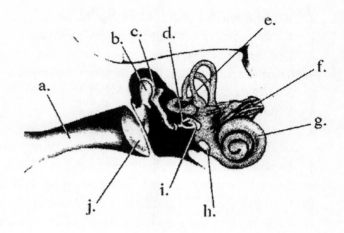

22. _____ texture gradients
23. _____ stereoscopic vision
24. _____ convergence
25. _____ continuity
26. _____ light and shadow
27. _____ common region
28. _____ relative size
29. _____ closure
30. _____ overlap
31. _____ retinal disparity
32. _____ linear perspective
33. _____ nearness
34. _____ similarity

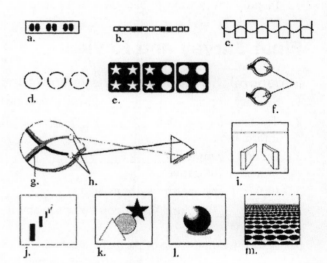

35. _____ reversible figure
36. _____ visual cliff
37. _____ binocular muscle cue
38. _____ mismatch
39. _____ Ponzo illusion
40. _____ Zulus
41. _____ top-down
42. _____ perceptual awareness
43. _____ Zener card
44. _____ ESP capacity

a. convergence
b. stereoscopic vision
c. run of luck
d. moon illusion
e. clairvoyance test
f. diminished Müller-Lyer illusion
g. infant depth perception
h. figure-ground
i. reality testing
j. perceptual expectancy

Short-Answer Questions

1. Explain how the senses act as data reduction systems.
2. Explain sensory coding and sensory localization.
3. Distinguish between the terms *sensation* and *perception*.
4. Trace the path of light from the time it enters the eye until it reaches the receptor cells.
5. Briefly describe the process of dark adaptation.
6. Differentiate between taste and flavour.
7. Explain why a blindfolded person with a bad cold would not be able to tell the difference between a bite of apple, a bite of raw potato, and a bite of raw onion.
8. Explain why many sensory events never reach conscious awareness.
9. Discuss the role of sensory gating in the perception of pain.
10. Distinguish between illusions and hallucinations.
11. Explain why most eyewitness testimony is inaccurate.
12. Identify seven ways to become a more accurate "eyewitness" to life.

Final Survey and Review

In general, how do sensory systems function?

1. Sensory organs _____ physical energies into nerve impulses.
2. The senses act as data _____ systems that select, analyze, and _____ sensory information.
3. A good example of _____ _____ is the identification of basic perceptual features in a stimulus pattern.
4. In fact, many sensory systems act as _____ detectors.
5. _____ and visual pop-out are examples of feature detection and sensory _____ in action.
6. Sensory response can be partially understood in terms of sensory _____ in the brain. That is, the _____ of the brain activated ultimately determines which type of sensory experience we have.

How is vision accomplished?

7. The visible spectrum consists of _____ radiation in a narrow range.
8. The visible spectrum ranges from violet, with a wavelength of _____ _____ , to red with a wavelength of _____ _____ .
9. _____ refers to a colour's name, which corresponds to its wavelength. Saturated or "pure" colours come from a narrow band of wavelengths. Brightness corresponds to the _____ of light waves.
10. The eye is in some ways like a camera. At its back lies an array of _____ , called rods and cones, that make up a light-sensitive layer called the _____ .
11. Vision is focused by the shape of the _____ and lens and by changes in the shape of the lens, called _____ .

12. Four common visual defects, correctable with glasses, are _____ (nearsightedness), hyperopia (farsightedness), presbyopia (loss of accommodation), and _____ (in which portions of vision are out of focus).

13. In the retina, the rods specialize in night vision, black and white reception, and _____ detection.

14. The cones, found exclusively in the _____ and otherwise toward the middle of the eye, specialize in colour vision, _____ (perception of fine detail), and daylight vision.

15. The rods supply much of our _____ vision. Loss of _____ vision is called tunnel vision.

16. The hypothesis that two separate _____ systems exist, one for movement (_____ - _____ - _____) and one to perceive (_____ - _____ - _____), is supported by a specific _____ study (the Scottish woman who suffered from carbon monoxide intoxication).

17. In the retina, colour vision is explained by the _____ theory. The theory says that three types of cones exist, each most sensitive to either red, green, or blue.

18. Three types of light-sensitive visual _____ are found in the cones; each is most sensitive to either red, green, or blue light.

19. Beyond the retina, the visual system analyzes colours into either-or messages. According to the _____ - _____ theory, colour information can be coded as either _____ _____ _____ , yellow, or blue, and black or white messages.

20. Total colour blindness is rare, but 8 percent of males and 1 percent of females are _____ - _____ colour blind or colour weak.

21. The _____ test is used to detect colour blindness.

22. Dark adaptation, an increase in sensitivity to light, is caused by increased concentrations of _____ _____ in the rods and the cones.

23. Most dark adaptation is the result of increased _____ concentrations in the rods.

What are the mechanisms of hearing?

24. Sound waves are the stimulus for hearing. Sound travels as waves of _____ (peaks) and _____ (valleys) in the air.

25. The pitch of a sound corresponds to the _____ of sound waves. Loudness corresponds to the _____ (height) of sound waves.

26. Sound waves are transduced by the eardrum, auditory _____ , oval window, cochlea, and ultimately, the hair cells in the organ of _____ .

27. The frequency theory says that the frequency of nerve impulses in the _____ _____ matches the frequency of incoming sounds (up to 4000 hertz).

28. Place theory says that high tones register near the _____ of the cochlea and low tones near its _____ .

29. Three basic types of deafness are nerve deafness, conduction deafness, and _____ deafness.

30. Conduction deafness can often be overcome with a hearing aid. Nerve deafness can sometimes be alleviated by _____ implants.

31. Stimulation deafness can be prevented by avoiding excessive exposure to loud sounds. Sounds above _____ _____ pose an immediate danger to hearing.

How do the chemical senses operate?

32. _____ and _____ are chemical senses responsive to airborne or liquefied molecules.

33. The _____ - _____ - _____ theory partially explains smell. In addition, the location of the olfactory receptors in the nose helps identify various scents.

34. The top outside edges of the tongue are responsive to _____ , _____ , _____ , and bitter tastes. It is suspected that a fifth taste quality called _____ also exists.

35. Taste also appears to be based in part on lock-and-key coding of _____ shapes.

What are the somesthetic senses and why are they important?

36. The somesthetic senses include the skin senses, vestibular senses, and _____ senses.

37. The skin senses include light touch, pressure, _____ , cold, and warmth. Sensitivity to each is related to the number of _____ found in an area of skin.

38. Distinctions can be made between _____ system pain, and _____ system pain.

39. Pain can be reduced by lowering anxiety and redirecting _____ to stimuli other than the pain stimulus.

40. Feeling that you have _____ over a stimulus tends to reduce the amount of pain you experience.

41. Various forms of motion sickness are related to messages received from the _____ system, which senses gravity and head movement.

42. The _____ organs detect the pull of gravity and rapid head movements.

43. The movement of fluid within the _____ canals, and the movement of the crista within each _____ , detects head movement and positioning.

44. According to sensory conflict theory, motion sickness is caused by a mismatch of _____ , _____ , and vestibular sensations. Motion sickness can be avoided by minimizing _____ _____ .

Why are we more aware of some sensations than others?

45. Incoming sensations are affected by sensory _____ (a decrease in the number of nerve impulses sent).

46. Selective _____ (selection and diversion of messages in the brain) and sensory gating (blocking or alteration of messages flowing toward the brain) also alter sensations.

47. Selective gating of pain messages apparently takes place in the spinal cord. _____ _____ theory proposes an explanation for many pain phenomena.

How do perceptual constancies affect our perceptions?

48. In vision, the _____ image changes from moment to moment, but the external world appears stable and undistorted because of perceptual _____ .

49. In size and shape constancy, the perceived sizes and shapes of objects remain the same even though their retinal images change size and shape. The apparent _____ of objects remains stable (a property called brightness constancy) because each reflects a constant _____ of _____ .

50. Perceptual constancies are partly _____ and partly _____ .

What basic principles do we use to group sensations into meaningful patterns?

51. The most basic organization of sensations is a division into _____ and _____ (object and background).

52. A number of factors, identified by the _____ psychologists, contribute to the organization of sensations. These are _____ , similarity, continuity, _____ , contiguity, common region, and combinations of the preceding.

53. Stimuli near one another tend to be perceptually grouped together. So, too, do stimuli that are similar in appearance. _____ refers to the fact that perceptions tend to be organized as simple, uninterrupted patterns.

54. _____ refers to nearness in time and space. Stimuli that fall in a defined area, or common region, also tend to be grouped together.

55. A perceptual organization may be thought of as an hypothesis held until evidence contradicts it. _____ patterns disrupt perceptual organization, especially figure-ground perceptions.

56. Perceptual organization shifts for _____ stimuli, which may have more than one interpretation. An example is _____ cube. Impossible _____ resist stable organization altogether.

How is it possible to see depth and judge distance?

57. Depth perception is the ability to perceive _____ - _____ space and judge distances.

58. Depth perception is present in basic form soon after birth as shown by testing with the _____ _____ and other methods. As soon as infants become active crawlers they refuse to cross the deep side of the _____ _____ .

59. Depth perception depends on the muscular cues of _____ (bending of the lens) and _____ (inward movement of the eyes).

60. A number of _____ cues, which will work in flat paintings, drawings, and photographs, also underlie normal depth perception.

61. Some of these cues are _____ _____ (the apparent convergence of parallel lines), relative size (more distant objects appear smaller), height in the picture plane, light and shadow (shadings of light), and overlap or _____ (one object overlaps another).

62. Additional pictorial cues include texture _____ (textures become finer in the distance), aerial haze (loss of colour and detail at large distances), and relative motion or motion _____ (differences in the apparent movement of objects when a viewer is moving).

63. All the pictorial cues are _____ depth cues (only one eye is needed to make use of them).

64. The moon illusion refers to the fact that the moon appears larger near the _____ .

65. The moon illusion appears to be explained by the _____ _____ hypothesis, which emphasizes the greater number of _____ _____ present when the moon is on the horizon.

How is perception altered by learning, expectations, and motives?

66. Perception is the process of assembling _____ into patterns that provide a usable _____ _____ of the world.

67. Organizing and interpreting sensations is greatly influenced by learned _____ _____ .
An example is the _____ room, which looks rectangular but is actually distorted so that objects in the room appear to change size.

68. Sensitivity to perceptual features is also partly learned. Studies of _____ vision show that even the most basic organization is subject to a degree of change.

69. Illusions are often related to perceptual habits. One of the most familiar of all illusions, the _____ - _____ illusion, involves two equal-length lines tipped with arrowheads and V's. This illusion seems to be related to perceptual learning based on experience with box-shaped buildings and rooms.

70. Linear perspective and size-distance _____ contribute to the Müller-Lyer illusion.

71. Personal _____ and emotionally significant stimuli often alter perceptions by changing the evaluation of what is seen or by altering attention to specific details.

72. Perceptions may be based on top-down or bottom-up _____ of information.

73. _____ - _____ perceptions begin with the organization of low-level features. In _____ - _____ processing, previous knowledge is used to rapidly organize sensory information.

74. Attention, prior experience, suggestion, and motives combine in various ways to create _____ _____ , or expectancies. A _____ _____ is a readiness to perceive in a particular way, induced by strong expectations.

How can I learn to perceive events more accurately?

75. Perception is an active _____ of events. This is one reason eyewitness testimony is surprisingly inaccurate.

76. In many crimes, eyewitness accuracy is further damaged by _____ focus. Similar factors, such as _____ , brief exposure times, cross-racial inaccuracies, and the wording of questions can lower eyewitness accuracy.

77. An underlying difficulty of perceptual accuracy comes from the innate ability of our perceptual system to _____ (_____ _____).

78. Perceptual accuracy is enhanced by reality testing, _____ , and conscious efforts to pay attention.

79. It is also valuable to break _____ _____ , to broaden frames of reference, to beware of perceptual sets, and to be aware of the ways in which motives and emotions influence perceptions.

Mastery Test

1. Sensory conflict theory attributes motion sickness to mismatches between what three systems?
   a. olfaction, kinesthesis, and audition
   b. vision, kinesthesis, and the vestibular system
   c. kinesthesis, audition, and the somesthetic system
   d. vision, gustation, and the skin senses

2. Which of the following types of colour blindness is most common?
   a. yellow-blue, male
   b. yellow-blue, female
   c. red-green, female
   d. red-green, male

3. Which of the following does not belong with the others?
   a. Pacinian corpuscle
   b. Merkle's disk
   c. organ of Corti
   d. free nerve endings

4. Which theory of colour vision best explains the fact that we do not see yellowish blue?
   a. trichromatic
   b. chromatic gating
   c. Ishihara hypothesis
   d. opponent process

5. Dark adaptation is closely related to concentrations of _____ in the _____.
   a. retinal, aqueous humour
   b. photopsin, cones
   c. rhodopsin, rods
   d. photons, optic nerve

6. Sensory analysis tends to extract perceptual _____ from stimulus patterns.
   a. thresholds
   b. features
   c. transducers
   d. amplitudes

7. The painkilling effects of acupuncture are partly explained by _____ theory.
   a. lock-and-key
   b. gate control
   c. opponent-process
   d. frequency

8. According to the _____ theory of hearing, low tones cause the greatest movement near the _____ of the cochlea.
   a. place, outer tip
   b. frequency, outer tip
   c. place, base
   d. frequency, base

9. Which of the following best represents the concept of a transducer?
   a. Translating English into Spanish.
   b. Copying a computer file from one floppy disk to another.
   c. Speaking into a telephone receiver.
   d. Turning water into ice.

10. Rods and cones are to vision as _____ are to hearing.
    a. auditory ossicles
    b. vibrations
    c. pinnas
    d. hair cells

11. You lose the ability to smell floral odours. This is called _____ and it is compatible with the _____ theory of olfaction.
    a. anosmia, lock-and-key
    b. anhedonia, place
    c. tinnitus, gate-control
    d. sensory adaptation, molecular

12. The main problem with current artificial vision systems is
    a. the retina's lack of an absolute threshold
    b. the danger of damaging the eyes while producing phosphenes
    c. their inability to transduce letters
    d. the rejection of implanted electrodes

13. Which two dimensions of colour are related to the wavelength of electromagnetic energy?
    a. hue and saturation
    b. saturation and brightness
    c. brightness and hue
    d. brightness and amplitude

14. The existence of the blind spot is explained by a lack of
    a. rhodopsin
    b. peripheral vision
    c. photoreceptors
    d. activity in the fovea

15. In vision, a loss of accommodation is most associated with aging of the
    a. iris
    b. fovea
    c. lens
    d. cornea

16. Visual acuity and colour vision are provided by the _____ found in large numbers in the _____ of the eye.
    a. cones, fovea
    b. cones, periphery
    c. rods, fovea
    d. rods, periphery

17. The Ames room creates a conflict between
    a. horizontal features and vertical features
    b. attention and habituation
    c. top-down and bottom-up processing
    d. shape constancy and size constancy

18. Weapon focus tends to lower eyewitness accuracy because it affects
    a. selective attention
    b. the adaptation level
    c. perceptions of contiguity
    d. dishabituation

19. The fact that Canadian tourists in London tend to look in the wrong direction before stepping into crosswalks is based on
    a. sensory localization
    b. perceptual habits
    c. sensory gating
    d. unconscious transference

20. Size constancy
    a. emerges at about four months of age
    b. is affected by experience with seeing objects of various sizes
    c. requires that objects be illuminated by light of the same intensity
    d. all of the preceding

21. Which of the following cues would be of greatest help to a person trying to thread a needle?
    a. light and shadow
    b. texture gradients
    c. linear perspective
    d. overlap

22. Size-distance invariances contribute to which of the following?
    a. Müller-Lyer illusion
    b. the stroboscopic illusion
    c. perceptual hallucinations
    d. changes in perceptual sets

23. The visual cliff is used primarily to test infant
    a. size constancy
    b. figure-ground perception
    c. depth perception
    d. adaptation to spatial distortions

24. Which of the following organizational principles is based on nearness in time and space?
    a. continuity
    b. closure
    c. contiguity
    d. size constancy

25. Which of the following is both a muscular and a monocular depth cue?
    a. convergence
    b. relative motion
    c. aerial perspective
    d. accommodation

26. A previously blind person has just had her sight restored. Which of the following perceptual experiences is she most likely to have?
    a. perceptual set
    b. size constancy
    c. linear perspective
    d. figure-ground

27. An artist manages to portray a face with just a few unconnected lines. Apparently the artist has capitalized on
    a. closure
    b. contiguity
    c. the reversible figure effect
    d. the principle of camouflage

28. The most basic source of stereoscopic vision is
    a. accommodation
    b. retinal disparity
    c. convergence
    d. stroboscopic motion

29. Necker's cube is a good example of
    a. an ambiguous stimulus
    b. an impossible figure
    c. camouflage
    d. a binocular depth cue

30. Which of the following is a binocular depth cue?
    a. accommodation
    b. convergence
    c. linear perspective
    d. motion parallax

31. Ambiguous stimuli allow us to hold more than one perceptual
    a. gradient
    b. parallax
    c. constancy
    d. hypothesis

32. Increased perceptual awareness is especially associated with
    a. dishabituation
    b. unconscious transference
    c. high levels of stress
    d. stimulus repetition without variation

33. According to researchers, which is the first colour that infants are able to perceive?
    a. red
    b. green
    c. yellow
    d. blue

34. If you lost your sense of touch you would probably (as shown by the case study of Ginette Lizotte of Quebec)
    a. not be able to walk because of lack of balance.
    b. be incapable of using any of your senses since they are all linked.
    c. not know how or whether you are moving without seeing where your body is.
    d. have constant physical pain.

Solutions

Recite and Review

1. nerve
2. data; analyze
3. perceptual
4. detectors
5. sensory
6. sensory; activated
7. visible
8. wavelength; wavelength
9. wavelength; narrow
10. rods; cones
11. shape; shape
12. nearsightedness; accommodation
13. rods
14. cones; colour
15. rods
16. vision for action; vision for perception
17. retina; cones
18. cones
19. either or; black or white
20. Total
21. colour blindness
22. increase; rods; cones
23. rods
24. peaks; valleys
25. pitch; height
26. eardrum; hair
27. frequency; frequency
28. high; low
29. nerve
30. Nerve
31. loud; shifts
32. smell; taste
33. location
34. bitter
35. coding
36. skin
37. pressure; number
38. reminding
39. lowering
40. reduce
41. head
42. gravity
43. fluid; crista
44. mismatch
45. reduction
46. gating
47. spinal cord
48. image; perceptual
49. constancy; constant
50. inborn; learned
51. object; background
52. organization; common
53. grouped; appearance
54. complete; time
55. hypothesis; organization
56. stimuli; cube
57. Depth
58. birth; crawlers
59. lens; eyes
60. cues; flat
61. parallel lines; smaller; picture
62. finer; motion; motion
63. one eye
64. larger
65. distance; horizon
66. patterns; model
67. habits; size
68. features
69. habits; buildings
70. size distance
71. emotionally significant
72. top down
73. features; organize
74. expectancies
75. inaccurate
76. focus; lower
77. perceptual; respond less
78. testing; attention
79. broaden

Connections

1. D
2. F
3. H
4. B
5. I
6. C
7. K
8. A
9. E
10. G
11. J
12. E
13. G
14. H
15. A
16. D
17. F
18. C
19. I
20. J
21. B
22. M
23. G
24. F
25. C
26. L
27. E
28. J
29. D
30. K
31. H
32. I
33. A
34. B
35. H
36. G
37. A
38. B
39. D
40. F
41. J
42. I
43. E
44. C

Short-Answer Questions

1. The senses select, analyze, and filter incoming sensory information to identify the most important data. As transducers,

they convert energy from the physical world into energy that the nervous system can process, understand, and interpret. The senses analyze incoming information to identify basic stimulus patterns (known as perceptual features). Examples of perceptual features include lines, shapes, edges, spots, colours, and patterns. The senses also act as detectors that are tuned to specific stimuli (feature detectors). For example, a frog's eye is very sensitive to small moving spots (think bugs), but not to small, unmoving objects. Frogs will starve to death when surrounded by dead bugs.

2. Sensory coding involves converting important information about the world into neural impulses so that the brain can process it. Sensory localization means that the type of sensation experienced depends on the part of the brain that is activated. The brain interprets activity in the visual cortex as the experience of sight, for example.

3. Sensation is activity in the sensory systems (vision, hearing, taste, smell, etc.) Perception is the organization of sensation into meaningful patterns such as perceptual constancies, perceptual grouping, perception of depth, etc.

4. Light passes through the cornea and enters the eye through the pupil. It passes through the lens, travels through the fluid in the eyeball and through four layers of cells (ganglion cells, amacrine cells, bipolar neurons, and horizontal cells) before reaching the rods and cones, which face the back of the eyeball.

5. Dark adaptation is increased sensitivity of the retina to low levels of light. It takes about half an hour for complete dark adaptation to take place. This is due to an increase in the production of rhodopsin.

6. There are taste buds on the tongue that are sensitive to four basic tastes: sweet, salt, sour, and bitter. In addition, there may be a fifth taste known as umami (a sort of broth-like taste). Flavour involves the smell, texture, and temperature of the food as well as the taste.

7. If individuals can't see or smell what they are eating, they will not be able to discriminate between three substances of similar texture.

8. Sensory adaptation and selective attention act as filters to limit incoming sensory information. Sensory adaptation is a decrease in sensory response to a stimulus (e.g., after a while you will not notice certain lingering odours). Selective attention means that certain stimuli are selected for further processing. Intensity, contrast, and change all help determine which incoming information will be processed first.

9. Sensory gating means that some messages are blocked before they ever get to the brain, so they are never processed. The gate control theory says that pain messages from slower speed nerve fibres (reminding pain) may be blocked by activity in large, faster speed nerve fibres. For example, using a counterirritant such as heat, ice, or a weak painful stimulus like a pinch may help control more severe pain.

10. An illusion is the consistent misjudgment of some aspect(s) of a stimulus (e.g. length, position, curvature, or direction). Many illusions are a result of perceptual learning, size constancy, shape constancy, continuity, or eye movements. Examples include moon illusion and the Müller-Lyer illusion. A hallucination is the perception of objects or events that are not there (e.g., seeing things, hearing voices).

11. Eyewitness accounts of an event are often inaccurate because what a person remembers seeing is rarely a replay of events that actually happened. Instead, a person may recall part of an event (that a person was dressed as a pirate at a costume party) and fill in the rest (that he wore an eye patch). Also, a person's confidence in the accuracy of an eyewitness account is no guarantee that the account really is accurate. Victims of crimes are not likely to be more reliable eyewitnesses, either, as they tend to focus their attention on the weapon used by the attacker rather than on dress, appearance, or other details. Sources of error include stress, the length of time the eyewitness was exposed to the event, information learned later on that is incorporated into the eyewitness account, attitudes and expectations, and the kinds of questions used to elicit the eyewitness account.

12. 1. Check the accuracy of your perceptions. 2. Break perceptual habits by doing things new ways. 3. Try out new experiences to broaden your frame of reference. 4. Be aware of stereotypes and biases. 5. Be aware that motives

and emotions may influence your perceptions. 6. Test reality on a regular basis (look for new evidence to check the accuracy of your perceptions). 7. Pay attention to what is around you.

Final Survey and Review

1. transduce
2. reduction; filter
3. sensory analysis
4. feature
5. Phosphenes; coding
6. localization; area
7. electromagnetic
8. 400 nanometres; 700 nanometres
9. Hue; amplitude
10. photoreceptors; retina
11. cornea; accommodation
12. myopia; astigmatism
13. motion
14. fovea; acuity
15. peripheral; peripheral
16. visual; vision for action; vision for perception; case
17. trichormatic
18. pigments
19. opponent; process; red or green
20. red; green
21. Ishihara
22. visual pigments
23. rhodopsin
24. compression; rarefaction
25. frequency; amplitude
26. ossicles; Corti
27. auditory; nerves
28. base; tip
29. stimulation
30. cochlear
31. 120 decibels
32. Olfaction; gustation
33. lock; and; key
34. sweet; salty; sour; umami
35. molecule
36. kinesthetic
37. pain; receptors
38. warning; reminding
39. attention
40. control
41. vestibular
42. otolith
43. semicircular; ampulla
44. visual; kinesthetic; sensory conflict
45. adaptation
46. attention
47. Gate control
48. retinal; constancies
49. brightness; proportion; light
50. native; empirical
51. figure; ground
52. Gestalt; nearness; closure
53. Closure
54. Contiguity
55. Camouflage
56. ambiguous; Necker's; figures
57. three; dimensional
58. visual cliff; visual cliff
59. accommodation; convergence
60. pictorial
61. linear perspective; interposition
62. gradients; parallax
63. monocular
64. horizon
65. apparent distance; depth cues
66. sensations; mental model
67. perceptual habits; Ames
68. inverted
69. Müller; Lyer
70. invariance
71. motives
72. processing
73. Bottom; up; top; down
74. perceptual sets; perceptual set
75. reconstruction
76. weapon; stress
77. habituate; respond less
78. dishabituation
79. perceptual habits

Mastery Test

1. B (p. 130)
2. D (p. 118)
3. C (p. 129)
4. D (p. 117)
5. C (p. 119)
6. B (p. 111)
7. B (p. 132)
8. A (p. 122)
9. C (p. 111)
10. D (p. 121)
11. A (p. 126)
12. D (p. 112)
13. A (pp. 111–113)
14. C (p. 115)
15. C (p. 113)
16. A (p. 111)
17. D (p. 145)
18. A (p. 151)
19. B (p. 144)
20. B (p. 134)
21. D (p. 141)
22. A (p. 146)
23. C (p. 139)
24. C (p. 136)
25. D (p. 139)
26. D (p. 135)
27. A (p. 136)
28. B (p. 139)
29. A (p. 137)
30. B (p. 139)
31. D (p. 137)
32. A (p. 152)
33. A (p. 118)
34. C (p. 128)

States of Consciousness

Chapter Overview

Consciousness consists of everything you are aware of at a given instant. Altered states of consciousness (ASCs) differ significantly from normal waking consciousness. Many conditions produce ASCs, which frequently have culturally defined meanings.

Sleep is an innate biological rhythm characterized by changes in consciousness and brain activity. Brain-wave patterns and sleep behaviours define four stages of sleep. The two most basic forms of sleep are rapid eye movement (REM) sleep and non-rapid eye movement (NREM) sleep. Dreams and nightmares occur primarily in REM sleep. Sleepwalking, sleeptalking, and night terrors are NREM events. Insomnia and other sleep disturbances are common, but generally treatable. Dreaming is emotionally restorative and it may help form adaptive memories. The psychodynamic view portrays dreams as a form of wish fulfillment; the activation-synthesis hypothesis says that dreaming is a physiological process with little meaning.

Hypnosis is characterized by narrowed attention and increased openness to suggestion. People vary in hypnotic susceptibility. Most hypnotic phenomena are related to the basic suggestion effect. Hypnosis can relieve pain and it has other useful effects, but it is not magic. Stage hypnotists simulate hypnosis in order to entertain.

Meditation can be used to alter consciousness, promote relaxation, and reduce stress. Two particular benefits of meditation are its ability to interrupt anxious thoughts and its ability to elicit the relaxation response. Sensory deprivation refers to any major reduction in external stimulation. Sensory deprivation also produces deep relaxation and a variety of perceptual effects. It can be used to help people enhance creative thinking and to change bad habits.

Psychoactive drugs are substances that alter consciousness. Most can be placed on a scale ranging from stimulation to depression, although some drugs are better classified as hallucinogens. The potential for abuse is high for drugs that lead to physical dependence, but psychological dependence can also be a serious problem. Drug abuse is often a symptom, rather than a cause, of personal maladjustment. It is supported by the immediate pleasure but delayed consequences associated with many psychoactive drugs and by cultural values that encourage drug abuse.

Various strategies, ranging from literal to highly symbolic, can be used to reveal the meanings of dreams. Dreaming—especially lucid dreaming—can be a source of creativity and it may be used for problem solving and personal growth.

Learning Objectives

After reading this chapter, students will be able to:

1. Describe the four stages of sleep.
2. Differentiate between REM and non-REM sleep and explain the functions of each.
3. Define the sleep disorders of insomnia and sleep apnea, and list the causes of each.
4. Explain the psychoanalytic and activation-synthesis theories of the nature and content of dreams.
5. Describe hypnosis and list its benefits and limitations.
6. Define meditation and list the benefits of meditation.
7. Explain the difference between drug dependence and drug tolerance.
8. Show how drugs affect the brain and explain psychological dependence.
9. Describe the effects of stimulants ("uppers"), sedatives ("downers"), and hallucinogens.
10. Show how dreams may be used to facilitate personal growth and understanding.

Practice Quizzes

Recite and Review

What is an altered state of consciousness?

Recite and Review: Page 158

1. States of _____ that differ from normal, alert, _____ consciousness are called altered states of consciousness (ASCs).
2. ASCs involved distinct shifts in the quality and _____ of mental activity.
3. Altered states are especially associated with _____ and _____ , hypnosis, meditation, _____ deprivation, and psychoactive drugs.
4. Cultural conditioning greatly affects what altered states a person recognizes, seeks, considers _____ , and attains.

What are the effects of sleep loss or changes in sleep patterns?

Recite and Review: Pages 158–161

5. Sleep is an innate biological _____ .
6. Our circadian rhythm works on a _____ -hour cycle and is controlled by an internal _____ clock.
7. Higher animals and people deprived of sleep experience _____ .
8. Moderate sleep loss mainly affects alertness and self-motivated performance on _____ or boring tasks.
9. Extended sleep _____ can (somewhat rarely) produce a _____ sleep-deprivation psychosis, marked by confusion, delusions, and possibly hallucinations.

10. Sleep patterns show some flexibility among individuals, but seven to eight hours remains average. The unscheduled human sleep-waking cycle averages _____ hours, but cycles of _____ and _____ tailor it to 24-hour days.

11. The amount of daily sleep _____ steadily from birth to old age and switches from multiple sleep-wake cycles to once-a-day sleep periods.

12. Once-a-day sleep patterns, with a 2-to-1 ratio of _____ and _____ , are most efficient for most people.

What are the different stages of sleep?

Recite and Review: Pages 162–164

13. Sleepiness is associated with the accumulation of a sleep hormone in the _____ and spinal cord.

14. Sleep occurs in _____ stages defined by changes in behaviour and brain _____ recorded with an electroencephalograph (EEG).

15. Stage 1, _____ _____ , has small irregular brain waves. In stage 2, sleep spindles appear. _____ waves appear in stage 3. Stage 4, or deep sleep, is marked by almost pure _____ waves.

16. Sleepers _____ between stages 1 and 4 (passing through stages 2 and 3) several times each night.

17. There are two basic sleep states, _____ sleep and non-REM (NREM) sleep.

18. REM sleep is much more strongly associated with _____ than NREM sleep is.

19. _____ and REMs occur mainly during stage 1 sleep but usually not during the first stage 1 period.

20. Dreaming is accompanied by sexual and _____ arousal but relaxation of the skeletal _____ . People who move about violently while asleep may suffer from _____ behaviour disorder.

What are the causes of sleep disorders and unusual sleep events?

Recite and Review: Pages 164–167

21. Insomnia, which is difficulty in getting to sleep or staying asleep, may be _____ or chronic.

22. When insomnia is treated with drugs, sleep quality is often _____ and drug-dependency _____ may develop.

23. Behavioural approaches to managing insomnia, such as relaxation, sleep restriction, _____ control, and paradoxical _____ are quite effective.

24. _____ (somnambulism) and sleeptalking occur during NREM sleep in stages 3 and 4.

25. Night terrors occur in _____ sleep, whereas nightmares occur in _____ sleep.

26. Nightmares can be eliminated by the method called imagery _____ .

27. Sleep _____ is believed to be one cause of sudden _____ death syndrome (SIDS).

Do dreams have meaning?

Recite and Review: Pages 167–169

28. People deprived of dream sleep show a _____ rebound when allowed to sleep without interruption. However, total sleep loss seems to be more important than loss of a single sleep _____ .

29. One of the more important functions of REM sleep appears to be the processing of adaptive _____ .

30. Calvin Hall found that most dream content is about _____ settings, people, and actions. Dreams more often involve negative _____ than positive _____ .

31. The Freudian, or psychodynamic, view is that dreams express unconscious _____ , frequently hidden by dream symbols.

32. Allan Hobson and Robert McCarley's _____ -synthesis model portrays dreaming as a physiological process. The brain, they say, creates dreams to explain _____ and motor messages that occur during REM sleep.

How is hypnosis done, and what are its limitations?

Recite and Review: Pages 170–173

33. Hypnosis is an altered state characterized by narrowed attention and _____ suggestibility.

34. The term _____ was first used by James Braid, an English doctor.

35. People vary in hypnotic susceptibility; _____ out of 10 can be hypnotized, as revealed by scores on the Stanford Hypnotic Susceptibility _____ .

36. The core of hypnosis is the _____ suggestion effect—a tendency to carry out suggested actions as if they were involuntary.

37. Hypnosis appears capable of producing relaxation, controlling _____ , and altering perceptions.

38. Stage hypnotism takes advantage of typical stage behaviour, _____ suggestibility, responsive subjects, disinhibition, and _____ to simulate hypnosis.

What is meditation? Does it have any benefits?

Recite and Review: Pages 173–175

39. Meditation refers to mental exercises that are used to alter _____ .

40. In receptive meditation, attention is _____ to include an awareness of one's entire moment-by-moment experience.

41. In concentrative meditation, attention is focused on a _____ object or thought.

42. Two major benefits of meditation are its ability to interrupt anxious thoughts and its ability to elicit the _____ response (the pattern of changes that occur in the body at times of deep relaxation).

43. Sensory deprivation takes place when there is a major reduction in the amount or variety of sensory _____ available to a person.

44. Prolonged sensory deprivation is stressful and disruptive, leading to _____ distortions.

45. Brief or mild sensory deprivation can enhance sensory sensitivity and induce deep _____ .

46. Sensory deprivation also appears to aid the breaking of long-standing _____ and promotes creative thinking. This effect is the basis for Restricted Environmental Stimulation Therapy (REST).

What are the effects of the more commonly used psychoactive drugs?

Recite and Review: Pages 176–190

47. A psychoactive drug is a substance that alters human _____ .

48. Most psychoactive drugs can be placed on a scale ranging from stimulation to _____ . Some, however, are best described as hallucinogens (drugs that alter _____ impressions).

49. Drugs may cause a physical dependence (_____) or a psychological dependence, or both.

50. The physically addicting drugs are heroin, morphine, codeine, methadone, barbiturates, alcohol, amphetamines, tobacco, and cocaine. All psychoactive drugs can lead to _____ dependence.

51. Stimulant drugs are easily abused because of the period of _____ that often follows stimulation. The greatest risks are associated with amphetamines, cocaine, and nicotine, but even _____ can be a problem.

52. "Designer drugs," such as MDMA, are chemical _____ of other drugs. Their long-term _____ effects are not known.

53. _____ includes the added risk of lung cancer, heart disease, and other health problems.

54. Barbiturates are _____ drugs whose overdose level is close to the intoxication dosage, making them dangerous drugs. Mixing barbiturates and alcohol may result in a fatal _____ interaction (in which the joint effect of two drugs exceeds the effects of adding one drug's effects to the other's).

55. Benzodiazepine tranquillizers, such as _____ , are used to lower anxiety. When abused, they have a strong _____ potential.

56. Alcohol is the most heavily abused drug in common use today. The development of a drinking problem is usually marked by an _____ phase of increasing consumption, a crucial phase, in which a _____ drink can set off a chain reaction, and a chronic phase, in which a person lives to drink and drinks to live.

57. Marijuana is a hallucinogen subject to a _____ dependence. Studies have linked chronic marijuana use with memory impairment, lung cancer, reproductive problems, immune system disorders, and other health problems.

58. Drug abuse is related to personal and social maladjustment, attempts to cope, and the _____ reinforcing qualities of psychoactive drugs.

How are dreams used to promote personal understanding?

Recite and Review: Psychology in Action

59. Freud held that the meaning of dreams is _____ by four dream _____ he called condensation, displacement, symbolization, and secondary elaboration.

60. Calvin Hall emphasizes the setting, cast, _____ , and emotions of a dream.

61. Rosalind Cartwright's view of dreams as feeling statements and Fritz Perls's technique of _____ for dream characters and objects are also helpful.

62. Dreams may be used for _____ problem solving, especially when dream control is achieved through lucid dreaming (a dream in which the dreamer feels capable of normal thought and action).

Connections

1. _____ Biological clock	a. over 9 hours
2. _____ Randy Gardner	b. infancy
3. _____ long sleepers	c. reflex muscle contraction
4. _____ sleep patterns	d. awake, alert
5. _____ short sleep cycles	e. circadian rhythm
6. _____ beta waves	f. interrupted breathing
7. _____ alpha waves	g. relaxed
8. _____ hypnic jerk	h. sleep deprivation
9. _____ apnea	i. sexual arousal
10. _____ REM sleep	j. 2 to 1 ratio

11. _____ REST	a. violent actions
12. _____ hypersomnia	b. fatal to infants
13. _____ REM behaviour disorder	c. unconscious meanings
14. _____ narcolepsy	d. sensory deprivation
15. _____ SIDS	e. designer drug
16. _____ dream symbols	f. sudden daytime REM sleep
17. _____ auto suggestion	g. relaxation
18. _____ MDMA	h. self-hypnosis
19. _____ flotation tank	i. excessive sleepiness

20. _____ drug tolerance	a. cocaine rush
21. _____ amphetamine	b. cancer agent
22. _____ dopamine	c. reduced response
23. _____ nicotine	d. sedative
24. _____ carcinogen	e. hallucinogen
25. _____ barbiturate	f. detoxification
26. _____ AAA	g. loss of pleasure
27. _____ alcohol treatment	h. stimulant
28. _____ THC	i. self-help group
29. _____ anhedonia	j. insecticide

Short-Answer Questions

1. Give three examples of altered states of consciousness.
2. Describe the four stages of sleep.
3. Explain REM and NREM sleep.
4. Briefly describe the effects of sleep deprivation.
5. Explain how the brain promotes sleep.
6. Describe the behavioural remedies for insomnia.
7. Explain how a stage hypnotist gets people to perform the way they do in front of an audience.
8. Trace the development of a drinking problem from a social drinker to an alcohol abuser to an alcoholic.

9. Describe the dangers, health risks, and health benefits of marijuana.

10. Describe the ways to increase recall of your dreams.

Final Survey and Review

What is an altered state of consciousness?

1. States of awareness that differ from normal, alert, waking _____ are called altered states of _____ (ASCs).

2. ASCs involve distinct shifts in the quality and pattern of _____ _____ .

3. Altered states are especially associated with sleep and dreaming, _____ , meditation, sensory _____ , and psychoactive drugs.

4. _____ conditioning greatly affects what altered states a person recognizes, seeks, considers normal, and attains.

What are the effects of sleep loss or changes in sleep patterns?

5. Sleep is an _____ _____ rhythm essential for survival.

6. Our circadian _____ works on a 24-hour cycle and is controlled by an internal _____ _____ .

7. Higher animals and people deprived of sleep experience involuntary _____ (a brief shift to sleep patterns in the brain).

8. Moderate sleep loss mainly affects _____ and self-motivated performance on routine or boring tasks.

9. Extended sleep loss can (somewhat rarely) produce a temporary sleep deprivation _____ , marked by confusion, _____ , and possibly hallucinations.

10. Sleep patterns show some flexibility, but seven to eight hours remains average. The unscheduled human _____ - _____ _____ averages 25 hours, but cycles of light and dark tailor it to 24-hour days.

11. The amount of daily sleep decreases steadily from birth to _____ _____ and switches from _____ sleep-wake cycles to once-a-day sleep periods.

12. Once-a-day sleep patterns, with a _____ - _____ - _____ ratio of sleep and waking, are most efficient for most people.

What are the different stages of sleep?

13. Sleepiness is associated with the accumulation of a sleep _____ in the brain and _____ _____ .

14. Sleep occurs in four stages defined by changes in behaviour and brain waves recorded with an _____ (EEG).

15. Stage 1, light sleep, has small irregular brain waves. In stage 2, sleep _____ appear. Delta waves appear in stage 3. Stage 4, or deep sleep, is marked by almost pure _____ _____ .

16. Sleepers alternate between stages _____ and _____ (passing through stages _____ and _____) several times each night.

17. There are two basic sleep states, _____ _____ movement (REM) sleep and non-REM (NREM) sleep.

18. _____ sleep is much more strongly associated with dreaming than _____ sleep is.

19. Dreams and REMs occur mainly during _____ _____ sleep, but usually not during the first _____ _____ period.

20. Dreaming is accompanied by sexual and emotional _____ but _____ of the skeletal muscles. People who move about violently while asleep may suffer from REM behaviour _____ .

What are the causes of sleep disorders and unusual sleep events?

21. Insomnia, which is difficulty in getting to sleep or staying asleep, may be temporary or _____ .

22. When insomnia is treated with drugs, sleep quality is often lowered and drug- _____ insomnia may develop.

23. Behavioural approaches to managing insomnia, such as relaxation, sleep _____ , stimulus control, and _____ intention are quite effective.

24. Sleepwalking (_____) and sleeptalking occur during _____ sleep in stages 3 and 4.

25. Night terrors occur in _____ sleep, whereas nightmares occur in _____ sleep.

26. Nightmares can be eliminated by the method called _____ _____ .

27. Sleep _____ is believed to be _____ cause of sudden infant death syndrome (SIDS).

Do dreams have meaning?

28. People deprived of dream sleep show a REM _____ when allowed to sleep without interruption. However, _____ sleep loss seems to be more important than loss of a single sleep stage.

29. One of the more important functions of _____ _____ appears to be the processing of adaptive memories.

30. Calvin _____ found that most dream content is about familiar settings, people, and actions. Dreams more often involve _____ emotions than _____ emotions.

31. The Freudian, or _____ , view is that dreams express unconscious wishes, frequently hidden by dream _____ .

32. Allan Hobson and Robert McCarley's activation- _____ model portrays dreaming as a physiological process. The brain, they say, creates dreams to explain sensory and _____ messages that occur during REM sleep.

How is hypnosis done, and what are its limitations?

33. Hypnosis is an altered state characterized by narrowed attention and increased _____ .

34. The term *hypnosis* was first used by James _____ , an English doctor.

35. People vary in hypnotic susceptibility; eight out of ten can be hypnotized, as revealed by scores on the _____ Hypnotic Susceptibility Scale.

36. The core of hypnosis is the basic _____ effect—a tendency to carry out suggested actions as if they were _____ .

37. Hypnosis appears capable of producing _____ , controlling pain, and altering perceptions.

38. _____ _____ takes advantage of typical stage behaviour, waking suggestibility, responsive subjects, disinhibition, and deception to _____ hypnosis.

What is meditation? Does it have any benefits?

39. _____ refers to mental exercises that are used to alter consciousness.

40. In _____ meditation, attention is broadened to include an awareness of one's entire moment-by-moment experience.

41. In _____ meditation, attention is focused on a single object or thought.

42. Two major benefits of meditation are its ability to interrupt anxious thoughts and its ability to elicit the _____ _____ (the pattern of changes that occur in the body at times of deep relaxation).

43. _____ deprivation takes place when there is a major reduction in the amount or variety of sensory _____ available to a person.

44. _____ sensory deprivation is stressful and disruptive, leading to perceptual distortions.

45. Brief or mild sensory _____ can induce deep _____ .

46. Sensory deprivation also appears to aid the breaking of long-standing habits and promotes creative thinking. This effect is the basis for _____ _____ Stimulation Therapy (REST).

What are the effects of the more commonly used psychoactive drugs?

47. A psychoactive drug is a substance that affects the brain in ways that alter _____ .

48. Most psychoactive drugs can be placed on a scale ranging from _____ to _____ . Some, however, are best described as _____ (drugs that alter sensory impressions).

49. Drugs may cause a physical _____ (addiction) or a psychological _____ , or both.

50. The _____ _____ drugs are heroin, morphine, codeine, methadone, barbiturates, alcohol, amphetamines, tobacco, and cocaine. All psychoactive drugs can lead to psychological dependence.

51. Stimulant drugs are easily abused because of the period of depression that often follows stimulation. The greatest risks are associated with amphetamines, _____ , and nicotine, but even caffeine can be a problem.

52. " _____ drugs," such as MDMA, are chemical variations of other drugs. Their long-term health effects are not known.

53. Nicotine (smoking) includes the added risk of _____ _____ , heart disease, and other health problems.

54. Barbiturates are depressant drugs whose overdose level is close to the intoxication dosage, making them dangerous drugs. Mixing barbiturates and _____ may result in a fatal drug _____ (in which the joint effect of two drugs exceeds the effects of adding one drug's effects to the other's).

55. _____ tranquillizers, such as Valium, are used to lower anxiety. When abused, they have a strong addictive potential.

56. _____ is the most heavily abused drug in common use today. The development of a drinking problem is usually marked by an initial phase of increasing consumption, a _____ phase,

in which a single drink can set off a chain reaction, and a chronic phase, in which a person lives to drink and drinks to live.

57. Marijuana is a _____ subject to a psychological dependence. Studies have linked chronic marijuana use with memory impairment, _____ cancer, reproductive problems, immune system disorders, and other health problems.

58. Drug abuse is related to personal and social _____ , attempts to cope, and the immediate reinforcing qualities of psychoactive drugs.

How are dreams used to promote personal understanding?

59. Freud held that the meaning of dreams is hidden by the dream processes he called _____ , displacement, symbolization, and _____ elaboration.

60. Calvin Hall emphasizes the _____ , _____ , plot, and emotions of a dream.

61. Rosalind Cartwright's view of dreams as _____ statements and Fritz Perl's technique of speaking for dream _____ and _____ are also helpful.

62. Dreams may be used for creative problem solving, especially when dream control is achieved through _____ dreaming (a dream in which the dreamer feels capable of normal thought and action).

Mastery Test

1. Delirium, ecstasy, and daydreaming all have in common the fact that they are
   a. forms of normal waking consciousness
   b. caused by sensory deprivation
   c. perceived as subjectively real
   d. ASCs

2. Alcoholics who quit drinking and people who have been prevented from dreaming typically experience
   a. sleep apnea
   b. REM rebound
   c. cataplexy
   d. sleep-deprivation psychosis

3. Which of the following does not belong with the others?
   a. nicotine
   b. caffeine
   c. cocaine
   d. codeine

4. Sleep spindles usually first appear in stage _____, whereas delta waves first appear in stage _____.
   a. 1, 2
   b. 2, 3
   c. 3, 4
   d. 1, 4

5. Which of the following most clearly occurs under hypnosis?
   a. unusual strength
   b. memory loss
   c. pain relief
   d. age regression

6. Alcohol, amphetamines, cocaine, and marijuana have in common the fact that they are all
   a. physically addicting
   b. psychoactive
   c. stimulants
   d. hallucinogens

7. Emotional arousal, blood pressure changes, and sexual arousal all primarily occur during
   a. REM sleep
   b. NREM sleep
   c. Delta sleep
   d. stage 4 sleep

8. The REST technique makes use of
   a. sensory deprivation
   b. hypodynamic imagery
   c. hallucinogens
   d. a CPAP mask

9. Mesmerism, hypnosis, hypnotic susceptibility scales, and stage hypnotism all rely in part on
   a. disinhibition
   b. rapid eye movements
   c. suggestibility
   d. imagery rehearsal

10. Shortened sleep-waking cycles overlook the fact that sleep
    a. must match a 3 to 1 ratio of time awake and time asleep
    b. is an innate biological rhythm
    c. is caused by a sleep-promoting substance in the blood
    d. cycles cannot be altered by external factors

11. Morning drinking appears during the _____ phase in the development of a drinking problem.
    a. initial
    b. crucial
    c. chronic
    d. rebound

12. Which of the following statements about sleep is true?
    a. Learning math or a foreign language can be accomplished during sleep.
    b. Some people can learn to do without sleep.
    c. Calvin Hall had hallucinations during a sleep deprivation experiment.
    d. Randy Gardner slept for 14 hours after ending his sleep deprivation.

13. Amphetamine is very similar in effects to
    a. narcotics and tranquillizers
    b. methaqualone
    c. codeine
    d. cocaine

14. Microsleeps would most likely occur
    a. in stage 4 sleep
    b. in a 3 to 1 ratio to microawakenings
    c. in conjunction with delusions and hallucinations
    d. during sleep deprivation

15. Adolescents who abuse drugs tend to be
    a. suffering from brain dysfunctions
    b. high in self-esteem but unrealistic about consequences
    c. maladjusted and impulsive
    d. similar in most respects to non-abusers

16. Sleepwalking, sleeptalking, and severe nightmares all have in common the fact that they
    a. are REM events
    b. happen only in children
    c. are sleep disorders
    d. can be controlled with imagery rehearsal

17. In its milder forms, sensory deprivation sometimes produces
    a. cataplectic images
    b. deep relaxation
    c. tryptophanic images
    d. REM symbolizations

18. The basic suggestion effect is closely related to
    a. hypnosis
    b. sensory enhancement after sensory deprivation
    c. hypersomnia
    d. the frequency of dreaming during REM sleep

19. A person who feels awake and capable of normal action while sleeping has experienced
    a. lucid dreaming
    b. the basic suggestion effect
    c. sleep drunkenness
    d. REM rebound

20. Which of the following is a hallucinogen?
    a. LSD
    b. THC
    c. hashish
    d. all of the preceding

21. The two most basic states of sleep are
    a. stage 1 sleep and stage 4 sleep
    b. REM sleep and NREM sleep
    c. Alpha sleep and delta sleep
    d. Alpha sleep and hypnic sleep

22. A mantra would most commonly be used in
    a. Perls' method of dream interpretation
    b. sensory deprivation research
    c. inducing hypnosis
    d. concentrative meditation

23. Learning to use a computer would most likely be slowed if you were _____ each night.
    a. deprived of a half hour of NREM sleep
    b. allowed to engage in extra REM sleep
    c. prevented from dreaming
    d. awakened three times at random

24. By definition, compulsive drug use involves
    a. dependence
    b. experimentation
    c. repeated overdoses
    d. anhedonia

25. A particularly dangerous drug interaction occurs when _____ and _____ are combined.
    a. alcohol, amphetamine
    b. barbiturates, nicotine
    c. alcohol, barbiturates
    d. amphetamine, codeine

26. Narcolepsy is an example of
    a. a night terror
    b. a sleep disorder
    c. a tranquillizer
    d. an addictive drug

27. Sleep restriction and stimulus control techniques would most likely be used to treat
    a. insomnia
    b. narcolepsy
    c. sleepwalking
    d. REM behaviour disorder

28. In addition to the nicotine they contain, cigarettes release
    a. dopamine
    b. tryptophan
    c. noradrenaline
    d. carcinogens

29. Disguised dream symbols are to psychodynamic dream theory as sensory and motor messages are to
    a. the Freudian theory of dreams
    b. the activation-synthesis hypothesis
    c. Fritz Perls's methods of dream interpretation
    d. paradoxical intention

30. According to a 1999 statistic from the Canadian Centre on Substance Abuse, how many Canadian deaths are due to smoking?
    a. 1 in 100
    b. 1 in 50
    c. 1 in 6
    d. 1 in 200

Solutions

Recite and Review

1. awareness; waking
2. *pattern*
3. sleep; dreaming; sensory
4. normal
5. rhythm
6. 24; biological
7. microsleeps
8. routine
9. loss; temporary
10. 25; light; dark
11. decreases
12. waking; sleep
13. brain
14. 4; waves
15. light sleep; Delta; delta
16. alternate
17. REM
18. dreaming
19. Dreaming
20. emotional; muscles; REM
21. temporary
22. lowered; insomnia
23. stimulus; intention
24. Sleepwalking
25. NREM; REM
26. rehearsal
27. apnea; infant
28. REM; stage
29. memories
30. familiar; emotions; emotions
31. wishes
32. activation; sensory
33. increased
34. hypnosis
35. 8; Scale
36. basic
37. pain
38. waking; deception
39. consciousness
40. widened
41. single
42. relaxation
43. stimulation
44. perceptual
45. relaxation
46. habits
47. consciousness
48. depression; sensory
49. addiction
50. psychological
51. depression; caffeine
52. variations; health
53. Nicotine
54. depressant; drug
55. valium; addictive
56. initial; single
57. psychological
58. immediate
59. hidden; processes
60. plot
61. speaking
62. creative

Connections

1. E
2. H
3. A
4. J
5. B
6. D
7. G
8. C
9. F
10. I
11. D
12. I
13. A
14. F
15. B
16. C
17. H
18. C
19. G
20. C
21. H
22. A
23. J
24. B
25. D
26. I
27. F
28. E
29. G

Short-Answer Questions

1. Sleep, dreaming, daydreaming, delirium, hypnosis, drug effects, and meditation are all altered states of consciousness. Altered states of consciousness also may be due to fatigue, sleep deprivation, sensory overload, monotonous stimulation, high fever, or sensory deprivation.

2. Stage 1 comprises light sleep, relaxed muscles, slowed heart rate, irregular breathing; EEG shows small, irregular waves. In stage 2 body temperature drops, and EEG shows sleep spindles. In stage 3 delta waves appear and sleep deepens. Stage 4 is deep sleep, and EEG shows primarily delta waves.

3. REM (rapid eye movement) sleep is associated with dreaming. Brain activity resembles waking patterns. There are signs of physical and sexual arousal (irregular heartbeat, erections in men, and increased blood to the genitals) although the body is very still. NREM sleep is mostly dreamless and increases after physical exertion. Nightmares, night terrors, and sleepwalking occur during non-REM sleep.

4. After two or three days of sleep deprivation, people can still perform complex tasks, but they may have trouble staying alert, paying attention, and doing simple or boring tasks.

Mood and memory may also be affected by small amounts of sleep loss. Sleep deprivation longer than three days may result in hallucinations and the inability to distinguish between waking nightmares and reality.

5. The brain has separate sleep and wakefulness systems. Activity (electrical and chemical) in one system promotes sleep, and a network of cells in the other system responds to chemicals that inhibit sleep. The two systems work in a back-and-forth pattern, switching from sleep to wakefulness. The brain never entirely shuts down during sleep; however, the pattern of brain activity changes with the different stages of sleep.

6. Avoid stimulants such as coffee and nicotine. Alcohol will also impair sleep quality. Deal with worries and/or concerns early in the evening; make a written plan for the next day. Learn relaxation techniques, both physical and mental. The day after a night of little or no sleep, do not sleep in, nap for more than an hour, sleep in the evening, or go to bed early. Do not disrupt your normal sleep rhythms. Link your bedroom with sleep; go to bed only when you feel tired, get up at the same time each morning, get up and leave the bedroom if you don't fall asleep quickly, do something else instead of lying in bed worrying about not falling asleep.

7. Stage hypnotists take advantage of the features of the stage setting to simulate hypnosis. These features include suggestibility (people cooperate because they don't want to spoil the act) and careful selection of subjects to eliminate people who don't follow suggestions. The hypnotist acts as director, the volunteers are the stars and centre of attention; the hypnotist uses tricks and deception to make the audience think that the subject's actions are unusual.

8. Signs of a developing problem include increasing consumption of alcohol coupled with concerns about the amount, morning drinking to help with a hangover, regretting behaviour or actions that leave a person feeling guilty or embarrassed, and blackouts. Eventually, a person may lose control of their drinking, so that one drink leads to another and another. People who are chronically dependent on alcohol drink compulsively and continuously. They may not eat and crave alcohol when they do not have it. Work, family, and social life deteriorate.

9. The dangers of short-term marijuana use include loss of attention and coordination, and changes in short-term memory. Long-term marijuana users may show small but long-lasting impairments in learning, memory, attention, and thinking. There may also be some negative effects on IQ scores. In humans, health risks include precancerous changes to cells in the lungs, lowering of sperm production, suppression of the immune system, changes to activity levels in the cerebellum (which affects balance), and effects on the part of the brain involved in memory. There is also evidence that children whose mothers smoked marijuana during pregnancy are less able to succeed in challenging activities. Although there is anecdotal evidence that smoking marijuana relieves the pain of glaucoma, increases the appetites of people with AIDS wasting syndrome, and reduces the nausea associated with chemotherapy, controlled scientific research has not yet been performed.

10. Keep a voice recorder or a pen and pad of paper beside the bed to write down your dreams. Try to wake up without an alarm, as you will most likely wake up after a period of REM sleep. When you wake up from a dream, lie with your eyes closed and try to remember as many details as possible. Try to record your dreams without opening your eyes (using a voice recorder). After you record a dream, try to recall additional details, including feelings, plot, characters, actions, etc. Keep a permanent dream diary in chronological order, and review your dreams often in order to identify recurrent themes, conflict, emotions, etc. Be aware that many drugs suppress dreaming (including alcohol, amphetamines, barbiturates, cocaine, and opiates).

Final Survey and Review

1. consciousness; consciousness
2. mental activity
3. hypnosis; deprivation
4. Cultural
5. innate biological
6. rhythm; biological clock
7. microsleeps
8. alertness
9. psychosis; delusions
10. sleep waking; cycle

11. old age; multiple
12. 2 to 1
13. hormone; spinal cord
14. electroencephalograph
15. spindles; delta waves
16. 1; 4; 2; 3
17. rapid eye
18. REM; NREM
19. stage 1; stage 1
20. arousal; relaxation; disorder
21. chronic
22. dependency
23. restriction; paradoxical
24. somnambulism; NREM
25. NREM; REM
26. imagery rehearsal
27. apnea; one
28. rebound; total
29. REM sleep
30. Hall; negative; positive
31. psychodynamic; symbols
32. synthesis; motor
33. suggestibility
34. Braid
35. Stanford
36. suggestion; involuntary
37. relaxation
38. Stage hypnotism; simulate
39. Meditation

40. receptive
41. concentrative
42. relaxation response
43. Sensory; stimulation
44. Prolonged
45. deprivation; relaxation
46. Restricted Environmental
47. consciousness
48. stimulation; depression; hallucinogens
49. dependence; dependence
50. physically addicting
51. cocaine
52. Designer
53. lung cancer
54. alcohol; interaction
55. Benzodiazepine
56. Alcohol; crucial
57. hallucinogen; lung
58. maladjustment
59. condensation; secondary
60. setting; cast
61. feeling; characters; objects
62. lucid

Mastery Test

1. D (p. 158)
2. B (p. 167)
3. D (p. 176)
4. B (p. 162)
5. C (p. 172)
6. B (p. 176)
7. A (p. 163)
8. A (p. 174)
9. C (p. 170)
10. B (p. 161)
11. A (p. 186)
12. D (p. 160)
13. D (p. 180)
14. D (p. 160)
15. C (p. 190)
16. C (p. 166)
17. B (p. 174)
18. A (p. 171)
19. A (p. 192)
20. D (p. 187)
21. B (p. 163)
22. D (p. 173)
23. C (p. 167)
24. A (p. 177)
25. C (p. 184)
26. B (p. 165)
27. A (p. 165)
28. D (p. 182)
29. B (p. 169)
30. C (p. 182)

Conditioning and Learning

Chapter Overview

Learning is a relatively permanent change in behaviour due to experience. Two basic forms of learning are classical conditioning and operant conditioning.

Classical conditioning is also called respondent or Pavlovian conditioning. Classical conditioning occurs when a neutral stimulus (NS) is associated with an unconditioned stimulus (US) (one that reliably elicits an unconditioned response). After many pairings of the NS and the US, the NS becomes a conditioned stimulus (CS) that elicits a conditioned response. Withdrawing the US leads to extinction (although some spontaneous recovery of conditioning may occur). It is apparent that stimulus generalization has occurred when a stimulus similar to the CS also elicits the conditioned response. In stimulus discrimination, people or animals learn to respond differently to two similar stimuli. Conditioning often involves simple reflex responses, but emotional conditioning is also possible. Aversive responses to food and the development of tolerance to drugs are also due to classical conditioning.

In operant conditioning (or instrumental learning), the consequences that follow a response alter the probability that it will be made again. Positive and negative reinforcers increase responding; punishment suppresses responding; non-reinforcement leads to extinction. Various types of reinforcers and different patterns of giving reinforcers greatly affect operant learning. Informational feedback (knowledge of results) also facilitates learning and performance. Antecedent stimuli (those that precede a response) influence operant learning, through stimulus generalization, discrimination, and stimulus control.

Learning, even simple conditioning, is based on acquiring information. Higher-level cognitive learning involves memory, thinking, problem solving, and language. At a simpler level, cognitive maps, latent learning, and discovery learning show that learning is based on acquiring information. Learning also occurs through observation and imitating models. Observational learning imparts large amounts of information that would be hard to acquire in other ways.

Operant principles can be applied to manage one's own behaviour and to break bad habits. A mixture of operant principles and cognitive learning underlies self-regulated learning—a collection of techniques to improve learning in school.

Learning Objectives

After reading this chapter, students will be able to:

1. Define learning.

2. Define conditioned stimulus, unconditioned stimulus, conditioned response, and unconditioned response.

3. Describe how classical conditioning occurs.

4. Explain stimulus generalization, stimulus discrimination, extinction, and spontaneous recovery in classical conditioning.

5. Explain how emotional responses and phobias may be affected by classical conditioning.

6. Explain operant conditioning.

7. Define shaping.

8. Distinguish between classical and operant conditioning.

9. Explain reinforcement. Show how positive and negative reinforcement can affect behaviour.

10. Give examples of primary and secondary reinforcers.

11. Describe the four schedules of partial reinforcement and show how each can affect behaviour.

12. Explain stimulus control. Describe the effects of operant stimulus generalization and discrimination.

13. Explain punishment. Describe the effects of punishment on behaviour.

14. Explain cognitive learning.

15. Show how learning can occur by imitation.

Practice Quizzes

Recite and Review

What is learning?

Recite and Review: Pages 198–199

1. Learning is a relatively permanent change in _____ due to experience. To understand learning we must study antecendents (events that _____ responses) and consequences (events that _____ responses).

2. Classical, or respondent, _____ and instrumental, or operant, _____ are two basic types of learning.

3. In classical conditioning, a previously _____ stimulus is associated with a stimulus that elicits a response. In operant conditioning, the pattern of voluntary _____ is altered by consequences.

How does classical conditioning occur?

Recite and Review: Pages 199–202

4. Classical conditioning, studied by Ivan Pavlov, occurs when a _____ stimulus (NS) is associated with an unconditioned stimulus (US). The US triggers a reflex called the unconditioned _____ (UR).

5. If the NS is consistently paired with the US, it becomes a conditioned _____ (CS) capable of producing a response by itself. This response is a conditioned (_____) response (CR).

6. During acquisition of classical conditioning, the conditioned stimulus must be consistently followed by the unconditioned _____ .

7. Higher-order conditioning occurs when a well-learned conditioned stimulus is used as if it were an unconditioned _____ , bringing about further learning.

8. When the CS is repeatedly presented alone, extinction takes place. That is, the _____ _____ is weakened or inhibited.

9. After extinction seems to be complete, a rest period may lead to the temporary reappearance of a conditioned response. This is called _____ _____ .

10. Through stimulus generalization, stimuli _____ to the conditioned stimulus will also produce a response.

11. Generalization gives way to _____ discrimination when an organism learns to respond to one stimulus, but not to similar stimuli.

12. From an informational view, conditioning creates expectancies (or expectations about events), which alter _____ patterns.

13. In classical conditioning, the CS creates an expectancy that the US will _____ it.

How are emotions affected by conditioning?

Recite and Review: Pages 203–206

14. Conditioning applies to visceral or emotional responses as well as simple _____ . As a result, _____ emotional responses (CERs) also occur.

15. Irrational fears called phobias may be CERs that are extended to a variety of situations by _____ generalization.

16. The conditioning of emotional responses can occur vicariously (_____) as well as directly. Vicarious classical conditioning occurs when we _____ another person's emotional responses to a stimulus.

17. Conditioned taste aversions develop when a _____ food is associated with an _____ reaction or _____ .

18. Drug tolerance comes from the body compensating (physiological responses) for the _____ of the drug. The process of injecting, _____ cues, and the paraphernalia used to prepare the drug will all become _____ with the compensatory physiological responses by _____ conditioning.

What is operant conditioning? How does it occur?

Recite and Review: Pages 206–211

19. Operant conditioning (or instrumental _____) occurs when a voluntary action is followed by a reinforcer.

20. Reinforcement in operant conditioning _____ the frequency or probability of a response. This result is based on what Edward L. Thorndike called the law of _____ .

21. An operant reinforcer is any event that follows a _____ and _____ its probability.

22. Learning in operant conditioning is based on the expectation that a response will have a specific _____ .

23. To be effective, operant _____ must be _____ contingent.

24. Delay of reinforcement reduces its effectiveness, but long _____ of responses may be built up so that a _____ reinforcer maintains many responses.

25. Superstitious behaviours (unnecessary responses) often become part of _____ chains because they appear to be associated with reinforcement.

26. In a process called shaping, complex _____ responses can be taught by reinforcing successive approximations (ever closer matches) to a final desired response.

27. If an operant response is not reinforced, it may extinguish (disappear). But after extinction seems complete, it may temporarily reappear (spontaneous _____).

28. In positive reinforcement, _____ or a pleasant event follows a response. In negative reinforcement, a response that _____ discomfort becomes more likely to occur again.

29. Punishment _____ responding. Punishment occurs when a response is followed by the onset of an aversive event or by the removal of a positive event (response _____).

What are the different kinds of operant reinforcement?

Recite and Review: Pages 211–216

30. Primary reinforcers are "natural," physiologically based rewards. Intracranial stimulation of " _____ centres" in the _____ can also serve as a primary reinforcer.

31. Secondary reinforcers are _____ . They typically gain their reinforcing value by association with primary reinforcers or because they can be _____ for primary reinforcers. Tokens and money gain their reinforcing value in this way.

32. Human behaviour is often influenced by social reinforcers, which are based on learned desires for attention and _____ from others.

33. Feedback, or knowledge of _____ , aids learning and improves performance.

34. Programmed instruction breaks learning into a series of small steps and provides immediate _____ .

35. Computer-assisted _____ (CAI) does the same, but has the added advantage of providing alternate exercises and information when needed.

36. Four variations of CAI are drill and _____ , instructional games, educational simulations, and interactive videodisc instruction.

Can patterns of reward influence our behaviour?

Recite and Review: Pages 216–219

37. Reward or reinforcement may be given continuously (after every _____), or on a schedule of _____ reinforcement. The study of schedules of reinforcement was begun by B. F. Skinner.

38. Partial reinforcement produces greater resistance to extinction. This is the partial reinforcement _____ .

39. The four most basic schedules of reinforcement are _____ ratio (FR), variable ratio (VR), _____ interval (FI), and variable interval (VI).

40. FR and VR schedules produce _____ rates of response. An FI schedule produces moderate rates of response with alternating periods of activity and inactivity. VI schedules produce _____ , steady rates of response and strong resistance to extinction.

41. Stimuli that _____ a reinforced response tend to control the response on future occasions (stimulus control).

42. Two aspects of stimulus control are generalization and _____ .

43. In generalization, an operant response tends to occur when stimuli _____ to those preceding reinforcement are present.

44. In discrimination, responses are _____ in the presence of discriminative stimuli associated with reinforcement and _____ in the presence of stimuli associated with non-reinforcement.

How does punishment affect behaviour?

Recite and Review: Pages 220–222

45. A punisher is any consequence that _____ the frequency of a target behaviour.

46. Punishment is most effective when it is _____ , consistent, and intense.

47. Mild punishment tends to only temporarily _____ responses that are also reinforced or were acquired by reinforcement.

48. The undesirable side effects of punishment include the conditioning of fear, the learning of _____ and avoidance responses, and the encouragement of aggression.

49. Reinforcement and non-reinforcement are a better way to change behaviour than punishment. When punishment is used, it should be _____ and combined with reinforcement of desired _____ .

What is cognitive learning?

Recite and Review: Pages 223–225

50. Cognitive learning involves higher mental processes, such as understanding, knowing, or anticipating. Evidence of cognitive learning is provided by cognitive _____ (internal representations of spatial relationships) and latent (hidden) _____ .

51. Discovery learning emphasizes insight and _____ , in contrast to rote learning.

Does learning occur by imitation?

Recite and Review: Pages 225–228

52. Much human learning is achieved through _____ , or modelling. Observational learning is influenced by the personal characteristics of the _____ and the success or failure of the _____ behaviour.

53. Television characters can act as powerful _____ for observational learning. Televised violence increases the likelihood of aggression by viewers.

Can we use the principles of conditioning to help solve practical problems?

Recite and Review: Psychology in Action

54. Operant principles can be readily applied to manage behaviour in everyday settings. Self-management of behaviour is based on self-reinforcement, self-recording, _____ , and behavioural contracting.

55. Prepotent, or frequent, high-probability _____ , can be used to reinforce low-frequency responses. This is known as the Premack _____ .

56. Attempts to break bad habits are aided by reinforcing alternate _____ , extinction, breaking _____ chains, and _____ cues or antecedents.

57. In school, self-regulated _____ typically involves all of the following: setting learning _____ , planning learning strategies, using self-instruction, monitoring progress, evaluating yourself, reinforcing _____ , and taking corrective action when required.

Connections

1.	_____ reflex response	a.	before responses
2.	_____ operant conditioning	b.	Pavlov's CS
3.	_____ antecedents	c.	after responses
4.	_____ meat powder	d.	higher-order conditioning
5.	_____ bell	e.	contraction of the pupil
6.	_____ salivation	f.	US missing
7.	_____ consequences	g.	UR
8.	_____ CS used as US	h.	Pavlov's US
9.	_____ extinction	i.	learning consequences

10.	_____ phobia	a.	conditioned emotional response (CER)
11.	_____ desensitization	b.	conditioning chamber
12.	_____ Skinner	c.	increased responding
13.	_____ shaping	d.	decreased responding
14.	_____ negative reinforcement	e.	social reinforcer
15.	_____ punishment	f.	Chimp-O-Mat
16.	_____ tokens	g.	approximations
17.	_____ approval	h.	resistance to extinction
18.	_____ partial reinforcement	i.	antecedent stimuli
19.	_____ stimulus control	j.	extinction of fear

20. _____ punishment
21. _____ expectancies
22. _____ knowledge of results (KR)
23. _____ computer-assisted instruction (CAI)
24. _____ discovery learning
25. _____ modelling
26. _____ self-instruction
27. _____ fixed ratio
28. _____ spontaneous recovery
29. _____ fixed interval

a. number of responses per reinforcer
b. reinforcement schedule
c. incomplete extinction
d. escape and avoidance
e. informational view
f. educational simulations
g. feedback
h. insight
i. self-regulated learning
j. imitation

Short-Answer Questions

1. Your friend thinks that his dog can see colours in the same way as a person. How could you use classical conditioning to prove whether or not this is true?

2. Two months ago, your friend Susan became very sick after consuming too much beer and peanuts. Now she can't even look at peanuts, let alone eat the peanut butter sandwich you brought her for lunch today. She says the smell makes her feel sick. How would you explain this using classical conditioning?

3. Compare and contrast positive and negative reinforcement, punishment and response cost.

4. Ms. Ashropova is a Grade 4 teacher who is having some problems managing her class. Although she yells at them a lot, she finds that, instead of behaving, they are acting up more than ever. Explain using the concept of social reinforcement.

5. How do secondary reinforcers become reinforcing?

6. How can parents use punishment effectively?

7. How could you use the principles of conditioning to change a habit?

Final Survey and Review

What is learning?

1. Learning is a relatively permanent change in behaviour due to experience. To understand learning we must study _____ (events that precede responses) and _____ (events that follow responses).

2. Classical, or _____ , conditioning and instrumental, or _____ , conditioning are two basic types of learning.

3. In classical conditioning, a previously _____ stimulus is associated with another stimulus that elicits a response. In operant conditioning, the pattern of voluntary responses is altered by _____ .

How does classical conditioning occur?

4. Classical conditioning, studied by _____ _____ , occurs when a neutral stimulus (NS) is associated with an _____ stimulus (US). The US triggers a _____ called the unconditioned response (UR).

5. If the NS is consistently paired with the US, it becomes a _____ stimulus (CS) capable of producing a response by itself. This response is a _____ (learned) response (CR).

6. During acquisition of classical conditioning, the conditioned stimulus must be consistently followed by the _____ _____ .

7. _____ - _____ conditioning occurs when a well-learned conditioned stimulus is used as if it were an unconditioned stimulus, bringing about further learning.

8. When the CS is repeatedly presented alone, _____ takes place (learning is weakened or inhibited).

9. After extinction seems to be complete, a rest period may lead to the temporary reappearance of a conditioned response. This is called _____ _____ .

10. Through stimulus _____ , stimuli similar to the conditioned stimulus will also produce a response.

11. Generalization gives way to stimulus _____ when an organism learns to respond to one stimulus, but not to similar stimuli.

12. From an _____ view, conditioning creates expectancies (or expectations about events), which alter response patterns.

13. In classical conditioning, the _____ creates an expectancy that the _____ will follow it.

How are emotions affected by conditioning?

14. Conditioning applies to visceral or emotional responses as well as simple reflexes. As a result, conditioned _____ _____ (CERs) also occur.

15. Irrational fears called _____ may be CERs that are extended to a variety of situations by stimulus _____ .

16. The conditioning of emotional responses can occur secondhand as well as directly. _____ classical conditioning occurs when we observe another person's emotional responses to a stimulus.

17. Conditioned taste _____ develop when a novel food is associated with an unpleasant reaction or _____ _____ (_____).

18. Drug tolerance comes from the body _____ (physiological responses) for the effects of a drug. The process of injecting, environmental cues, and paraphernalia used to prepare the drug will be _____ to the _____ _____ _____ responses by classical conditioning.

What is operant conditioning? How does it occur?

19. Operant conditioning (or _____ learning) occurs when a voluntary action is followed by a reinforcer.

20. Reinforcement in operant conditioning increases the frequency or _____ of a response. This result is based on what Edward L. _____ called the law of effect.

21. An operant reinforcer is any event that follows a _____ and _____ its probability.

22. Learning in operant conditioning is based on the _____ that a response will have a specific effect.

23. To be effective, operant reinforcers must be response _____ .

24. Delay of reinforcement _____ its effectiveness, but long chains of responses may be built up so that a single _____ maintains many responses.

25. _____ behaviours (unnecessary responses) often become part of response chains because they appear to be associated with reinforcement.

26. In a process called _____ , complex operant responses can be taught by reinforcing successive _____ (ever closer matches) to a final desired response.

27. If an operant response is not reinforced, it may _____ (disappear). But after extinction seems complete, it may temporarily reappear (_____ recovery).

28. In _____ reinforcement, reward or a pleasant event follows a response. In _____ reinforcement, a response that ends discomfort becomes more likely to occur again.

29. Punishment decreases responding. Punishment occurs when a response is followed by the onset of an _____ event or by the removal of a _____ event (response cost).

What are the different kinds of operant reinforcement?

30. _____ reinforcers are "natural," physiologically based rewards. Intracranial _____ of "pleasure centres" in the brain can also serve as a reinforcers of this type.

31. _____ reinforcers are learned. They typically gain their reinforcing value by association with _____ reinforcers or because they can be exchanged for _____ reinforcers. Tokens and money gain their reinforcing value in this way.

32. Human behaviour is often influenced by _____ reinforcers, which are based on learned desires for attention and approval from others.

33. Feedback, or _____ of results, aids learning and improves performance.

34. Programmed _____ breaks learning into a series of small steps and provides immediate feedback.

35. _____ - _____ _____ (CAI) does the same, but has the added advantage of providing alternate exercises and information when needed.

36. Four variations of _____ are drill and practice, instructional games, educational simulations, and interactive videodisc instruction.

Can patterns of reward influence our behaviour?

37. Reward or reinforcement may be given continuously (after every response), or on a _____ of partial reinforcement like those studied by B. F. _____ .

38. Partial reinforcement produces greater resistance to _____ . This is the _____ reinforcement effect.

39. The four most basic schedules of reinforcement are fixed and variable _____ (FR and VR) and fixed and variable _____ (FI and VI).

40. _____ and _____ schedules produce high rates of responding. An _____ schedule produces moderate rates of responding with alternating periods of activity and inactivity. VI schedules produce slow, steady rates of responding and strong resistance to _____ .

41. Stimuli that precede a reinforced response tend to control the response on future occasions. This is called _____ _____ .

42. Two aspects of stimulus control are _____ and discrimination.

43. In _____ , an operant response tends to occur when stimuli similar to those preceding reinforcement are present.
44. In _____ , responses are given in the presence of stimuli associated with reinforcement and withheld in the presence of stimuli associated with non-reinforcement.

How does punishment affect behaviour?

45. A _____ is any consequence that lowers the frequency of a target behaviour.
46. Punishment is most effective when it is immediate, _____ , and intense.
47. Mild punishment tends to only temporarily suppress responses that are also _____ in some way.
48. The undesirable side effects of punishment include the conditioning of fear; the learning of escape and _____ responses; and the encouragement of _____ against others.
49. _____ and _____ are a better way to change behaviour than punishment.

What is cognitive learning?

50. Cognitive learning involves higher mental processes, such as understanding, knowing, or anticipating. Evidence of cognitive learning is provided by _____ _____ (internal representations of spatial relationships) and _____ (hidden) learning.
51. Discovery learning emphasizes insight and understanding, in contrast to _____ learning.

Does learning occur by imitation?

52. Much human learning is achieved through observation, or _____ . _____ learning is influenced by the personal characteristics of the model and the success or failure of the model's behaviour.
53. Television characters can act as powerful models for _____ learning. Televised violence increases the likelihood of aggression by viewers.

Can we use the principles of conditioning to help solve practical problems?

54. Operant principles can be readily applied to manage behaviour in everyday settings. Self-management of behaviour is based on self-reinforcement, self-recording, feedback, and behavioural _____ .
55. Prepotent, or frequent, high-probability responses, can be used to _____ low-frequency responses. This is known as the _____ principle.
56. Attempts to break bad habits are aided by reinforcing _____ responses, extinction, breaking response _____ , and removing cues or _____ .
57. In school, self-regulated learning typically involves all of the following: setting learning goals, planning learning _____ , using self-instruction, monitoring progress, evaluating yourself, _____ successes, and taking corrective action when required.

Mastery Test

1. Tokens are a good example of
   a. secondary reinforcers
   b. the effects of ICS on behaviour
   c. non-contingent reinforcers
   d. generalized reinforcers

2. The principle of feedback is of particular importance to
   a. CERs
   b. ICS
   c. CAI
   d. higher-order conditioning

3. As a coffee lover, you have become very efficient at carrying out the steps necessary to make a cup of espresso. Your learning is an example of
   a. response chaining
   b. spontaneous recovery
   c. vicarious reinforcement
   d. secondary reinforcement

4. To teach a pet dog to use a new dog door, it would be helpful to use
   a. the Premack principle
   b. shaping
   c. respondent conditioning
   d. delayed reinforcement

5. To test for the presence of classical conditioning you would omit the
   a. CS
   b. US
   c. CR
   d. S+

6. To teach a child to say "Please" when she asks for things, you should make getting the requested item
   a. the CS
   b. a token
   c. a negative reinforcer
   d. response-contingent

7. Money is to secondary reinforcer as food is to
   a. ICS
   b. prepotent responses
   c. primary reinforcer
   d. negative reinforcer

8. Whether or not a model is reinforced has a great impact on
   a. discovery learning
   b. latent learning
   c. observational learning
   d. self-regulated learning

9. One thing that classical and operant conditioning have in common is that both
   a. were discovered by Pavlov
   b. involve an expectation
   c. are affected by the consequences of making a response
   d. permanently change behaviour

10. To shape the behaviour of a teacher in one of your classes you would probably have to rely on
    a. tokens
    b. primary reinforcers
    c. negative attention seeking
    d. social reinforcers

11. The concept that best explains persistence at gambling is
    a. partial reinforcement
    b. continuous reinforcement
    c. fixed interval reinforcement
    d. fixed ratio reinforcement

12. Which of the following is *not* a common side effect of mild punishment?
    a. escape learning
    b. avoidance learning
    c. aggression
    d. accelerated extinction

13. Research suggests that TV violence
    a. causes viewers to be more aggressive
    b. makes aggression more likely
    c. has no effect on the majority of viewers
    d. vicariously lowers aggressive urges

14. Which of the following types of learning is most related to the consequences of making a response?
    a. Pavlovian conditioning
    b. classical conditioning
    c. operant conditioning
    d. respondent conditioning

15. Which combination would most likely make a CER into a phobia?
    a. CER-discrimination
    b. CER-desensitization
    c. CER-response cost
    d. CER-generalization

16. A loud, unexpected sound causes a startle reflex; thus, a loud sound could be used as a _____ in conditioning.
    a. NS
    b. CR
    c. UR
    d. US

17. Antecedents are to _____ as consequences are to _____.
    a. discriminative stimuli, reinforcers
    b. shaping, response chaining
    c. conditioned stimuli, cognitive maps
    d. punishment, negative reinforcement

18. The use of self-recording to change personal behaviour is closely related to the principle of
    a. response chaining
    b. feedback
    c. two-factor reinforcement
    d. stimulus control

19. _____ typically only temporarily suppresses reinforced responses.
    a. Negative reinforcement
    b. Extinction
    c. Mild punishment
    d. Stimulus generalization

20. In general, the highest rates of responding are associated with
    a. delayed reinforcement
    b. variable reinforcement
    c. interval reinforcement
    d. fixed ratio reinforcement

21. A child who has learned, through classical conditioning, to fear sitting in a dentist's chair becomes frightened when he is placed in a barber's chair. This illustrates the concept of
    a. stimulus generalization
    b. spontaneous recovery
    c. higher-order discrimination
    d. vicarious conditioning

22. The informational view of learning places emphasis on the creation of mental
    a. expectancies
    b. reinforcement schedules
    c. contracts
    d. antecedents

23. For some adults, blushing when embarrassed or ashamed is probably a _____ first formed in childhood.
    a. conditioned stimulus
    b. CAI
    c. discriminative stimulus
    d. CER

24. Learning to obey traffic signals is related to the phenomenon called
    a. stimulus control
    b. spontaneous recovery
    c. escape learning
    d. modelling

25. Involuntary responses are to _____ conditioning as voluntary responses are to _____ conditioning.
    a. classical, respondent
    b. classical, operant
    c. operant, classical
    d. operant, instrumental

26. Negative attention seeking by children demonstrates the impact of _____ on behaviour.
    a. operant extinction
    b. social reinforcers
    c. response costs
    d. prepotent responses

27. Which consequence increases the probability that a response will be repeated?
    a. punishment
    b. response cost
    c. non-reinforcement
    d. negative reinforcement

28. The conditioning of taste aversions usually involves what kind of conditioned stimulus?
    a. oddly coloured food
    b. unfamiliar and rarely eaten food
    c. both familiar and novel food
    d. it's not the food but the context you are in (e.g., who you are with) that will produce the aversion.

Solutions

Recite and Review

1. behaviour; precede; follow
2. conditioning; conditioning
3. neutral; responses
4. neutral; response
5. stimulus; learned
6. stimulus
7. stimulus
8. conditioned response
9. spontaneous recovery
10. similar
11. stimulus
12. response
13. follow
14. reflexes; conditioned
15. stimulus
16. secondhand; observe
17. novel; unpleasant; UR
18. effects; environmental; associated; classical
19. learning
20. increases; effect
21. response; increases
22. effect
23. reinforcement; response
24. chains; single
25. response
26. operant
27. recovery
28. reward; ends
29. decreases; cost
30. pleasure; brain
31. learned; exchanged
32. approval
33. results
34. feedback
35. instruction
36. practice
37. response; partial
38. effect
39. fixed; fixed
40. high; slow
41. precede
42. discrimination
43. similar
44. given; withheld
45. decreases
46. immediate
47. suppress
48. escape
49. mild; responses
50. maps; learning
51. understanding
52. imitation; model; model's
53. models
54. feedback
55. responses; principle
56. responses; response; removing
57. learning; goals; successes

Connections

1. E
2. I
3. A
4. H
5. B
6. G
7. C
8. D
9. F
10. A
11. J
12. B
13. G
14. C
15. D
16. F
17. E
18. H
19. I
20. D
21. E
22. G
23. F
24. H
25. J
26. I
27. A
28. C
29. B

Short-Answer Questions

1. Since you don't want to examine your friend's dog's eye under an electron microscope to look for the presence of cones, you need another way to tell if the dog can see colours. Classical conditioning can be used to determine whether a dog can see colour in the following way. If the dog can tell the difference between two colours, you should be able to establish a conditioned response to one colour, but not the other. A light of one colour (Light A) could be paired with food in the dog's mouth, while a light of another colour (Light B) is never paired with the food. If the dog begins to salivate to Light A but never to Light B (assuming that the lights are equal intensity, among other things), we can be fairly certain that the dog cannot discriminate between the two colours.

2. Susan's aversion to the peanut butter sandwich is an example of a conditioned taste aversion. The conditioned stimulus is the peanuts, the unconditioned stimulus is the beer, or whatever made her sick in the first place, the unconditioned response was getting sick on the beer and the conditioned response is the nausea she now feels when you offer her the peanut butter sandwich.

3. Both positive and negative reinforcement strengthen a response. Positive reinforcement involves a positive outcome (something you like or want) and

negative reinforcement involves the removal of an unpleasant or aversive stimulus (as when a pill takes away a headache). In either case, the behaviour is strengthened. Punishment is defined as an event that follows a response and makes it less likely to happen again. If you take a pill for your headache and it makes it worse, you will probably not take that pill again. Response cost is the removal of a reinforcer in order to eliminate a behaviour. If you come home too late too often, you might be punished by being grounded, or lose the use of the family car.

4. Social reinforcers are reinforcers that satisfy peoples' desire for attention and approval. In other words, they are reinforcers provided by other people. If Ms. Ashropova is paying attention to the students in her class only when they misbehave, she is reinforcing misbehaviour. Since most elementary school children want, need, and like the teacher's attention, it is no surprise that they misbehave in order to get it. Ms. Ashropova would probably have better results if she rewarded the desired behaviour instead.

5. Secondary reinforcers become reinforcing in two ways. First, they may become reinforcing because they are associated with primary reinforcers. If a dog is praised ("good boy") at the same time he is given a treat, the praise will become a secondary reinforcer. Other secondary reinforcers, such as money, are reinforcing because they can be exchanged for things that you need or want.

6. Avoid the use of punishment whenever possible; positive reinforcement usually works better. If possible, punish immediately. Use the minimum punishment necessary to suppress the behaviour. Be consistent, and punish with respect.

7. First, identify the behaviour that you want to change. Next, get a baseline measure of how often you engage in the behaviour, or how much time you spend doing it. Then, establish a realistic goal for change. If you are currently studying ten minutes per week for your psychology course, it is unrealistic to think that you will spend three hours per day on it any time soon. Establish daily, weekly, and/or monthly goals as well, depending on the behaviour you wish to change. Then decide how you will reward yourself for meeting a daily, weekly, or monthly target. Keep accurate records of the behaviour as you do it. If you meet a goal, reward yourself, but be honest. If your reward for an hour spent studying is a TV show you really like, don't watch it if you studied only 20 minutes. Last, change or adapt the plan as you go along. If something doesn't work, don't do it.

Final Survey and Review

1. antecedents; consequences
2. respondent; operant
3. neutral; consequences
4. Ivan Pavlov; unconditioned; reflex
5. conditioned; conditioned
6. unconditioned stimulus
7. Higher order
8. extinction
9. spontaneous recovery
10. generalization
11. discrimination
12. informational
13. CS; US
14. emotional responses
15. phobias; generalization
16. Vicarious
17. aversions; unconditioned response; UR
18. compensating; associated; compensatory or physiological
19. instrumental
20. probability; Thorndike
21. response; increases
22. expectation
23. contingent
24. decreases; reinforcer
25. Superstitious
26. shaping; approximations
27. extinguish; spontaneous
28. positive; negative
29. aversive; positive
30. Primary; stimulation
31. Secondary; primary; primary
32. social
33. knowledge
34. instruction
35. Computer Assisted; Instruction
36. CAI
37. schedule; Skinner
38. extinction; partial
39. ratio; interval
40. FR; VR; FI; extinction
41. stimulus control
42. generalization
43. generalization
44. discrimination
45. punisher
46. consistent
47. reinforced
48. avoidance; aggression
49. Reinforcement; non-reinforcement
50. cognitive maps; latent
51. rote
52. modelling; Observational

53. observational
54. contracting
55. reinforce; Premack
56. alternate; chains; antecedents
57. strategies; reinforcing

Mastery Test

1. A (p. 212)
2. C (p. 214)
3. A (p. 208)
4. B (p. 209)
5. B (p. 200)
6. D (p. 208)
7. C (p. 211)
8. C (p. 226)
9. B (p. 208)
10. D (p. 213)
11. A (p. 216)
12. D (p. 221)
13. B (p. 227)
14. C (p. 199)
15. D (p. 204)
16. D (p. 201)
17. A (p. 218)
18. B (p. 229)
19. C (p. 220)
20. D (p. 216)
21. A (p. 202)
22. A (p. 201)
23. D (p. 203)
24. A (p. 218)
25. B (p. 207)
26. B (p. 213)
27. D (p. 210)
28. B (p. 205)

Memory

Chapter Overview

Memory systems encode and store information for later retrieval. A popular model divides memory into three systems: sensory memory, short-term memory (STM), and long-term memory (LTM). Sensory memory stores exact copies of sensory information for very brief periods. STM is limited to about seven bits of information, but chunking and recoding allow more information to be stored. LTM has nearly unlimited storage. Short-term memories last only a short time; long-term memories are relatively permanent. Long-term memories can be further divided into declarative memories (which may be semantic or episodic) and procedural memories.

Explicit memories are revealed by recall, recognition, and relearning tasks. Implicit memories are revealed by priming. Eidetic imagery (photographic memory) is fairly common in children, but rare among adults. Many people have internal memory images and some have exceptional memory based on internal imagery. Exceptional memory capacity is based on both learned strategies and natural abilities.

Forgetting is most rapid immediately after learning. Some "forgetting" is based on a failure to encode information. Short-term forgetting is partly explained by the decay (weakening) of memory traces. Some long-term forgetting may also occur this way. Some forgetting is related to a lack of memory cues. Much forgetting is related to interference among memories. Clinical psychologists believe that memories are sometimes repressed (unconsciously held out of awareness). Some also believe that repressed childhood memories of abuse can be "recovered." However, there is often no way to separate true memories from fantasies.

In the brain, memory traces (engrams) must be consolidated before they become relatively permanent. The hippocampus is a structure involved in memory consolidation. Information appears to be stored in the brain through changes in nerve cells.

Memory can be improved by the use of mnemonic systems and by attention to factors that affect memory, such as overlearning, serial position, organization, and the like.

Learning Objectives

After reading this chapter, students will be able to:

1. Trace the path of incoming information from the environment to long-term memory.
2. Describe the features of each type of memory.

3. Show how recoding and rehearsing can affect short-term memory.

4. Explain how memories may be changed or updated.

5. Describe how memories are organized.

6. Explain procedural, declarative, semantic, and episodic memory.

7. Show how recall, recognition, and relearning can be used to measure memory.

8. Explain forgetting and describe the common causes of forgetting.

9. Explain how memories are formed in the brain and identify the brain structures involved.

10. Give examples of techniques that can be used to improve memory and explain why they work.

Practice Quizzes

Recite and Review

Is there more than one type of memory?

Recite and Review: Pages 236–239

1. Memory is an active _____ . _____ is first encoded (changed into the form in which it will be retained).

2. Next it is _____ in memory. Later it must be retrieved to be put to use.

3. Humans appear to have _____ interrelated memory systems. These are sensory memory, _____ - _____ memory, and _____ - _____ memory.

4. Sensory memory holds an _____ copy of what is seen or heard, in the form of an icon (_____) or echo (sound sensation).

5. Short-term memories tend to be stored as _____ . Long-term memories are stored on the basis of _____ , or importance.

6. STM acts as a _____ storehouse for small amounts of information. It provides a working memory where thinking, mental arithmetic, and the like take place. LTM acts as a _____ storehouse for meaningful information.

7. Sensory memory is exact, but very brief, lasting only a few _____ or less. Through selective attention, some information is transferred to _____ .

What are the features of each type of memory?

Recite and Review: Pages 239–243

8. The digit-span test reveals that STM has an average upper limit of about seven _____ of information. However, this can be extended by chunking, or recoding information into _____ units or groups.

9. Short-term memories are brief and very sensitive to _____ , or interference; however, they can be prolonged by maintenance rehearsal (silent _____).

10. Elaborative rehearsal, which emphasizes meaning, helps transfer information from _____ to LTM. Elaborative rehearsal links new information with existing _____ .

11. LTM seems to have an almost unlimited storage capacity. However, LTM is subject to constructive processing, or ongoing revision and _____ . As a result, people often have pseudo-memories (_____ memories) that they believe are true.

12. LTM is highly _____ to allow retrieval of needed information. The pattern, or structure, of memory networks is the subject of current memory research. Network _____ portray LTM as a system of linked ideas.

Is there more than one type of long-term memory?
Recite and Review: Pages 243–245

13. Within long-term memory, declarative memories for _____ seem to differ from procedural memories for _____ .

14. _____ memories may be further categorized as semantic memories or episodic memories.

15. Semantic memories consist of basic factual knowledge that is almost immune to _____ .

16. Episodic memories record _____ experiences that are associated with specific times and places.

How is memory measured?
Recite and Review: Pages 246–248

17. The tip-of-the-tongue _____ shows that memory is not an all-or-nothing event. Memories may be revealed by _____ , recognition, or relearning.

18. In recall, memory proceeds without specific cues, as in an _____ exam. Recall of listed information often reveals a serial position effect (_____ items on the list are most subject to errors).

19. A common test of _____ is the multiple-choice question. _____ is very sensitive to the kinds of distractors (wrong choices) used.

20. In relearning, "forgotten" material is learned again, and memory is indicated by a _____ score.

21. Recall, recognition, and relearning mainly measure explicit _____ that we are aware of having. Other techniques, such as priming, are necessary to reveal implicit _____ , which are unconscious.

22. _____ can facilitate the retrieval of an implicit memory by making use of _____ to trigger hidden memories.

What are "photographic" memories?
Recite and Review: Pages 248–251

23. Eidetic imagery (photographic memory) occurs when a person is able to project an _____ onto an external surface. Such images allow brief, nearly complete recall by some children.

24. Eidetic imagery is rarely found in _____ . However, many adults have internal images, which can be very vivid and a basis for remembering.

25. Exceptional memory can be learned by finding ways to directly store information in _____ . Learning has no effect on the limits of _____ . Some people may have naturally superior memory abilities that exceed what can be achieved through learning.

What causes forgetting?

Recite and Review: Pages 252–256

26. Forgetting and memory were extensively studied by Herman Ebbinghaus, whose _____ of forgetting shows that forgetting is typically most rapid immediately _____ learning.

27. Ebbinghaus used nonsense syllables to study memory. The forgetting of _____ material is much _____ than shown by his curve of forgetting.

28. Failure to encode _____ is a common cause of "forgetting."

29. Forgetting in sensory memory and STM probably reflects decay of memory _____ in the nervous system. Decay or _____ of memories may also account for some LTM loss, but most forgetting cannot be explained this way.

30. Often, forgetting is cue dependent. The power of cues to trigger memories is revealed by state-dependent _____ , in which bodily _____ at the time of learning and of retrieval affect memory.

31. Much _____ in both STM and LTM can be attributed to interference of memories with one another.

32. When recent learning _____ with retrieval of prior learning, retroactive interference has occurred. If old memories interfere with new memories, proactive interference has occurred.

How accurate are everyday memories?

Recite and Review: Pages 257–258

33. Repression is the _____ of painful, embarrassing, or traumatic memories.

34. Repression is thought to be unconscious, in contrast to suppression, which is a _____ attempt to avoid thinking about something.

35. Experts are currently debating the validity of childhood memories of _____ that reappear after apparently being repressed for decades.

36. Canadian researchers have shown that preschoolers can be susceptible to _____ when the interviewer is _____ , when asked detailed questions, and when false events are suggested many times.

37. Independent evidence has verified that some recovered memories are _____ . However, others have been shown to be _____ .

38. In the absence of confirming or disconfirming _____ , there is currently no way to separate true memories from fantasies. Caution is advised for all concerned with attempts to retrieve supposedly hidden memories.

39. Flashbulb memories, which seem especially vivid, are created at emotionally significant times. While such memories may not be accurate, we tend to place great _____ in them.

What happens in the brain when memories are formed?

Recite and Review: Pages 259–261

40. Retrograde _____ and the effects of electroconvulsive _____ (ECS) may be explained by the concept of consolidation.

41. Consolidation theory holds that engrams (permanent _____ _____) are formed during a critical period after learning. Until they are consolidated, long-term memories are easily destroyed.

42. The hippocampus is a _____ structure associated with the consolidation of memories.

43. The search within the brain for engrams has now settled on changes in individual _____ cells.

44. The best-documented changes are alterations in the amounts of transmitter _____ released by nerve cells.

How can memory be improved?

Recite and Review: Pages 261–264 & Psychology in Action

45. Memory can be improved by using feedback, recitation, and rehearsal, by selecting and _____ information, and by using the progressive _____ method, spaced practice, overlearning, and active search strategies.

46. The effects of serial _____ , sleep, review, cues, and elaboration should also be kept in mind when studying or memorizing.

47. Mnemonic systems, such as the _____ method, use mental images and unusual associations to link new information with familiar memories already stored in _____ . Such strategies give information personal meaning and make it easier to recall.

Connections

1. _____ echoes and icons
2. _____ working memory
3. _____ seven information bits
4. _____ chunking
5. _____ revised memories
6. _____ memory structure
7. _____ pseudo-memories
8. _____ self-reference effect

a. STM
b. constructive processing
c. network model
d. sensory memory
e. false memories
f. recoding
g. better recall
h. magic number

9. _____ selective attention
10. _____ long-term memory
11. _____ incoming information
12. _____ encoding for LTM
13. _____ sensory memory
14. _____ short-term memory
15. _____ rehearsal buffer

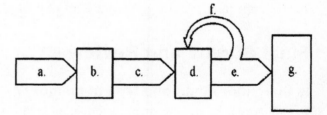

16. _____ semantic memory
17. _____ long-term memory
18. _____ procedural memory
19. _____ sensory memory
20. _____ episodic memory
21. _____ short-term memory
22. _____ declarative memory

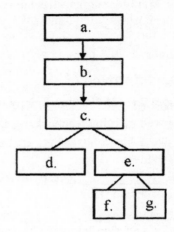

Short-Answer Questions

1. How is information transferred from sensory memory to short-term memory?
2. What is a pseudo-memory? How are they formed?
3. Distinguish between implicit and explicit memories.
4. What effect does hypnosis have on memory?
5. Describe cue-dependent forgetting.
6. Explain the effects of interference on forgetting.
7. What is a flashbulb memory? Can you give an example from yourown experience?
8. Describe the role of consolidation in the formation of new memories.
9. What are the four basic principles of mnemonics?
10. Describe three ways to remember a list of things in order.

Final Survey and Review

Is there more than one type of memory?

1. Memory is an active system. Information is first _____ (changed into the form in which it will be retained).
2. Next it is stored in memory. Later it must be _____ to be put to use.
3. Humans appear to have three interrelated memory systems. These are _____ memory, _____ - _____ memory, and long-term memory.
4. Sensory memory holds an exact copy of what is seen or heard, in the form of an _____ (image) or _____ (sound sensation).
5. _____ - _____ memories tend to be stored as sounds. _____ - _____ memories are stored on the basis of meaning, or importance.

6. _____ acts as a temporary storehouse for small amounts of information. It provides a _____ memory where thinking, mental arithmetic, and the like take place. LTM acts as a permanent storehouse for _____ information.

7. _____ memory is exact, but very brief, lasting only a few seconds or less. Through _____ _____ , some information is transferred to STM.

What are the features of each type of memory?

8. The _____ - _____ test reveals that STM has an average upper limit of about seven bits of information. However, this can be extended by chunking, or _____ information into larger units or groups.

9. Short-term memories are brief and very sensitive to interruption, or _____ ; however, they can be prolonged by _____ rehearsal (silent repetition).

10. _____ rehearsal, which emphasizes meaning, helps transfer information from STM to LTM.

11. LTM seems to have an almost unlimited storage capacity. However, LTM is subject to _____ processing, or ongoing revision and updating. As a result, people often have _____ - _____ (false memories) that they believe are true.

12. LTM is highly organized to allow retrieval of needed information. The pattern, or structure, of memory _____ is the subject of current memory research. _____ models portray LTM as a system of linked ideas.

Is there more than one type of long-term memory?

13. Within long-term memory, _____ memories for facts seem to differ from _____ memories for skills.

14. Declarative memories may be further categorized as _____ memories or _____ memories.

15. _____ memories consist of basic factual knowledge that is almost immune to forgetting.

16. _____ memories record personal experiences that are associated with specific times and places.

How is memory measured?

17. The _____ -of-the- _____ state shows that memory is not an all-or-nothing event. Memories may be revealed by recall, _____ , or relearning.

18. In _____ , memory proceeds without specific cues, as in an essay exam. Remembering a list of information often reveals a _____ _____ effect (middle items on the list are most subject to errors).

19. A common test of recognition is the _____ -choice question. Recognition is very sensitive to the kinds of _____ (wrong choices) used.

20. In _____ , "forgotten" material is learned again, and memory is indicated by a savings score.

21. Recall, recognition, and relearning mainly measure _____ memories that we are aware of having. Other techniques, such as priming, are necessary to reveal _____ memories, which are unconscious.

What are "photographic" memories?

22. _____ _____ (photographic memory) occurs when a person is able to project an image onto an external surface. Such images allow brief, nearly complete recall by some children.

23. _____ _____ is rarely found in adults. However, many adults have internal images, which can be very vivid and a basis for remembering.

24. _____ memory can be learned by finding ways to directly store information in LTM. Learning has no effect on the _____ of STM. Some people may have naturally superior memory abilities that exceed what can be achieved through learning.

What causes forgetting?

25. Forgetting and memory were extensively studied by Herman _____ , whose curve of forgetting shows that forgetting is typically most rapid immediately after learning.

26. He used _____ syllables to study memory. The forgetting of meaningful material is much slower than shown by his curve of forgetting.

27. Failure to _____ information is a common cause of "forgetting."

28. Forgetting in _____ memory and _____ probably reflects decay of memory traces in the nervous system. Decay or disuse of memories may also account for some _____ loss, but most forgetting cannot be explained this way.

29. Often, forgetting is _____ dependent. The power of _____ to trigger memories is revealed by _____ - _____ learning, in which bodily states at the time of learning and of retrieval affect memory.

30. Much forgetting in both STM and LTM can be attributed to _____ of memories with one another.

31. When recent learning interferes with retrieval of prior learning, _____ interference has occurred. If old memories interfere with new memories, _____ interference has occurred.

How accurate are everyday memories?

32. _____ is the motivated forgetting of painful, embarrassing, or traumatic memories.

33. _____ is thought to be unconscious, in contrast to _____ , which is a conscious attempt to avoid thinking about something.

34. Experts are currently debating the validity of childhood memories of abuse that reappear after apparently being _____ for decades.

35. Preschoolers can be influenced by suggestion if the interviewer is biased, if they are asked _____ questions, and if false events are suggested _____ .

36. Independent evidence has verified that some _____ memories are true. However, others have been shown to be false.

37. In the absence of confirming or disconfirming evidence, there is currently no way to separate true memories from _____ . Caution is advised for all concerned with attempts to retrieve supposedly hidden memories.

38. _____ memories, which seem especially vivid, are created at emotionally significant times. While such memories may not be _____ , we tend to place great confidence in them.

What happens in the brain when memories are formed?

39. _____ amnesia and the effects of _____ shock (ECS) may be explained by the concept of consolidation.

40. Consolidation theory holds that _____ (permanent memory traces) are formed during a critical period after learning. Until they are _____ , long-term memories are easily destroyed.

41. The _____ is a brain structure associated with the consolidation of memories.

42. The search within the brain for engrams has now settled on changes in individual _____
_____ .

43. The best-documented changes are alterations in the amounts of _____ chemicals released by nerve cells.

How can memory be improved?

44. Memory can be improved by using _____ (knowledge of results), recitation, and rehearsal, by _____ and organizing information, and by using the progressive part method, spaced practice, overlearning, and active _____ strategies.

45. The effects of _____ position, sleep, review, cues, and _____ (connecting new information to existing knowledge) should also be kept in mind when studying or memorizing.

46. _____ systems, such as the keyword method, use mental images and unusual associations to link new information with familiar memories already stored in LTM. Such strategies give information personal meaning and make it easier to recall.

Mastery Test

1. The meaning and importance of information has a strong impact on
   a. sensory memory
   b. eidetic memory
   c. long-term memory
   d. procedural memory

2. Pseudo-memories are closely related to the effects of
   a. repression
   b. suppression
   c. semantic forgetting
   d. constructive processing

3. The occurrence of _____ implies that consolidation has been prevented.
   a. retrograde amnesia
   b. hippocampal transfer
   c. suppression
   d. changes in the activities of individual nerve cells

4. Most of the techniques used to recover supposedly repressed memories involve
   a. redintegration and hypnosis
   b. suggestion and fantasy
   c. reconstruction and priming
   d. coercion and fabrication

5. Most daily memory chores are handled by
   a. sensory memory and LTM
   b. STM and working memory
   c. STM and LTM
   d. STM and declarative memory

6. Three key processes in memory systems are
   a. storage, organization, recovery
   b. encoding, attention, reprocessing
   c. encoding, storage, retrieval
   d. retrieval, reprocessing, reorganization

7. Procedural memories are to skills as _____ memories are to facts.
   a. declarative
   b. short-term
   c. redintegrative
   d. eidetic

8. An ability to answer questions about distances on a map you have seen only once implies that some memories are based on
   a. constructive processing
   b. redintegration
   c. internal images
   d. episodic processing

9. Sally gives John her phone number after class. Unfortunately, when John decides to call her the next day, he cannot remember her number. The most likely explanation for this is
   a. engram decay
   b. disuse
   c. cue-dependent forgetting
   d. encoding failure

10. Icons and echoes are found in
    a. sensory memory
    b. short-term memory
    c. long-term memory
    d. working memory

11. Priming is most often used to elicit
    a. semantic memories
    b. episodic memories
    c. implicit memories
    d. eidetic memories

12. Elizabeth is able to project the image of a moving horse onto a blank piece of paper and trace around it. She has
    a. sensory memories
    b. eidetic imagery
    c. flashbulb memories
    d. mnemonic imagery

13. Chunking may be used to increase the capacity of
    a. sensory memory
    b. STM
    c. LTM
    d. declarative memory

14. There is currently no way to tell if a "recovered" memory is true or false unless independent _____ exists.
    a. evidence
    b. amnesia
    c. elaboration
    d. consolidation

15. Essay tests require the use of
    a. recall
    b. recognition
    c. relearning
    d. priming

16. A savings score is a measure of
    a. recall
    b. recognition
    c. relearning
    d. priming

17. _____ rehearsal helps link new information to existing memories by concentrating on meaning.
    a. Redintegrative
    b. Constructive
    c. Maintenance
    d. Elaborative

18. Serge learns a list of 20 English vocabulary words. On a test, he makes the most mistakes on the words in the middle of the list. This is due to the
    a. feeling of knowledge
    b. serial position effect
    c. tip-of-the-tongue state
    d. semantic forgetting curve

19. According to the curve of forgetting, the greatest decline in the amount recalled occurs during the _____ after learning.
    a. first hour
    b. second day
    c. third to sixth days
    d. retroactive period

20. Most memory researchers believe that long-term memories are
    a. stored in the hippocampus
    b. relatively permanent
    c. unaffected by later input
    d. permanent only for facts

21. Which of the following is most likely to improve the accuracy of recall?
    a. hypnosis
    b. constructive processing
    c. the serial position effect
    d. memory cues

22. To qualify as repression, forgetting must be
    a. retroactive
    b. proactive
    c. unconscious
    d. explicit

23. Which of the following typically is NOT a good way to improve memory?
    a. cramming
    b. overlearning
    c. rehearsal
    d. recall strategies

24. One thing that is clearly true about flashbulb memories is that
    a. they are unusually accurate
    b. we place great confidence in them
    c. they apply primarily to public tragedies
    d. they are recovered by using visualization and hypnosis

25. One common mnemonic strategy is the
    a. serial position technique
    b. feeling of knowing tactic
    c. network procedure
    d. keyword method

26. An adult hockey fanatic in your family knows all the names of hockey players and their sweater numbers since the beginning of the NHL. This individual's capacity shows
    a. that memory skills can be learned
    b. what one can do with eidetic memory
    c. that such feats can be accomplished only with procedural knowledge (memory)
    d. the importance of sensory memory in memorizing information

27. Which of the following is NOT considered a part of long-term memory?
    a. echoic memory
    b. semantic memory
    c. episodic memory
    d. declarative memory

28. You are very thirsty. Suddenly you remember a time years ago when you became very thirsty while hiking. This suggests that your memory is
    a. proactive
    b. state dependent
    c. still not consolidated
    d. eidetic

29. After memorizing five lists of words you recall fewer items on the last list than a person who memorized only list number five. This observation is explained by
    a. reactive processing
    b. reconstructive processing
    c. proactive interference
    d. retroactive interference

Solutions

Recite and Review

1. system; Information
2. stored
3. three; short; term; long; term
4. exact; image
5. sounds; meaning
6. temporary; permanent
7. seconds; STM
8. bits; larger
9. interruption; repetition
10. STM; memories
11. updating; false
12. organized; models
13. facts; skills
14. Declarative
15. forgetting
16. personal
17. state; recall
18. essay; middle
19. recognition; Recognition
20. savings
21. memories; memories
22. Priming; cues
23. image
24. adults
25. LTM; STM
26. curve; after
27. meaningful; slower
28. information
29. traces; disuse
30. learning; states
31. forgetting
32. interferes
33. forgetting
34. conscious
35. abuse
36. suggestion; biased
37. true; false
38. evidence
39. confidence
40. amnesia; shock
41. memory traces
42. brain
43. nerve
44. chemicals
45. organizing; part
46. position
47. keyword; LTM

Connections

1. D
2. A
3. H
4. F
5. B
6. C
7. E
8. G
9. C
10. G
11. A
12. E
13. B
14. D
15. F
16. F or G
17. C
18. D
19. A
20. F or G
21. B
22. E

Short-Answer Questions

1. Selective attention controls what information moves from sensory to short-term memory.

2. A pseudo-memory is a false memory that a person believes is accurate. They are more likely to occur in response to very negative experiences than to neutral or positive experiences. They are a problem in eyewitness identification as well; if people see a picture of a suspect, they are more likely to identify the suspect in a lineup. Pseudo-memories are formed because memory is a constructive process; that is, we are constantly updating or reorganizing memories to take new information into account.

3. Implicit memories are outside conscious awareness. For example, experienced keyboarders can find all the keys on a keyboard even if they can't identify them on a blank drawing. Explicit memories are past experiences that you deliberately call to mind, as when writing an exam or remembering an event.

4. Hypnosis has occasionally been used to help people recall events. However, researchers have found that hypnotized people are more likely to use imagination to fill in any memory gaps, and are more confident that their memories are accurate even when they are not. Hypnosis actually facilitates the production of false memories. Even if hypnotized people produce more information, there is no way to tell which memories are true and which are not.

5. Memories may be "forgotten" because appropriate cues are not available to help us recall them. A memory may be available (stored in memory) but not accessible (you can't access it) until you are given a cue to facilitate recall (as in a multiple-choice test).

6. Interference is the tendency for memories to impair the recall of other memories. Retroactive interference occurs when new memories interfere with the recall of old memories. Proactive

interference occurs when old memories interfere with the recall of new memories.

7. A flashbulb memory is an especially vivid, detailed memory that is formed at a time of high emotion. Depending on age, a person may have a flashbulb memory of the *Titanic*, the *Challenger* disaster, the winning goal in the seventh game of the 1972 Canada–Russia hockey series, etc. Although they are vivid and detailed, flashbulb memories are not always accurate.

8. Consolidation is the process by which the brain forms new long-term memories. Anything that disrupts consolidation (head injury, seizure, or ECS) will result in a loss of memory for things that preceded the event (retrograde amnesia). The hippocampus is especially important in this process.

9. 1. Use mental images (vivid is better). 2. Make information meaningful. 3. Make the information familiar; link it with what you already know. 4. Form unusual, bizarre, or exaggerated mental associations.

10. 1. Form a chain of associations connecting each item to the one before it. 2. Attach each item in order to items found along a familiar path (like from the front door to the fridge); when you want to recall the list, take a walk. 3. Use a system or rhyme (for example, Roy G. Biv denotes the colours of the visible spectrum, or Mrs. Vandertamp

is a list of the French verbs that take étre in the passé compose.)

Final Survey and Review

1. encoded
2. retrieved
3. sensory; short term
4. icon; echo
5. Short term; Long term
6. STM; working; meaningful
7. Sensory; selective; attention
8. digit; span; recoding
9. interference; maintenance
10. Elaborative
11. constructive; pseudo memories
12. networks; Network
13. declarative; procedural
14. semantic; episodic
15. Semantic
16. Episodic
17. tip; tongue; recognition
18. recall; serial; position
19. multiple; distractors
20. relearning
21. explicit; implicit
22. Eidetic; imagery
23. Eidetic; imagery
24. Exceptional; limits
25. Ebbinghaus
26. nonsense
27. encode
28. sensory; STM; LTM
29. cue; cues; state dependent
30. interference
31. retroactive; proactive
32. Repression
33. Repression; suppression
34. repressed
35. specific; repeatedly
36. recovered
37. fantasies
38. Flashbulb; accurate
39. Retrograde; electroconvulsive
40. engrams; consolidated
41. hippocampus
42. nerve; cells
43. transmitter
44. feedback; selecting; search
45. serial; elaboration
46. Mneumonic

Mastery Test

1. C (p. 238)
2. D (p. 242)
3. A (p. 259)
4. B (p. 258)
5. C (p. 238)
6. C (p. 236)
7. A (p. 244
8. C (p. 248)
9. D (p. 253)
10. A (p. 237)
11. C (p. 248)
12. B (p. 249)
13. B (p. 240)
14. A (p. 258)
15. A (p. 246)
16. C (p. 247)
17. D (p. 240)
18. B (p. 246)
19. A (p. 252)
20. B (p. 241)
21. D (p. 262)
22. C (p. 257)
23. A (p. 264)
24. B (p. 258)
25. D (p. 266)
26. A (p. 250)
27. A (p. 244)
28. B (p. 255)
29. C (p. 256)

Cognition and Intelligence

Chapter Overview

Thinking is the mental manipulation of images, concepts, and language (or symbols). Most people use internal images (including kinesthetic images) for thinking. A concept is a generalized idea of a class of objects or events. We learn concepts from positive and negative instances, and from rules. Different types of concepts are used. Prototypes are often used to identify concepts. Language translates events into symbols, which are combined using the rules of grammar and syntax. True languages are productive. Studies suggest that, with training, primates are capable of some language use.

The solution to a problem may be arrived at mechanically (by trial and error or by rote). Solutions developed through understanding usually begin with discovering the general properties of an answer. Problem solving is frequently aided by analogies and heuristics, which can guide and narrow the search for solutions. When understanding leads to a rapid solution, insight has occurred. Insight can be blocked by fixations. Work on artificial intelligence has focused on computer simulations and expert systems. Human expertise is based on organized knowledge and acquired strategies.

Intelligence refers to a general capacity to act purposefully, think rationally, and deal effectively with the environment. In practice, intelligence is operationally defined by creating tests. The first practical individual intelligence test was assembled by Alfred Binet. A modern version is the Stanford-Binet Intelligence Scale. A second major intelligence test is the Wechsler Adult Intelligence Scale. Culture-fair and group intelligence tests are also available. Intelligence is expressed as an intelligence quotient (IQ) or as a deviation IQ. The distribution of IQ scores approximates a normal curve. Intelligence reflects the combined effects of heredity and environment.

People with IQs in the gifted or "genius" range tend to be superior in many respects. Many children are gifted or talented in other ways. The terms *mentally retarded* and *developmentally disabled* apply to persons who have an IQ below 70 or who lack various adaptive behaviours. About 50 percent of the cases of mental retardation are organic; the remaining cases are of undetermined cause (many are thought to be familial).

Intuitive thinking often leads to errors. Wrong conclusions may be drawn when an answer seems highly representative of what we already believe is true. A second problem involves ignoring the base rate of an event. Clear thinking is usually aided by stating or framing a problem in broad terms. Major sources of thinking errors include rigid mental sets, faulty logic, and oversimplifications. Various strategies, including brainstorming, tend to enhance creative problem solving.

Learning Objectives

After reading this chapter, students will be able to:

1. Define cognition. Distinguish between images and concepts. Explain how concepts are formed.

2. Describe the characteristics of a true language.

3. Describe three approaches to problem solving. Distinguish between general and functional solutions.

4. Discuss the common barriers to problem solving. Give examples of each.

5. Define artificial intelligence and show how it relates to cognition.

6. Discuss the difficulties in using intuition to solve problems.

7. Distinguish between the Stanford-Binet and Wechsler tests of intelligence. Explain what is meant by a culture-fair test.

8. Explain the concept of mental age.

9. Describe the relationship between intelligence and achievement.

10. Discuss sex differences in intelligence.

11. Discuss the causes of mental retardation.

12. Describe the relationship between heredity, environment, and intelligence.

Practice Quizzes

Recite and Review

What is the nature of thought?

Recite and Review: Pages 272–273

1. Cognitive psychology is the study of human _____ processing (thinking, language, and problem solving).

2. Thinking is the manipulation of _____ representations of external problems or situations.

3. Three basic units of thought are images, concepts, and _____ or symbols.

In what ways are images related to thinking?

Recite and Review: Pages 273–275

4. Most people have internal images of one kind or another. Images may be based on information stored in memory or they may be _____ .

5. The size of images used in problem solving may _____ . Images may be three-dimensional and they may be rotated in _____ to answer questions.

6. Many of the systems in the brain that are involved in processing _____ images work in reverse to create mental images.

How are concepts learned? Are there different kinds of concepts?

Recite and Review: Pages 275–277

7. A concept is a generalized idea of a _____ of objects or events.

8. Forming concepts may be based on experiences with _____ and negative instances.

9. Concepts may also be acquired by learning rules that define the _____ .

10. In practice, we frequently use prototypes (general _____ of the concept class) to identify concepts.

11. Concepts may be classified as conjunctive (" _____ " concepts), disjunctive (" _____ - _____ " concepts), relational concepts, or exemplars (past _____).

12. The denotative meaning of a word or concept is its exact _____ . Connotative meaning is _____ or emotional.

13. Connotative meaning can be measured with the semantic differential. Most connotative meaning involves the dimensions _____ - _____ , strong-weak, and active-passive.

What is the role of language in thinking?

Recite and Review: Pages 277–280

14. Language allows events to be encoded into _____ for easy mental manipulation.

15. Language is built out of phonemes (basic speech _____) and morphemes (speech sounds collected into _____ units).

16. Thinking in language is influenced by _____ . The study of meaning is called semantics.

17. Language carries meaning by combining a set of symbols or signs according to a set of _____ (grammar), which includes _____ about word rules (syntax).

18. Various sentences are created by applying transformation _____ to simple statements.

19. A true language is productive, and can be used to generate new ideas or possibilities. American Sign Language (ASL) and other _____ languages used by deaf people are true languages.

Can animals be taught to use language?

Recite and Review: Pages 280–282

20. Animal communication is relatively limited because it lacks symbols that can be rearranged easily. As a result, it does not have the productive quality of _____ language.

21. Attempts to teach chimpanzees ASL and other non-verbal systems suggest to some that primates are capable of language use. However, others believe that the chimps are merely using _____ responses to get food and other reinforcers.

22. Studies that make use of lexigrams (_____ word-symbols) provide the best evidence yet of animal language use.

What do we know about problem solving?

Recite and Review: Pages 282–287

23. The solution to a problem may be found mechanically (by trial and error or by _____ application of rules). However, mechanical solutions are frequently inefficient or ineffective, except where aided by _____ .

24. Solutions by understanding usually involves a _____ comprehension of the problem. Using _____ has been shown to help find solutions.

25. Problem solving is frequently aided by heuristics. These are strategies that typically _____ the search for solutions.

26. When understanding leads to a rapid _____ , insight has occurred. Three elements of insight are _____ encoding, selective combination, and selective comparison.

27. Insights and other problem-solving attempts can be blocked by fixation (a tendency to repeat _____ solutions).

28. Functional fixedness is a common _____ , but emotional blocks, cultural values, learned conventions, and perceptual _____ are also problems.

What is artificial intelligence?
Recite and Review: Pages 287–288

29. Artificial intelligence refers to computer _____ that can perform tasks that require _____ when done by people.

30. Two principal areas of artificial intelligence research are _____ simulations and expert systems.

31. Expert human problem solving is based on organized _____ and acquired strategies, rather than some general improvement in thinking ability.

How accurate is intuition?
Recite and Review: Pages 288–291

32. Intuitive thinking often leads to _____ . Wrong conclusions may be drawn when an answer seems highly representative of what we already believe is _____ . (That is, when people apply the representativeness heuristic.)

33. A second problem is ignoring the base rate (or underlying _____) of an event.

34. Clear thinking is usually aided by stating or framing a problem in _____ terms.

How is human intelligence defined and measured?
Recite and Review: Pages 291–295

35. Intelligence refers to one's general capacity to act purposefully, think _____ , and deal effectively with the _____ .

36. In practice, writing an intelligence test provides an operational _____ of intelligence.

37. The first practical _____ _____ was assembled in 1904, in Paris, by Alfred Binet.

38. A modern version of Binet's test is the Stanford-Binet _____ _____ , Fourth Edition.

39. The Stanford-Binet measures _____ reasoning, quantitative reasoning, abstract/visual reasoning, and short-term _____ .

40. Intelligence is expressed in terms of an intelligence _____ (IQ). IQ is defined as mental age (MA) divided by chronological age (CA) and then multiplied by _____ .

41. An "average" IQ of _____ occurs when mental age _____ chronological age.

42. Modern IQ tests no longer calculate _____ directly. Instead, the final score reported by the test is a deviation IQ, which gives a person's _____ intellectual standing in his or her age group.

43. A second major intelligence test is the Wechsler _____ Intelligence Scale, Third Edition (WAIS-III). The WAIS-III measures both verbal and performance (_____) intelligence.

44. Intelligence tests have also been produced for use with _____ of people. The Scholastic Assessment Test (SAT), measures a variety of _____ aptitudes and it can be used to estimate intelligence.

How do IQ scores relate to achievement and thinking ability?

Recite and Review: Pages 296–303

45. When graphed, the distribution (percentage of people receiving each score) of IQ scores approximates a normal (_____ -shaped) _____ .

46. While researchers agree that men and women do not differ in _____ intelligence, a debate still exists as to whether specific differences are due to _____ or due to biological influences in men and women.

47. People with IQs above 140 are considered to be in the _____ or "genius" range.

48. Studies done by Lewis Terman showed that the gifted tend to have a higher _____ between IQ score and real-world success.

49. By criteria other than _____ , a large proportion of children might be considered gifted or talented in one way or another.

50. Howard Gardner believes that _____ IQ tests define intelligence too narrowly. According to Gardner, intelligence consists of abilities in language, logic and _____ , _____ and spatial thinking, music, kinesthetic skills, intrapersonal skills, interpersonal skills, and naturalist skills.

51. The terms *mentally* _____ and *developmentally disabled* are applied to those whose IQ falls below _____ or who lack various adaptive behaviours.

52. Further classifications of retardation are _____ (50–55 to 70), moderate (35–40 to 50–55), _____ (20–25 to 35–40), and profound (below 20–25).

53. About _____ percent of the cases of mental retardation are organic, being caused by _____ injuries, fetal damage, metabolic disorders, or genetic abnormalities. The remaining cases are of undetermined cause.

54. Many cases of subnormal intelligence are thought to be the result of familial retardation (a low level of _____ stimulation in the home, poverty, and poor nutrition).

55. Studies of family relationships in humans, especially comparisons between fraternal twins and identical twins (who have identical _____), also suggest that intelligence is partly _____ .

56. However, environment is also important, as revealed by changes in tested intelligence induced by _____ environments and improved education.

57. _____ therefore reflects the combined effects of heredity and environment.

58. Differences in the average IQ scores for various racial groups are based on environmental differences, not _____ (or _____).

What can be done to improve thinking and promote creativity?

Recite and Review: Psychology in Action

59. _____ sets can act as major barriers to creative _____ .

60. Creativity can be enhanced by defining problems _____ , by establishing a creative atmosphere, restating a problem in _____ ways, by allowing _____ for incubation, by seeking _____ input, by taking sensible risks, and by looking for analogies.

61. Brainstorming, in which the production and criticism of ideas are kept _____ , also tends to enhance creative problem solving.

Connections

1. _____ cognition
2. _____ language
3. _____ examplar
4. _____ mental rotation
5. _____ reverse vision
6. _____ stored images
7. _____ kinesthetic imagery
8. _____ concept
9. _____ prototype
10. _____ connotative meaning

a. 3-D images
b. remembered perceptions
c. images created by brain
d. mental class
e. implicit actions
f. thinking
g. ideal or model
h. emotional meaning
i. representation of past experiences
j. symbols and rules

11. _____ word meanings
12. _____ morpheme
13. _____ phoneme
14. _____ "hidden" grammar rules
15. _____ Washoe
16. _____ insight
17. _____ Kanzi
18. _____ trial-and-error
19. _____ heuristic
20. _____ fixation

a. meaningful unit
b. ASL
c. semantics
d. lexigrams
e. language sound
f. mechanical solution
g. thinking strategy
h. blind to alternatives
i. sudden solution
j. transformation rules

21. _____ Binet
22. _____ identical twins
23. _____ IQ
24. _____ deviation IQ
25. _____ fluid reasoning
26. _____ memory test
27. _____ WAIS
28. _____ culture-fair test
29. _____ group test
30. _____ normal curve

a. same genes
b. relative standing
c. Wechsler test
d. first intelligence test
e. ethnic minority
f. Scholastic Assessment Test (SAT)
g. bell shape
h. digit span
i. MA/CA X 100
j. reasoning ability

31. _____ fixation	a.	knowledge plus rules
32. _____ expert systems	b.	many types of solutions
33. _____ fluency	c.	underlying odds
34. _____ flexibility	d.	affects decisions
35. _____ originality	e.	many solutions
36. _____ base rate	f.	blind to alternatives
37. _____ framing	g.	novelty of solutions

Short-Answer Questions

1. Distinguish between images, concepts, and language.
2. Why are mental images useful in problem solving?
3. In what ways do bees, pigeons, and humans appear to think alike? In what ways do they differ?
4. What is meant by the term *relational concept*? Give an example to illustrate your answer.
5. What is meant by the term *conjunctive concept*? Give an example to illustrate your answer.
6. What is meant by the term *disjunctive concept*? Give an example to illustrate your answer.
7. Describe the research into teaching chimpanzees to use language.
8. Show how insight can be used to solve problems.
9. What is meant by the term *heuristic*? Give an example to illustrate your answer.
10. Explain how studies of twins can be used to support both sides of the heredity-environment controversy as it relates to intelligence.

Final Survey and Review

What is the nature of thought?

1. _____ psychology is the study of human information processing (thinking, _____ , and problem solving).
2. Thinking is the manipulation of internal _____ of external problems or situations.
3. Three basic units of thought are _____ , _____ , and language or _____ .

In what ways are images related to thinking?

4. Most people have internal images of one kind or another. Images may be based on _____ _____ in memory or they may be created.
5. The _____ of images used in problem solving may change. Images may be three-dimensional and they may be _____ in space to answer questions.
6. Many of the systems in the _____ that are involved in processing _____ images work in reverse to create _____ images.

How are concepts learned? Are there different kinds of concepts?

7. A concept is a _____ idea of a class of objects or events.

8. Forming concepts may be based on experiences with positive and _____ _____ .

9. Concepts may also be acquired by learning _____ that define the concept.

10. In practice, we frequently use _____ (general models of the concept class) to identify concepts.

11. Concepts may be classified as _____ ("and" concepts), _____ ("either-or" concepts), relational concepts, or _____ (past experiences).

12. The _____ meaning of a word or concept is its exact definition. _____ meaning is personal or emotional.

13. Connotative meaning can be measured with the _____ differential. Most connotative meaning involves the dimensions good-bad, _____ - _____ , and _____ - _____ .

What is the role of language in thinking?

14. Language allows events to be _____ into symbols for easy mental manipulation.

15. Language is built out of _____ (basic speech sounds) and _____ (speech sounds collected into meaningful units).

16. Thinking in language is influenced by meaning. The study of meaning is called _____ .

17. Language carries meaning by combining a set of symbols or signs according to a set of rules (_____), which includes rules about word order (_____).

18. Various sentences are created by applying _____ rules to simple statements.

19. A true language is _____ , and can be used to generate new ideas or possibilities. _____ _____ Language (ASL) and other gestural languages used by deaf people are true languages.

Can animals be taught to use language?

20. _____ communication is relatively limited because it lacks symbols that can be rearranged easily. As a result, it does not have the _____ quality of human language.

21. Attempts to teach chimpanzees ASL and other non-verbal systems suggest to some that _____ are capable of language use. However, others believe that the chimps are merely using operant responses to get food and other _____ .

22. Studies that make use of _____ (geometric word-symbols) provide the best evidence yet of animal language use.

What do we know about problem solving?

23. The solution to a problem may be found _____ (by trial and error or by rote application of rules). However, _____ solutions are frequently inefficient or ineffective, except where aided by computer.

24. Solutions by _____ usually involves a deeper comprehension of the problem. Using _____ can help find solutions.

25. Problem solving is frequently aided by _____ . These are strategies that typically narrow the search for solutions.

26. When understanding leads to a rapid solution, _____ has occurred. Three elements of _____ are selective _____ , selective combination, and selective comparison.

27. Insights and other problem solving attempts can be blocked by _____ (a tendency to repeat wrong solutions).

28. _____ fixedness is a common fixation, but emotional _____, cultural _____, learned conventions, and perceptual habits are also problems.

What is artificial intelligence?

29. Artificial intelligence refers to _____ _____ that can perform tasks that require intelligence when done by _____ .

30. Two principal areas of artificial intelligence research are computer simulations and _____ _____ .

31. Expert human problem solving is based on _____ knowledge and acquired _____ , rather than some general improvement in thinking ability.

How accurate is intuition?

32. Intuitive thinking often leads to errors. Wrong conclusions may be drawn when an answer seems highly _____ of what we already believe is true. (That is, when people apply the representativeness _____ .)

33. A second problem is ignoring the _____ _____ (or underlying probability) of an event.

34. Clear thinking is usually aided by stating or _____ a problem in broad terms.

How is human intelligence defined and measured?

35. Intelligence refers to one's general capacity to act _____ , _____ rationally, and deal effectively with the environment.

36. In practice, writing an intelligence test provides an _____ definition of intelligence.

37. The first practical intelligence test was assembled in 1904, in Paris, by _____ _____ .

38. A modern version of that test is the _____ - _____ Intelligence Scale, Fourth Edition.

39. The Stanford-Binet measures verbal reasoning, _____ reasoning, _____ /visual reasoning, and short-term memory.

40. Intelligence is expressed in terms of an intelligence quotient (IQ). IQ is defined as _____ _____ (MA) divided by _____ _____ (CA) and then multiplied by 100.

41. An "average" IQ of 100 occurs when _____ age equals _____ age.

42. Modern IQ tests no longer calculate IQ directly. Instead, the final score reported by the test is a _____ _____ , which gives a person's relative intellectual standing in his or her age group.

43. A second major intelligence test is the _____ Adult Intelligence Scale-III (WAIS-III). The WAIS-III measures both _____ and _____ (non-verbal) intelligence.

44. Intelligence tests have also been produced for use with groups of people. The _____ _____ Test (SAT), measures a variety of mental _____ and it can be used to estimate intelligence.

How do IQ scores relate to achievement and thinking ability?

45. When graphed, the _____ (percentage of people receiving each score) of IQ scores approximates a _____ (bell-shaped) curve.

46. While researchers _____ that men and women do not differ in overall intelligence, a debate still exists as to whether _____ differences are due to learning or biological influences.

47. People with IQs above _____ are considered to be in the gifted or "genius" range.

48. Studies done by Lewis _____ showed that the _____ tend to have a higher correlation between IQ score and real world _____ .

49. By criteria other than IQ, a large proportion of children might be considered _____ or _____ in one way or another.

50. Howard _____ believes that traditional IQ tests define intelligence too narrowly. According to Gardner, intelligence consists of abilities in _____ , logic and math, visual and spatial thinking, _____ , kinesthetic skills, intrapersonal skills, interpersonal skills, and _____ skills.

51. The terms *mentally retarded* and _____ *disabled* are applied to those whose IQ falls below 70 or who lack various _____ behaviours.

52. Further classifications of retardation are mild (50–55 to 70), _____ (35–40 to 50–55), severe (20–25 to 35–40), and _____ (below 20–25).

53. About 50 percent of the cases of mental retardation are _____ , being caused by birth injuries, fetal damage, metabolic disorders, or _____ abnormalities. The remaining cases are of undetermined cause.

54. Many cases of subnormal intelligence are thought to be the result of _____ retardation (a low level of intellectual stimulation in the home, poverty, and poor nutrition).

55. Studies of family relationships in humans, especially comparisons between _____ twins and _____ twins, suggest that intelligence is partly hereditary.

56. However, _____ is also important, as revealed by changes in tested intelligence induced by stimulating _____ and improved education.

57. Intelligence therefore reflects the combined effects of _____ and _____ .

58. Differences in the average IQ scores for various racial groups are based on _____ differences, not heredity.

What can be done to improve thinking and promote creativity?

59. Mental _____ can act as major barriers to _____ thinking.

60. Creativity can be enhanced by defining problems broadly, by establishing a creative atmosphere, by allowing time for _____ , by restating a problem in different ways, by seeking varied _____ , by taking sensible _____ , and by looking for analogies.

61. _____ , in which the production and criticism of ideas is kept separate, also tends to enhance creative problem solving.

Mastery Test

1. The mark of a true language is that it must be
   a. spoken
   b. productive
   c. based on spatial grammar and syntax
   d. capable of encoding conditional relationships

2. Computer simulations and expert systems are two major applications of
   a. AI
   b. ASL
   c. brainstorming
   d. problem framing

3. Failure to wear automobile seat belts is an example of
   a. allowing too much time for incubation
   b. framing a problem broadly
   c. ignoring base rates
   d. recognition that two events occurring together are more likely than either one alone

4. One thing that images, concepts, and symbols all have in common is that they are
   a. morphemes
   b. internal representations
   c. based on reverse vision
   d. translated into micromovements

5. To decide if a container is a cup, bowl, or vase, most people compare it to
   a. a prototype
   b. its connotative meaning
   c. a series of negative instances
   d. a series of relevant phonemes

6. _____ is generally all or nothing.
   a. insight
   b. fixation
   c. automatic processing
   d. rote problem solving

7. "Either-or" concepts are
   a. conjunctive
   b. disjunctive
   c. relational
   d. prototypical

8. Which term does not belong with the others?
   a. selective comparison
   b. functional fixedness
   c. learned conventions
   d. emotional blocks

9. Which intelligence test includes separate verbal and performance subtests?
   a. WAIS
   b. Gardner 8
   c. QSST
   d. Standard-Binet

10. Mental retardation is defined by deficiencies in
    a. aptitudes and self-help skills
    b. intelligence and scholastic aptitudes
    c. language and spatial thinking
    d. IQ and adaptive behaviours

11. A John is 12. His IQ is 100. His MA is
    a. 8
    b. 12
    c. 10
    d. 15

12. The difference between prime beef and dead cow is primarily a matter of
    a. syntax
    b. conjunctive meaning
    c. semantics
    d. the productive nature of language

13. Culture-fair tests attempt to measure intelligence without being affected by a person's
    a. verbal skills
    b. cultural background
    c. educational level
    d. all of the preceding

14. Working backward from the solution to the problem describes a
    a. syllogism
    b. heuristic
    c. prototype
    d. dimension of the semantic differential

15. Language allows events to be _____ into _____.
    a. translated, concepts
    b. fixated, codes
    c. rearranged, lexigrams
    d. encoded, symbols

16. "A triangle must be a closed shape with three sides made of straight lines." This statement is an example of a
    a. prototype
    b. positive instance
    c. conceptual rule
    d. disjunctive concept

17. Among animals trained to use language, Kanzi has been unusually accurate at
    a. using proper syntax
    b. substituting gestures for lexigrams
    c. expressing conditional relationships
    d. forming chains of operant responses

18. The largest number of people are found in which IQ range?
    a. 80–89
    b. 90–109
    c. 110–119
    d. below 70

19. Looking for analogies and delaying evaluation are helpful strategies for increasing
    a. creative problem-solving
    b. mental rotation
    c. functional fixedness
    d. concept formation

20. Questions about vocabulary, comprehension, and absurdities would be found in which ability area of the Stanford-Binet?
    a. knowledge
    b. quantitative reasoning
    c. abstract/visual reasoning
    d. short-term memory

21. According to Noam Chomsky, surface sentences are created by applying _____ to simple sentences.
    a. encoding grammars
    b. transformation rules
    c. conditional prototypes
    d. selective conjunctions

22. Which of the following animals (this category includes humans) has mental images and is capable of rotating them?
    a. bees
    b. pigeons
    c. humans
    d. all of the above

Solutions

Recite and Review

1. information
2. internal
3. language
4. created
5. change; space
6. visual
7. class
8. positive
9. concept
10. models
11. and; either or; experiences
12. definition; personal
13. good; bad
14. symbols
15. sounds; meaningful
16. meaning
17. order; rules
18. rules
19. gestural
20. human
21. operant
22. geometric
23. rote; computer
24. deeper; analogies
25. narrow
26. solution; selective
27. wrong
28. fixation; habits
29. programs; intelligence
30. computer
31. knowledge
32. errors; true
33. probability
34. broad
35. rationally; environment
36. definition
37. intelligence test
38. Intelligence Scale
39. verbal; memory
40. quotient; 100
41. 100; equals
42. IQs; relative
43. Adult; non-verbal
44. groups; mental
45. bell; curve
46. overall; learning
47. gifted
48. correlation
49. IQ
50. traditional; math; visual
51. retarded; 70
52. mild; severe
53. 50; birth
54. intellectual
55. genes; heredity
56. stimulating
57. Intelligence
58. genetics; heredity
59. Mental; thinking
60. broadly; different; time; varied
61. separate

Connections

1. F
2. J
3. I
4. A
5. C
6. B
7. E
8. D
9. G
10. H
11. C
12. A
13. E
14. J
15. B
16. I
17. D
18. F
19. G
20. H
21. D
22. A
23. I
24. B
25. J
26. H
27. C
28. E
29. F
30. G
31. F
32. A
33. E
34. B
35. G
36. C
37. D

Short-Answer Questions

1. Images are mental representations (pictures) of objects or events. They may be "viewed" in three dimensions and rotated, and may have sounds or smells associated with them. Concepts are mental representations of a set of objects or events (such as *cup* or *professor*). Language is used to communicate information. Not all forms of communication are languages, however. Languages have a set of symbols (words or signs), a set of rules for combining those words or signs (grammar), and can generate new thoughts or ideas.

2. Mental images can be used to solve many problems. For example, you can picture your new apartment with different arrangements of furniture rather than actually moving everything around. This saves wear and tear on the floor, and on you. You can also use mental images to change feelings ("cheer up"), or behaviour (imagine yourself as a non-smoker). You can mentally rehearse asking a teacher for a

grade review or a person for a date.

3. Bees, pigeons, and people can all recognized learned patterns even if they are rotated. However, as far as research has shown, only people are capable of seeing relationships or connections between objects.

4. A relational concept is based on how one objects relates to another—above, below, left, right, and sister are all relational concepts.

5. A conjunctive concept is one that is defined by the presence of two or more features in common ("and" concepts).

6. A disjunctive concept is one that is defined by the presence of at least one of several possible features ("either/or" concepts). These are harder to learn than either relational or conjunctive concepts.

7. Early attempts to teach chimps to speak were not especially successful. Since then, chimpanzees have been taught to associate some of the signs of ASL with objects, actions, or events using operant conditioning and imitation. In addition to learning a number of signs, the chimps have also been able to construct simple sentences using these signs. However, in all these studies, there have problems with the animal's use of syntax (word order). More recently, Kanzi, a pygmy chimpanzee, has been taught to communicate using both gestures and a buttons on a computer keyboard. Kanzi can also understand a number of spoken sentences. Kanzi's sentences follow correct word order, and, like children, he has

picked up some of the rules of grammar.

8. Solutions obtained by insight are usually clear and happen quickly once insight has occurred. Insight involves selecting relevant information while ignoring distractions, selectively combining unrelated bits of information, and selectively comparing new problems with those already solved.

9. An heuristic is a "rule" or strategy for identifying and evaluating possible solutions to a problem, in order to reduce the number of alternatives. This raises the odds of finding a successful solution. There are a number of different heuristics that can be used in a variety of situations, including working backward from the solution to the problem, representing the problem in different ways, and testing possible solutions to clarify what information is needed.

10. Evidence in favour of heredity—the IQs of identical twins are more correlated than the IQs of fraternal twins, which are more correlated than the IQs of non-twin siblings. When identical twins are reared apart, the same relationships hold, although the correlation is lower. There is also evidence that, especially for younger children, environmental factors play a key role in intelligence.

Final Survey and Review

1. Cognitive; language
2. representations
3. images; concepts; symbols
4. information stored
5. size; rotated
6. brain; visual; mental
7. generalized
8. negative instances
9. rules
10. prototypes
11. conjunctive; disjunctive; exemplars
12. denotive; Connotative
13. semantic; strong; weak; active; passive
14. encoded
15. phonemes; morphemes
16. sematics
17. grammar; syntax
18. transformation
19. productive; American Sign
20. Animal; productive
21. primates; reinforcers
22. lexigrams
23. mechanically; mechanical
24. understanding; analogies
25. heuristics
26. insight; insight; encoding
27. fixation
28. Functional; blocks; values
29. computer programs; people
30. expert systems
31. organized; strategies
32. representative; heuristic
33. base rate
34. framing
35. purposefully; think
36. operational
37. Alfred Binet
38. Stanford Binet
39. quantitative; abstract
40. mental age; chronological age
41. mental; chronological
42. deviation IQ
43. Wechsler; verbal; performance
44. Scholastic Assessment; aptitudes
45. distribution; normal
46. agree; specific
47. 140
48. Terman; gifted; success
49. gifted; talented

50. Gardner; language; music; naturalist
51. developmentally; adaptive
52. moderate; profound
53. organic; genetic
54. familial
55. fraternal; identical
56. environment; environments
57. heredity; environment
58. environmental
59. sets; creative
60. incubation; input; risks
61. Brainstorming

Mastery Test

1. B (p. 279)
2. A (p. 287)
3. C (p. 289)
4. B (p. 272)
5. A (p. 276)
6. A (p. 286)
7. B (p. 276)
8. A (p. 283)
9. A (p. 294)
10. D (p. 298)
11. B (p. 293)
12. C (p. 278)
13. D (p. 295)
14. B (p. 285)
15. D (p. 277)
16. C (p. 276)
17. A (p. 281)
18. B (p. 294)
19. A (p. 305)
20. A (p. 292)
21. B (p. 279)
22. D (p. 274)

Motivation and Emotion

Chapter Overview

Motivation typically involves needs, drives, goals, and goal attainment. Three types of motives are primary motives, stimulus motives, and secondary motives. Most primary motives maintain homeostasis.

Hunger is influenced by the stomach, blood sugar levels, metabolism in the liver, fat stores in the body, activity in the hypothalamus, diet, and other factors. Eating disorders are serious and sometimes fatal problems. Behavioural dieting uses self-control techniques to change basic eating patterns and habits.

Thirst and other basic motives are affected by many factors, but they are primarily controlled by the hypothalamus. Pain avoidance is episodic and partially learned. The sex drive is non-homeostatic.

Sexual arousal is related to stimulation of the body's erogenous zones, but arousal is strongly influenced by mental factors. There is little difference in male and female sexual responsiveness. Sexual orientation refers to whether a person is heterosexual, homosexual, or bisexual. A combination of hereditary, biological, social, and psychological influences combine to produce one's sexual orientation. Human sexual response can be divided into four phases: (1) excitement; (2) plateau; (3) orgasm; and (4) resolution, which apply to both males and females and to people of all sexual orientations.

The stimulus motives include drives for information, exploration, manipulation, and sensory input. Drives for stimulation are partially explained by arousal theory. Optimal performance on a task usually occurs at moderate levels of arousal. Circadian rhythms are closely tied to sleep, activity, and energy cycles.

Social motives, which are learned, account for much of the diversity of human motivation. The need for achievement is a social motive correlated with success in many situations.

Maslow's hierarchy of motives categorizes needs as basic or growth oriented. Self-actualization, the highest and most fragile need, is reflected in meta-needs. In many situations, extrinsic motivation can lower intrinsic motivation, enjoyment, and creativity.

Emotions are linked to basic adaptive behaviours. Other major elements of emotion are bodily changes, emotional expressions, and emotional feelings. Physiological changes during emotion are caused by adrenaline and the autonomic nervous system (ANS). The sympathetic branch of the ANS arouses the body and the parasympathetic branch quiets it. Basic emotional expressions are unlearned. Facial expressions are central to emotion. Body gestures and movements (body language) also express feelings. A variety of theories have been proposed to explain emotion.

Subjective well-being (happiness) is a combination of general life satisfaction and positive emotions. Making progress toward your goals is associated with happiness, especially if the goals express your personal interests and values.

Learning Objectives

After reading this chapter, students will be able to:

1. Define motivation and explain the roles of needs, drives, and incentives in motivated behaviour.

2. Give examples of the three main types of motives.

3. Define homeostasis and explain its role in motivation.

4. Describe the brain mechanisms that control hunger. Explain how external cues, and environmental and social influences can affect eating.

5. Identify the biological factors involved in the sex drive.

6. Define sexual orientation. Distinguish between heterosexual, homosexual, and bisexual orientations.

7. Explain the relationship between arousal and motivation.

8. Describe the characteristics of people with high need for achievement.

9. Identify the five levels of Maslow's hierarchy of needs.

10. Distinguish between intrinsic and extrinsic motivation.

11. Identify the three major elements of emotion.

12. Describe the role of the autonomic nervous system in emotional arousal.

13. Explain how a polygraph works.

14. Differentiate between Cannon-Bard, James-Lange, and Schachter's cognitive theories of emotion.

15. Explain what is meant by the term *emotional intelligence*.

Practice Quizzes

Recite and Review

What is motivation? Are there different types of motives?
Recite and Review: Pages 312–315

1. Motives _____ , sustain, and direct _____ .

2. Motivation typically involves the sequence _____ , drive, _____ , and goal attainment.

3. Behaviour can be activated either by needs that _____ or by goals that _____ .

4. The attractiveness of a _____ and its ability to initiate action are related to its incentive value (its value above and beyond its capacity to fill a _____).

5. Three principal types of motives are primary motives, stimulus motives, and _____ motives.

6. Most _____ motives operate to maintain a _____ state of bodily equilibrium called homeostasis.

What causes hunger? Overeating? Eating disorders?

Recite and Review: Pages 315–323

7. Hunger is influenced by a complex interplay between distention (fullness) of the _____ , hypoglycemia (low _____ sugar), and metabolism in the _____ .

8. The most direct control of eating is exerted by the hypothalamus, which has areas that act like _____ and _____ systems for hunger and eating.

9. The lateral hypothalamus acts as a _____ system; the ventromedial hypothalamus is part of a satiety system; the paraventricular nucleus influences both hunger and _____ .

10. Other factors influencing hunger are the set point for the proportion of _____ in the body, external eating cues, and the attractiveness and variety of _____ .

11. Hunger is also influenced by emotions, learned _____ preferences and _____ aversions, and cultural values.

12. A person is considered overweight if 25 percent or more of their body weight is made up of _____ and is considered obese if this proportion is more than _____ percent.

13. Anorexia nervosa (self-inflicted _____) and bulimia nervosa (_____ and purging) are two prominent eating disorders.

14. Reverse anorexia is seen in some well-muscled _____ who, unlike anorexics, have the unreal perception that their body is too _____ .

15. These eating disorders tend to involve conflicts about self-image, self-control, and _____ .

Is there more than one type of thirst? In what ways are pain avoidance and the sex drive unusual?

Recite and Review: Pages 323–324

16. Like hunger, thirst and other basic motives are affected by a number of _____ factors, but are primarily under the central control of the hypothalamus in the _____ .

17. Thirst may be either intracellular (when _____ is lost from inside _____) or extracellular (when _____ is lost from the spaces between _____).

18. Pain avoidance is unusual because it is episodic (associated with particular conditions) as opposed to occurring in regular _____ .

19. Pain is best described as a _____ that responds to both pain intensity and the _____ components (i.e., memory, what the wound looks like, etc.) that surround the event.

20. Pain avoidance and pain tolerance are partially _____ (influenced by training).

21. The sex drive in many lower animals is related to estrus (or "heat") in _____ . The sex drive is unusual in that it is non-homeostatic (relatively _____ of needs in the body).

22. Sex _____ in both males and females may be related to bodily levels of androgens.

What are the typical patterns of human sexual response?

Recite and Review: Pages 325–326

23. Sexual arousal is related to stimulation of the body's erogenous zones (areas that produce erotic _____), but cognitive elements such as _____ and images are equally important.

24. There is little difference in sexual _____ between males and females.

25. Evidence suggests that sexual activity peaks at a _____ age for females than it does for males, although this difference is diminishing.

26. Sexual orientation refers to one's degree of emotional and erotic attraction to members of the same _____ , opposite _____ , or both _____ .

27. A person may be heterosexual, _____ , or bisexual.

28. A combination of hereditary, biological, social, and psychological influences combine to produce one's _____ _____ .

29. There is _____ _____ chance of an exclusively homosexual person changing sexual orientation.

30. In a series of landmark studies, William _____ and Virginia Johnson directly observed sexual response in a large number of adults.

31. Human sexual response can be divided into four phases: (1) _____ , (2) plateau, (3) _____ , and (4) resolution.

32. Males experience a refractory period after _____ and ejaculation. Only 5 percent of men are _____ -orgasmic.

How does arousal relate to motivation?

Recite and Review: Pages 327–330

33. The stimulus drives reflect needs for information, exploration, manipulation, and _____ input.

34. Drives for stimulation are partially explained by arousal theory, which states that an ideal level of _____ _____ will be maintained if possible.

35. The desired level of _____ or stimulation varies from person to person.

36. Optimal performance on a task usually occurs at _____ levels of arousal. This relationship is described by an inverted U function.

37. The Yerkes-Dodson law further states that for _____ tasks the ideal arousal level is higher, and for _____ tasks it is lower.

38. Circadian _____ within the body are closely tied to sleep, activity levels, and energy cycles. Time-zone travel and shift work can seriously disrupt _____ and bodily rhythms.

39. If you anticipate a _____ in body rhythms, you can gradually preadapt to your new _____ over a period of days.

What are social motives? Why are they important?

Recite and Review: Pages 330–333

40. _____ motives are learned through socialization and cultural conditioning.

41. One of the most prominent social motives is the _____ for achievement (nAch).

42. High nAch is correlated with _____ in many situations, with occupational choice, and with moderate _____ taking.

43. Self-confidence affects _____ because it influences the challenges you will undertake, the _____ you will make, and how long you will _____ when things don't go well.

Are some motives more basic than others?

Recite and Review: Pages 333–335

44. Maslow's hierarchy (rank ordering) of motives categorizes needs as _____ and growth oriented.

45. _____ needs in the hierarchy are assumed to be prepotent (dominant) over _____ needs.

46. _____ -actualization, the highest and most fragile need, is reflected in meta- _____ .

47. In many situations, extrinsic motivation (that which is induced by obvious _____ rewards) can reduce intrinsic motivation, enjoyment, and creativity.

What happens during emotion? Can "lie detectors" really detect lies?

Recite and Review: Pages 336–340

48. Emotions are linked to many basic adaptive _____ , such as attacking, retreating, feeding, and reproducing.

49. Other major elements of emotion are physiological changes in the body, emotional expressions, and emotional _____ .

50. The following are considered to be primary emotions: fear, surprise, _____ , disgust, _____ , anticipation, joy, and acceptance. Other emotions seem to represent mixtures of the primaries.

51. Physical changes associated with emotion are caused by the action of adrenaline, a _____ released into the bloodstream, and by activity in the autonomic _____ _____ (ANS).

52. The sympathetic _____ of the ANS is primarily responsible for arousing the body, the parasympathetic _____ for quieting it.

53. Sudden death due to prolonged and intense emotion is probably related to parasympathetic _____ (excess activity). Heart attacks caused by sudden intense emotion are more likely due to sympathetic _____ .

54. The polygraph, or "lie detector," measures _____ _____ by monitoring heart rate, blood pressure, breathing rate, and the galvanic skin response (GSR).

55. Asking a series of _____ and irrelevant questions may allow the detection of _____ , but overall, the accuracy of the lie detector has been challenged by many researchers.

How accurately are emotions expressed by "body language" and the face?

Recite and Review: Pages 340–342

56. Basic emotional expressions, such as smiling or baring one's teeth when angry, appear to be _____ .

57. Facial expressions of _____ , anger, disgust, _____ , and happiness are recognized by people of all cultures.

58. Body gestures and movements (body language) also express _____ , mainly by communicating emotional _____ .

59. Three dimensions of _____ expressions are pleasantness-unpleasantness, attention-rejection, and activation.

60. The study of _____ _____ is known as kinesics.

How do psychologists explain emotions?

Recite and Review: Pages 342–347

61. The James-Lange theory of emotion says that emotional experience _____ an awareness of the bodily reactions of emotion.

62. In contrast, the Cannon-Bard theory says that bodily reactions and emotional experience occur _____ _____ _____ _____ and that emotions are organized in the brain.

63. Schachter's cognitive theory of emotion emphasizes the importance of _____ , or interpretations, applied to feelings of bodily arousal.

64. Also important is the process of attribution, in which bodily _____ is attributed to a particular person, object, or situation.

65. The facial feedback hypothesis holds that sensations and information from emotional _____ help define what emotion a person is feeling.

66. Contemporary views of emotion place greater emphasis on how _____ are appraised. Also, all of the elements of emotion are seen as interrelated and interacting.

67. Emotional intelligence can be seen as the equivalent of Howard Gardner's intelligence. This _____ intelligence refers to skills such as empathy, self-control, _____ , sensitivity to the feelings of others, _____ , and self-motivation.

What factors contribute most to a happy and fulfilling life?

Recite and Review: Psychology in Action

68. Subjective well-being (_____) occurs when _____ emotions outnumber _____ emotions and a person is satisfied with his or her life.

69. Happiness is only mildly related to _____ , education, marriage, religion, age, sex, and work. However, people who have an extroverted, optimistic _____ do tend to be happier.

70. People who are making progress toward their long-term _____ tend to be happier. This is especially true if the _____ have integrity and personal meaning.

Connections

1. _____ physiological needs
2. _____ safety and security
3. _____ self-actualization
4. _____ lateral hypothalamus
5. _____ basic needs
6. _____ esteem and self-esteem
7. _____ paraventricular nucleus
8. _____ growth needs
9. _____ love and belonging
10. _____ ventromedial hypothalamus

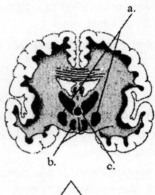

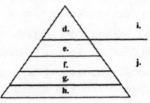

11. _____ need
12. _____ incentive value
13. _____ secondary motives
14. _____ homeostasis
15. _____ satiety system
16. _____ feeding system
17. _____ hunger and satiety
18. _____ weight cycling
19. _____ estrus
20. _____ circadian

a. steady state
b. lateral hypothalamus
c. internal deficiency
d. learned goals
e. estrogen levels
f. yo-yo dieting
g. about a day
h. paraventricular nucleus
i. ventromedial hypothalamus
j. goal desirability

21. _____ changes eating habits
22. _____ need for achievement
23. _____ facial expressions
24. _____ mood
25. _____ sympathetic branch
26. _____ attribution
27. _____ body language
28. _____ sadness
29. _____ anxiety
30. _____ emotional intelligence

a. standards of excellence
b. prolonged mild emotion
c. assigning causes to events
d. behavioural dieting
e. emotional competence
f. emotion
g. appraisal of threat
h. facial feedback hypothesis
i. kinesics
j. fight or flight

Short-Answer Questions

1. Explain how the set point is related to obesity.
2. How do external cues affect eating?
3. How are behavioural techniques used to help people lose weight?
4. Identify the causes of anorexia.
5. What treatments are available to help people with eating disorders?
6. Identify the four phases of Masters and Johnson's sexual response cycle.
7. Describe four ways to reduce test anxiety.
8. How is nAch related to risk taking?
9. How accurate is a lie detector? What are its limitations?
10. Briefly discuss cultural differences in the expression of emotion.
11. Explain the facial feedback hypothesis.

Final Survey and Review

What is motivation? Are there different types of motives?

1. Motives initiate (begin), _____ (perpetuate), and _____ activities.
2. Motivation typically involves the sequence need, _____ , response, and goal _____ (need reduction).
3. Behaviour can be activated either by _____ (push) or by _____ (pull).
4. The attractiveness of a goal and its ability to initiate action are related to its _____ .
5. Three principal types of motives are _____ motives, _____ motives, and _____ motives.
6. Most primary motives operate to maintain a steady state of bodily equilibrium called _____ .

What causes hunger? Overeating? Eating disorders?

7. Hunger is influenced by a complex interplay between _____ (fullness) of the stomach, _____ (low blood sugar), metabolism in the liver, and fat stores in the body.
8. The most direct control of eating is exerted by the _____ , which has areas that act like feeding (start) and _____ (stop) systems for hunger and eating.
9. The _____ hypothalamus acts as a feeding system; the _____ hypothalamus is part of a satiety system; the paraventricular _____ influences both hunger and satiety.
10. Other factors influencing hunger are the _____ _____ for the proportion of fat in the body, external eating _____ , and the attractiveness and variety of diet.
11. Hunger is also influenced by emotions, learned taste preferences, taste _____ and _____ values.
12. A person is considered _____ if 25 percent or more of their body weight is made up of fat and _____ if this proportion is at least 30 percent.
13. _____ nervosa (self-inflicted starvation) and _____ nervosa (gorging and purging) are two prominent eating disorders.

14. _____ anorexia is seen in some well-muscled bodybuilders who have the belief that their bodies are too small.

15. These eating disorders tend to involve conflicts about _____ , self-control, and anxiety.

Is there more than one type of thirst? In what ways are pain avoidance and the sex drive unusual?

16. Like hunger, thirst and other basic motives are affected by a number of bodily factors, but are primarily under the central control of the _____ in the brain.

17. Thirst may be either _____ (when fluid is lost from inside cells) or _____ (when fluid is lost from the spaces between cells).

18. Pain avoidance is unusual because it is _____ (associated with particular conditions) as opposed to _____ (occurring in regular cycles).

19. Pain is best described as a system (_____) that responds to both pain _____ and psychological components (i.e., _____ , what wound looks like, etc.).

20. Pain _____ and pain _____ are partially learned.

21. The sex drive in many lower animals is related to _____ (or "heat") in females. The sex drive is unusual in that it is non- _____ (relatively independent of body needs).

22. Sex drive in both males and females may be related to bodily levels of _____ .

What are the typical patterns of human sexual response?

23. Sexual arousal is related to stimulation of the body's _____ zones (areas that produce erotic pleasure), but _____ elements such as thoughts and images are equally important.

24. There is little _____ in sexual behaviour between males and females.

25. Evidence suggests that the sex drive peaks at a later age for _____ than it does for _____ , although this difference is diminishing.

26. Sexual _____ refers to one's degree of emotional and erotic attraction to members of the same sex, opposite sex, or both sexes.

27. A person may be _____ , homosexual, or _____ .

28. A combination of _____ , biological, _____ , and psychological influences combine to produce one's sexual orientation.

29. As a group, _____ men and women do not differ psychologically from _____ .

30. In a series of landmark studies, William Masters and Virginia _____ directly observed sexual response in a large number of adults.

31. Human sexual response can be divided into four phases: (1) excitement, (2) _____ , (3) orgasm, and (4) _____ .

32. Males experience a _____ period after orgasm and ejaculation. Only 5 percent of men are multi- _____ .

How does arousal relate to motivation?

33. The _____ drives reflect needs for information, _____ , manipulation, and sensory input.

34. Drives for stimulation are partially explained by _____ _____ , which states that an ideal level of bodily arousal will be maintained if possible.

35. The desired level of arousal or _____ varies from person to person.

36. Optimal performance on a task usually occurs at moderate levels of arousal. This relationship is described by an _____ _____ function.

37. The _____ - _____ law further states that for simple tasks the ideal arousal level is higher, and for complex tasks it is lower.

38. _____ rhythms within the body are closely tied to sleep, activity levels, and energy cycles. Travel across _____ _____ and shift work can seriously disrupt sleep and bodily rhythms.

39. If you anticipate a change in body rhythms, you can gradually _____ to your new schedule over a period of days.

What are social motives? Why are they important?

40. Social motives are learned through _____ and cultural conditioning.

41. One of the most prominent social motives is the need for _____ (nAch).

42. _____ nAch is correlated with success in many situations, with occupational choice, and with _____ risk taking.

43. _____ - _____ affects motivation because it influences the challenges you will undertake, the effort you will make, and how long you will persist when things don't go well.

Are some motives more basic than others?

44. Maslow's _____ (rank ordering) of motives categorizes needs as basic and _____ oriented.

45. Lower needs in the hierarchy are assumed to be _____ (dominant) over higher needs.

46. Self- _____ , the highest and most fragile need, is reflected in _____ -needs.

47. In many situations, _____ motivation (that which is induced by obvious external rewards) can reduce _____ motivation, enjoyment, and creativity.

What happens during emotion? Can "lie detectors" really detect lies?

48. Emotions are linked to many basic _____ behaviours, such as attacking, retreating, feeding, and reproducing.

49. Other major elements of emotion are physiological changes in the body, emotional _____ , and emotional feelings.

50. The following are considered to be _____ emotions: fear, surprise, sadness, disgust, anger, anticipation, joy, and acceptance.

51. Physical changes associated with emotion are caused by the action of _____ , a hormone released into the bloodstream, and by activity in the _____ nervous system (ANS).

52. The _____ branch of the ANS is primarily responsible for arousing the body, the _____ branch for quieting it.

53. Sudden death due to prolonged and intense emotion is probably related to _____ rebound (excess activity). Heart attacks caused by sudden intense emotion are more likely due to _____ arousal.

54. The _____ , or "lie detector," measures emotional arousal by monitoring heart rate, blood pressure, breathing rate, and the _____ skin response (GSR).

55. Asking a series of _____ and _____ questions may allow the detection of lies, but overall, the accuracy of the lie detector has been challenged by many researchers.

How accurately are emotions expressed by "body language" and the face?

56. Basic emotional _____ , such as smiling or baring one's teeth when angry, appear to be unlearned.

57. _____ expressions of fear, anger, disgust, sadness, and happiness are recognized by people of all cultures.

58. Body _____ and movements (body language) also express feelings, mainly by communicating emotional tone.

59. Three dimensions of facial expressions are pleasantness-unpleasantness, attention-rejection, and _____ .

60. The study of body language is known as _____ .

How do psychologists explain emotions?

61. The _____ -Lange theory of emotion says that emotional experience follows an awareness of the bodily reactions of emotion.

62. In contrast, the _____ -Bard theory says that bodily reactions and emotional experience occur at the same time and that emotions are organized in the brain.

63. Schachter's _____ theory of emotion emphasizes the importance of labels, or interpretations, applied to feelings of bodily _____ .

64. Also important is the process of _____ , in which bodily arousal is attributed to a particular person, object, or situation.

65. The _____ _____ hypothesis holds that sensations and information from emotional expressions help define what emotion a person is feeling.

66. Contemporary views of emotion place greater emphasis on how situations are _____ (evaluated). Also, all of the elements of emotion are seen as interrelated and interacting.

67. _____ intelligence can be seen as the equivalent of Howard Gardner's personal intelligence. It involves skills such as _____ , self-control, self-awareness, sensitivity to the feelings of others, persistence and _____ - _____ .

What factors contribute most to a happy and fulfilling life?

68. _____ _____ - _____ (happiness) occurs when positive emotions outnumber negative emotions and a person is satisfied with his or her life.

69. Happiness is only mildly related to wealth, education, marriage, religion, age, sex, and work. However, people with _____ , optimistic personalities do tend to be happier.

70. People who are making progress toward their long-term goals tend to be happier. This is especially true if the goals have _____ and personal _____ .

Mastery Test

1. Which of the following is NOT one of the signs of emotional arousal recorded by a polygraph?
   a. heart rate
   b. blood pressure
   c. pupil dilation
   d. breathing rate

2. Plain water is most satisfying when a person has _____ thirst.
   a. intracellular
   b. hypothalamic
   c. extracellular
   d. homeostatic

3. When expectations of a friendly first date clash with an attempted seduction the problem can be attributed to differences in
   a. gender identity
   b. erogenous confrontation
   c. gender myths
   d. sexual scripts

4. Strong external rewards tend to undermine
   a. extrinsic motivation
   b. intrinsic motivation
   c. prepotent motivation
   d. stimulus motivation

5. Activity in the ANS is directly responsible for which element of emotion?
   a. emotional feelings
   b. emotional expressions
   c. physiological changes
   d. misattributions

6. The first two phases of the sexual response cycle are
   a. excitement, arousal
   b. arousal, orgasm
   c. excitement, plateau
   d. stimulation, arousal

7. Motivation refers to the ways in which activities are initiated, sustained, and
   a. acquired
   b. valued
   c. directed
   d. aroused

8. The feeling of thirst is a/an
   a. need
   b. drive
   c. deprivation
   d. incentive value

9. Which facial expression is NOT recognized by people of all cultures?
   a. anger
   b. disgust
   c. surpise
   d. fear

10. Learning to weaken eating cues is useful in
    a. self-selection feeding
    b. yo-yo dieting
    c. rapid weight cycling
    d. behavioural dieting

11. Jet lag occurs when a traveller's _____ are out of synchrony with local time.
    a. biorhythms
    b. circadian rhythms
    c. sensation-seeking patterns
    d. opponent processes

12. Which theory holds that emotional feelings, physical arousal, and behaviour occur at the same time?
    a. James-Lange
    b. Cannon-Bard
    c. cognitive
    d. attribution

13. Compared with people in North America, people in Asian cultures are less likely to express which emotion?
    a. anger
    b. jealousy
    c. curiosity
    d. fear

14. Binge eating is most associated with
    a. bulimia nervosa
    b. bait shyness
    c. low levels of NPY
    d. anorexia nervosa

15. Desirable goals are high in
    a. need reduction
    b. incentive value
    c. homeostatic valence
    d. motivational "push"

16. _____ is to pain avoidance as _____ is to the sex drive.
    a. Non-homeostatic, episodic
    b. Episodic, non-homeostatic
    c. Non-homeostatic, cyclic
    d. Cyclic, non-homeostatic

17. A specialist in kinesics could be expected to be most interested in
    a. facial blends
    b. circadian rhythms
    c. sensation seeking
    d. primary motives

18. Coping statements are a way to directly correct which part of test anxiety?
    a. overpreparation
    b. under-arousal
    c. excessive worry
    d. compulsive rehearsal

19. The desires for exploration and activity are categorized as
    a. primary drives
    b. secondary motives
    c. stimulus drives
    d. extrinsic motives

20. Sudden death following a period of intense fear may occur when _____ slows the heart to a stop.
    a. sympathetic overload
    b. adrenaline poisoning
    c. opponent-process feedback
    d. parasympathetic rebound

21. Research on well-being suggests that a good life is one that combines happiness and
    a. financial success
    b. educational achievement
    c. an introverted personality
    d. achieving meaningful goals

22. You could induce eating in a laboratory rat by activating the
    a. lateral hypothalamus
    b. corpus callosum
    c. rat's set point
    d. ventromedial hypothalamus

23. People think cartoons are funnier if they see them while holding a pen crosswise in their teeth. This observation supports
    a. the James-Lange theory
    b. the Cannon-Bard theory
    c. Schachter's cognitive theory
    d. the facial feedback hypothesis

24. Basic biological motives are closely related to
    a. nAch
    b. homeostasis
    c. activity in the thalamus
    d. levels of melatonin in the body

25. Self-actualization is to _____ needs as safety and security are to _____ needs.
    a. growth, basic
    b. basic, meta-
    c. prepotent, basic
    d. meta-, extrinsic

26. Which of the following is NOT a basic element of emotion?
    a. physiological changes
    b. emotional expressions
    c. emotional feelings
    d. misattributions

27. Even though you just had a big dinner, you eat two pieces of cake. This is an example of the
    _____ of food.
    a. anxiety value
    b. incentive value
    c. metabolic value
    d. secondary value

28. According to the Yerkes-Dodson law, optimum performance occurs at _____ levels of
    arousal for simple tasks and _____ levels of arousal for complex tasks.
    a. higher, lower
    b. lower, higher
    c. minimum, high
    d. average, high

29. Contemporary models of emotion place greater emphasis on _____, or the way situations
    are evaluated.
    a. appraisal
    b. attribution
    c. feedback
    d. emotional tone

30. Which Canadian ethnic group is more at risk of developing type 2 diabetes due to obesity?
    a. Italian
    b. French
    c. Jewish
    d. Native

31. According to Canadian researcher Ronald Melzack our pain system is best described as a combination of
    a. only pain avoidance
    b. both pain level and psychological components
    c. psychological components and perception of experience
    d. pain tolerance and pain avoidance

32. Kim is extremely empathetic, is able to manage his own emotions, and uses his emotions consistently. He probably has a high level of
    a. body kinesthesis
    b. street smarts
    c. emotional intelligence
    d. cognitive dissonance

Solutions

Recite and Review

1. initiate; behaviour
2. need; reponse
3. push; pull
4. goal; need
5. secondary
6. primary; steady
7. stomach; blood; liver
8. start; stop
9. feeding; satiety
10. fat; diet
11. taste; taste
12. fat; 30
13. starvation; gorging
14. bodybuilders; small
15. anxiety
16. bodily; brain
17. fluid; cells; fluid; cells
18. cycles
19. system; psychological
20. learned
21. females; independent
22. drive
23. pleasure; thoughts
24. responsiveness
25. later
26. sex; sex; sexes
27. homosexual
28. sexual orientation
29. very little
30. Masters
31. excitement; orgasm
32. orgasm; multi
33. sensory
34. physical arousal
35. arousal
36. moderate
37. simple; complex
38. rhythms; sleep
39. change; schedule
40. Social
41. need
42. success; risk
43. motivation; effort; persist
44. basic
45. Lower; higher
46. Self; needs
47. external
48. behaviours
49. feelings
50. sadness; anger
51. hormone; nervous system
52. branch; branch
53. rebound; arousal
54. emotional arousal
55. relevant; lying
56. unlearned
57. fear; sadness
58. feelings; tone
59. facial
60. body language
61. follows
62. at the same time
63. labels
64. arousal
65. expressions
66. situations
67. personal; self-awareness; persistence
68. happiness; positive; negative
69. wealth; personality
70. goals; goals

Connections

1. H
2. G
3. D
4. A
5. J
6. E
7. C
8. I
9. F
10. B
11. C
12. J
13. D
14. A
15. I
16. B
17. H
18. F
19. E
20. G
21. D
22. A
23. H
24. B
25. J
26. C
27. I
28. F
29. G
30. E

Short-Answer Questions

1. Set point—the proportion of body fat that is maintained by changes in hunger and eating. When body fat stores go below this set point, a person will feel hungry and eat more often. Set point can be altered by a number of different things, including nicotine (which lowers set point; this is why people tend to gain weight when they stop smoking). If the set point is raised, people will gain weight. If it is lowered, they will lose.

2. External cues such as the availability of food, attractiveness of food, the presence of other people, other things people do while eating (watching TV, studying) can all act as triggers for eating. Becoming aware of these external cues is one of the steps in behavioural dieting.

3. Behavioural techniques can help people avoid yo-yo dieting by helping them learn their eating habits, weaken personal eating

cues, develop techniques to control eating, and avoid too many snacks.

4. Causes of anorexia include a distorted body image and exaggerated fear of becoming fat. Anorexic teenaged girls are obedient daughters and may seek perfect weight control as well. Another hypothesis is that anorexia is a disorder of an evolutionary suppression mechanism that protected women from the risks of child-bearing during times of uncertain food supply.

5. Treatments for anorexia include a medically supervised diet to help the person gain weight along with counselling to deal with the emotional aspects of the situation. Treatments for bulimia include behavioural techniques to monitor food intake and extinction techniques to stop the gorge-purge cycle. Cognitive-behavioural approaches focus on changing thinking patterns and beliefs about body shape and image as well as the actual behaviours. Peer support groups designed to increase self-esteem and change negative attitudes toward eating are also helpful.

6. Excitement phase—beginning stages of sexual arousal; plateau—second stage, physical arousal intensifies; orgasm—climax and release of sexual excitement; resolution—return to prearoused state.

7. Preparation—improve study skills, overprepare, start studying well in advance; relaxation—learn to relax before an exam, study with a supportive study partner; rehearsal—practise coping with upsetting or unforeseen events before the exam (plan what you will do if you run out of time, go blank, etc); restructuring thoughts—list distracting or self-defeating thoughts you might have during an exam, then plan alternative thoughts to put in place of the upsetting ones.

8. People high in nAch have high standards and set high goals for themselves. They take calculated risks because easy-to-achieve goals offer no sense of satisfaction. They also avoid situations where winning will be due to luck rather than skill.

9. A lie detector measures changes in heart rate, blood pressure, breathing, and sweating. It records general emotional arousal, but it can't tell the difference between fear, anxiety, and lying. Although supporters of the use of lie detectors claim up to 95 percent accuracy rates, research shows that accuracy is substantially reduced when people thought about past emotional situations when they answered irrelevant questions. Its accuracy is also affected by tranquillizers and self-inflicted pain.

10. Although the basic expressions of emotion are the same across cultures, there are differences in the expression of anger (common in Western cultures, less common in Asian cultures with the emphasis on group harmony). Depression is less likely to be diagnosed in China since such problems are not considered socially acceptable.

11. The facial feedback hypothesis suggests that people interpret their emotional states based on feedback they get from the muscles of their faces. That is, the brain recognizes the feedback it gets when you smile and interprets it as the emotion of happiness. This hypothesis is supported by the fact that people who made angry faces showed increased heart rate and skin temperature.

Final Survey and Review

1. sustain; direct
2. drive; attainment
3. needs; goals
4. incentive
5. primary; stimulus; secondary
6. homeostasis
7. distention; hypoglycemia
8. hypothalamus; satiety
9. lateral; ventromedial; nucleus
10. set point; cues
11. aversions; cultural
12. overweight; obese
13. Anorexia; bulimia
14. Reverse
15. self-image
16. hypothalamus
17. intracellular; extracellular
18. episodic; cyclic
19. neuromatrix; intensity; memory
20. avoidance; tolerance
21. estrus; homeostatic
22. androgens
23. erogenous; cognitive
24. difference
25. females; males
26. orientation
27. heterosexual; bisexual
28. heredity; social
29. homosexual; heterosexuals
30. Johnson
31. plateau; resolution
32. refractory; orgasmic
33. stimulus; exploration
34. arousal; theory

35. stimulation
36. inverted; U
37. Yerkes Dodson
38. Circadian; time zones
39. preadapt
40. socialization
41. achievement
42. High; moderate
43. Self; confidence
44. hierarchy; growth
45. prepotent
46. actualization; meta
47. extrinsic; intrinsic
48. adaptive
49. expressions
50. primary
51. adrenaline; autonomic
52. sympathetic; parasympathetic
53. parasympathetic; sympathetic
54. polygraph; galvanic
55. relevant; irrelevant
56. expressions
57. Facial
58. gestures
59. activation
60. kinesics
61. James
62. Cannon
63. cognitive; arousal
64. attribution
65. facial feedback
66. appraised
67. Emotional; empathy; self; motivation
68. Subjective well; being
69. extroverted
70. integrity; meaning

Mastery Test

1. C (p. 339)
2. A (p. 323)
3. D (p. 325)
4. B (p. 335)
5. C (p. 328)
6. C (p. 326)
7. C (p. 312)
8. B (p. 312)
9. C (p. 341)
10. D (p. 319)
11. B (p. 329)
12. B (p. 343)
13. A (p. 341)
14. A (p. 321)
15. B (p. 313)
16. B (p. 323)
17. A (p. 342)
18. C (p. 329)
19. C (p. 327)
20. D (p. 338)
21. D (p. 349)
22. A (p. 316)
23. D (p. 345)
24. B (p. 314)
25. A (p. 333)
26. D (p. 336)
27. B (p. 313)
28. A (p. 328)
29. A (p. 345)
30. D (p. 318)
31. B (p. 324)
32. C (p. 346)

Personality

Chapter Overview

Personality refers to unique and enduring behaviour patterns. Character is personality evaluated. Temperament refers to the hereditary and physiological aspects of one's emotional nature. Personality traits are lasting personal qualities. Personality types are categories defined by groups of shared traits. Behaviour is also influenced by self-concept. Personality theories combine various ideas and principles to explain personality.

Allport's trait theory classifies traits as common, individual, cardinal, central, or secondary. Cattell's trait theory attributes visible surface traits to the existence of 16 underlying source traits. The five-factor model reduces traits to five dimensions. Traits appear to interact with situations to determine behaviour. Behavioural genetics suggests that heredity influences personality traits.

Like other psychodynamic approaches, Sigmund Freud's psychoanalytic theory emphasizes unconscious forces and conflicts within the personality. Behavioural theories of personality emphasize learning, conditioning, and the immediate effects of the environment. Social learning theory adds cognitive elements, such as perception, thinking, and understanding to the behavioural view. Many differences between males and females are based on social learning. Psychological androgyny is related to greater behavioural adaptability and flexibility. Humanistic theory emphasizes subjective experiences and needs for self-actualization.

Techniques typically used for personality assessment are interviews, direct observation, questionnaires, and projective tests.

Shyness is a mixture of social inhibition and social anxiety. It is marked by heightened public self-consciousness and a tendency to regard one's shyness as a lasting trait. Shyness can be lessened by changing self-defeating beliefs and by improving social skills.

Learning Objectives

After reading this chapter, students will be able to:

1. Define personality.
2. Distinguish between central and source traits. Give examples of the five key dimensions of personality.
3. Describe Freud's theory of personality. Summarize Freud's five psychosexual stages of personality development.

4. Explain the behavioural view of the structure of personality. Describe the relationship between self-reinforcement and self-esteem.

5. Identify the four critical situations that may have a lasting influence on personality.

6. Describe the humanistic view of personality.

7. Define self-actualizaton and describe the personality characteristics of a self-actualized person.

8. Explain Roger's self-theory of personality.

9. Describe the four basic methods that psychologists use to assess personality.

10. Distinguish between objective and projective tests and give examples of each.

Practice Quizzes

Recite and Review

What do psychologists mean by the term *personality*? What core concepts make up the field of personality?

Recite and Review: Pages 356–359

1. Personality is made up of one's unique and relatively stable _____ patterns.

2. Character is personality that has been judged or _____ . That is, it is the possession of desirable qualities.

3. Temperament refers to the _____ and physiological aspects of one's emotional nature.

4. Personality traits are lasting personal qualities that are inferred from _____ .

5. A personality type is a style of personality defined by having a group of related _____ or similar characteristics.

6. Two widely recognized personality _____ are an introvert (shy, self-centred person) and an extrovert (bold, outgoing person).

7. Behaviour is influenced by self-concept, which is a person's perception of his or her own _____ traits.

8. _____ theories combine interrelated assumptions, ideas, and principles to explain personality.

9. Four major types of personality theories are _____ , psychodynamic, behaviouristic, and humanistic.

What are personality traits? Are some traits more basic than others? Do traits predict how someone will act in the future?

Recite and Review: Pages 359–364

10. Trait _____ attempt to specify qualities of personality that are most lasting or characteristic of a person.

11. Gordon Allport made useful distinctions between common traits (which are shared by most members of a culture) and _____ traits (characteristics of a single person).

12. Allport also identified cardinal traits (a trait that influences nearly all of a person's activities), central traits (core traits of personality), and _____ traits (superficial traits).

13. The theory of Raymond Cattell attributes visible _____ traits to the existence of 16 underlying source traits (which he identified using factor _____).

14. Source traits are measured by the Sixteen _____ _____ Questionnaire (16 PF).

15. The outcome of the 16 PF and other personality tests may be graphically presented as a _____ profile.

16. The five-factor model of personality reduces traits to five _____ dimensions of personality.

17. The five factors are extroversion, _____ , conscientiousness, neuroticism, and openness to _____ .

18. _____ interact with situations to determine behaviour.

19. Heredity is responsible for 25 to 50 percent of the variation in personality _____ .

20. Studies of separated _____ twins suggest that heredity contributes significantly to adult personality traits. Overall, however, personality is shaped as much, or more, by differences in environment.

How do psychodynamic theories explain personality?

Recite and Review: Pages 365–369

21. Psychodynamic theories focus on the inner workings of personality, especially hidden or _____ forces and internal conflicts.

22. According to Sigmund Freud's psychoanalytic theory, personality is made up of the id, _____ , and superego.

23. The id operates on the pleasure _____ . The ego is guided by the reality _____ .

24. The _____ is made up of the conscience and the ego ideal.

25. Libido, derived from the _____ instincts, is the primary _____ running the personality.

26. Conflicts within the personality may cause neurotic _____ or moral _____ and motivate use of ego-defence mechanisms.

27. The personality operates on three levels, the _____ , preconscious, and unconscious.

28. The id is completely _____ ; the ego and superego can operate at all three levels of awareness.

29. The Freudian view of personality development is based on a series of psychosexual _____ : the _____ , anal, phallic, and genital.

30. Fixations (unresolved emotional conflicts) at any stage can leave a lasting imprint on _____ .

31. Freud pioneered the idea that feeding, toilet training, and early sexual experiences leave an imprint on _____ .

What do behaviourists emphasize in their approach to personality?

Recite and Review: Pages 369–374

32. Behavioural theories of personality emphasize _____ , conditioning, and immediate effects of the environment.

33. Learning theorists generally stress the effects of prior learning and _____ determinants of behaviour.

34. Learning theorists Dollard and Miller consider _____ the basic core of personality. _____ express the combined effects of drive, cue, response, and _____ .

35. _____ learning theory adds cognitive elements, such as perception, thinking, and understanding to the behavioural view of personality.

36. Examples of social learning concepts are the _____ situation (the situation as it is perceived), expectancies (expectations about what effects a response will have), and reinforcement _____ (the subjective value of a reinforcer or activity).

37. Self-efficacy shapes our lives by influencing our choice of _____ .

38. Some social learning theorists treat "conscience" as a case of _____ -reinforcement.

39. The behaviouristic view of personality development holds that social reinforcement in four situations is critical. The critical situations are _____ , toilet or cleanliness training, sex training, and _____ or aggression training.

40. Identification (feeling emotionally connected to a person) and _____ (mimicking another person's behaviour) are of particular importance in sex (or gender) training.

41. Research conducted by Sandra Bem indicates that roughly one-third of all persons are androgynous (they possess both _____ and _____ traits).

42. Androgyny is measured with the Bem _____ _____ Inventory (BSRI).

43. _____ males have difficulty expressing _____ , playfulness, and concern.

44. Highly _____ females find it difficult to be independent and assertive.

45. Psychological _____ appears related to greater adaptability or flexibility in behaviour.

How do humanistic theories differ from other perspectives on personality?
Recite and Review: Pages 375–379

46. Humanistic theory views human nature as _____ , and emphasizes subjective experience, _____ choice, and needs for self-actualization.

47. Abraham Maslow's study of self-actualizers identified characteristics they share, ranging from efficient perceptions of reality to frequent _____ _____ (temporary moments of self-actualization).

48. Carl Rogers's theory views the _____ as an entity that emerges when experiences that match the self- _____ are symbolized (admitted to consciousness), while those that are incongruent are excluded.

49. The incongruent person has a highly unrealistic _____ - _____ and/or a mismatch between the _____ - _____ and the ideal self.

50. The congruent or _____ functioning person is flexible and open to experiences and feelings.

51. In the development of personality, humanists are primarily interested in the emergence of a _____ - _____ and in self-evaluations.

52. As parents apply conditions of _____ (standards used to judge thoughts, feelings, and actions) to a child, the child begins to do the same.

53. Internalized conditions of worth contribute to incongruence, they damage _____ self-regard, and they disrupt the organismic _____ process.

How do psychologists measure personality?

Recite and Review: Pages 379–386

54. Techniques typically used for personality assessment are _____ , observation, questionnaires, and projective _____ .

55. Structured and unstructured _____ provide much information, but they are subject to _____ bias and misperceptions. The halo effect may also _____ accuracy.

56. Direct observation, sometimes involving situational tests, behavioural assessment, or the use of _____ scales, allows evaluation of a person's actual _____ .

57. Personality questionnaires, such as the _____ _____ Personality Inventory-2 (MMPI-2), are objective and _____ , but their validity is open to question.

58. Honesty tests, which are essentially personality _____ , are widely used by businesses to make hiring decisions. Their validity is hotly debated.

59. Projective tests ask a subject to project thoughts or feelings onto an ambiguous _____ or unstructured situation.

60. The Rorschach, or _____ test, is a well-known projective technique. A second is the _____ Apperception Test (TAT).

61. The validity and objectivity of projective tests are quite _____ . Nevertheless, projective techniques are considered useful by many clinicians, particularly as part of a _____ battery.

What causes shyness? What can be done about it?

Recite and Review: Psychology in Action

62. Shyness is a mixture of _____ inhibition and _____ anxiety.

63. Shy persons tend to lack social skills and they feel social anxiety (because they believe they are being _____ by others).

64. Shy persons also have a self-defeating bias in their _____ (they tend to blame _____ for social failures).

65. Shyness is marked by heightened _____ self-consciousness (awareness of oneself as a _____ object) and a tendency to regard shyness as a lasting trait.

66. Shyness can be lessened by changing self-defeating _____ and by improving _____ skills.

Connections

1. _____ character	a. heart-attack risk
2. _____ trait	b. system of concepts
3. _____ Type A	c. personality judged
4. _____ cardinal trait	d. traits of Big Five
5. _____ choleric	e. source traits
6. _____ phlegmatic	f. culturally typical
7. _____ facet traits	g. sluggish
8. _____ 16 PF	h. universal dimensions
9. _____ common traits	i. relates to all of a person's activities
10. _____ Big Five	j. lasting personal quality

11. _____ trait-situation	a. mouth
12. _____ Thanatos	b. pride
13. _____ Eros	c. genitals
14. _____ conscience	d. female conflict
15. _____ ego ideal	e. interaction
16. _____ oral stage	f. male conflict
17. _____ anal stage	g. death instinct
18. _____ phallic stage	h. elimination
19. _____ Oedipus	i. life instinct
20. _____ Electra	j. guilt

21. _____ habits	a. interview problem
22. _____ androgyny	b. evaluation fears
23. _____ Maslow	c. shoot-don't-shoot
24. _____ Rogers	d. personality questionnaire
25. _____ social learning	e. same score each time
26. _____ halo effect	f. fully functioning person
27. _____ MMPI	g. self-actualization
28. _____ reliability	h. BSRI
29. _____ social anxiety	i. cognitive behaviourism
30. _____ situational test	j. learned behaviour patterns

Short-Answer Questions

1. Show how self-esteem may be affected by cultural differences.

2. What is meant by the term *common traits*?

3. What is meant by the term *cardinal traits*?

4. What evidence suggests that personality traits are inherited?

5. Briefly explain how personality might be learned.

6. Using Freud's psychodynamic theory, explain why feeding and toilet training are important in the development of personality.

7. Using the behaviouristic view of personality development, explain why feeding and toilet training may be important in the development of personality.
8. What is the role of social reinforcement in the development of personality?
9. What is the role of imitation in the development of personality?
10. What is the role of identification in the development of personality?
11. How does androgyny relate to adaptability?
12. Compare Freud's and Roger's views of the structure of personality.
13. What can be done to reduce shyness?

Final Survey and Review

What do psychologists mean by the term *personality*? What core concepts make up the field of personality?

1. _____ is made up of one's unique and relatively stable behaviour _____ .
2. _____ is personality that has been judged or evaluated. That is, it is the possession of desirable qualities.
3. _____ refers to the hereditary and physiological aspects of one's emotional nature.
4. Personality _____ are lasting personal qualities that are inferred from behaviour.
5. A personality _____ is a style of personality defined by having a group of related traits or similar characteristics.
6. Two widely recognized personality types are an _____ (shy, self-centred person) and an _____ (bold, outgoing person).
7. Behaviour is influenced by _____ - _____ , which is a person's perception of his or her own personality traits.
8. Personality _____ combine interrelated assumptions, ideas, and principles to explain personality.
9. Four major types of personality theories are trait, _____ , behaviouristic, and _____ .

What are personality traits? Are some personality traits more basic or important than others? Do traits predict how someone will act in the future?

10. _____ theories attempt to specify qualities of personality that are most lasting or characteristic of a person.
11. Gordon _____ made useful distinctions between _____ traits (which are shared by most members of a culture) and individual traits (characteristics of a single person).
12. He also identified _____ traits (a trait that influences nearly all of a person's activities), _____ traits (core traits of personality), and secondary traits (superficial traits).
13. The theory of Raymond _____ attributes visible surface traits to the existence of 16 underlying _____ traits (which he identified using _____ analysis).
14. _____ _____ are measured by the Sixteen Personality Factor Questionnaire (16 PF).
15. The outcome of the 16 PF and other personality tests may be graphically presented as a trait _____ .

16. The _____ - _____ model of personality reduces traits to five universal dimensions of personality.

17. They are _____ , agreeableness, conscientiousness, _____ , and openness to experience.

18. Traits _____ with _____ to determine behaviour.

19. Heredity is responsible for _____ to _____ percent of the variation in personality traits.

20. Studies of separated identical twins suggest that _____ contributes significantly to adult personality traits. Overall, however, personality is shaped as much, or more, by differences in _____ .

How do psychodynamic theories explain personality?

21. Psychodynamic theories focus on the inner workings of _____ , especially hidden or unconscious forces and internal _____ .

22. According to Sigmund Freud's _____ theory, personality is made up of the _____ , ego, and _____ .

23. The id operates on the _____ principle. The ego is guided by the _____ principle.

24. The superego is made up of the _____ and the _____ ideal.

25. _____ , derived from the life _____ , is the primary energy running the personality.

26. Conflicts within the personality may cause _____ anxiety or _____ anxiety and motivate use of ego-defence mechanisms.

27. The personality operates on three levels, the conscious, _____ , and _____ .

28. The _____ is completely unconscious; the _____ and _____ can operate at all three levels of awareness.

29. The Freudian view of personality development is based on a series of _____ stages: the oral, anal, _____ , and genital.

30. _____ (unresolved emotional conflicts) at any stage can leave a lasting imprint on personality.

31. Freud's theory pioneered the idea that _____ , _____ training, and early sexual experiences leave an imprint on personality.

What do behaviourists emphasize in their approach to personality?

32. _____ theories of personality emphasize learning, conditioning, and immediate effects of the environment.

33. Learning theorists generally stress the effects of prior learning and situational _____ of behaviour.

34. Learning theorists Dollard and Miller consider habits the basic core of personality. Habits express the combined effects of _____ , _____ , response, and reward.

35. Social learning theory adds _____ elements, such as perception, thinking, and understanding to the behavioural view of personality.

36. Examples of social learning concepts are the psychological situation (the situation as it is perceived), _____ (expectations about what effects a response will have), and _____ value (the subjective value of a reinforcer or activity).

37. _____ - _____ plays a key role in shaping our lives by influencing our choice of activities.

38. Some social learning theorists treat "conscience" as a case of self- _____ .

39. The behaviouristic view of personality development holds that social reinforcement in four situations is critical. The critical situations are feeding, _____ _____ , sex training, and anger or _____ training.

40. _____ (feeling emotionally connected to a person) and imitation (mimicking another person's behaviour) are of particular importance in sex (or gender) training.

41. Research conducted by Sandra Bem indicates that roughly one- _____ of all persons are _____ (they possess both masculine and feminine traits).

42. Androgyny is measured with the _____ Sex Role _____ (BSRI).

43. Masculine men have difficulty expressing _____ and _____ .

44. Feminine women find that being _____ and _____ is difficult.

45. Psychological androgyny appears related to greater _____ or flexibility in behaviour.

How do humanistic theories differ from other perspectives on personality?

46. Humanistic theory views human nature as good, and emphasizes _____ experience, free choice, and needs for self- _____ .

47. Abraham _____ study of _____ - _____ identified characteristics they share, ranging from efficient perceptions of reality to frequent peak experiences.

48. Carl Rogers's theory views the self as an entity that emerges when experiences that match the self-image are _____ (admitted to consciousness), while those that are _____ are excluded.

49. The _____ person has a highly unrealistic self-image and/or a mismatch between the self-image and the _____ self.

50. The _____ or fully functioning person is flexible and open to experiences and feelings.

51. In the development of personality, humanists are primarily interested in the emergence of a self-image and in _____ - _____ .

52. As parents apply _____ of worth (standards used to judge thoughts, feelings, and actions) to a child, the child begins to do the same.

53. Internalized _____ _____ _____ contribute to incongruence, they damage positive self-regard, and they disrupt the _____ valuing process.

How do psychologists measure personality?

54. Techniques typically used for personality assessment are interviews, direct _____ , questionnaires, and _____ tests.

55. Structured and _____ interviews provide much information, but they are subject to interviewer _____ and misperceptions. The halo effect may also lower the accuracy of an interview.

56. Direct observation, sometimes involving _____ tests, _____ assessment, or the use of rating scales, allows evaluation of a person's actual behaviour.

57. _____ questionnaires, such as the Minnesota Multiphasic Personality _____ -2 (MMPI-2), are objective and reliable, but their _____ is open to question.

58. _____ tests, which are essentially personality questionnaires, are widely used by businesses to measure integrity and make hiring decisions.

59. _____ tests ask subjects to react to an ambiguous stimulus or unstructured situation.

60. The _____ , or inkblot test, is a well-known projective technique. A second is the Thematic _____ Test (TAT).

61. The _____ and objectivity of projective tests are quite low. Nevertheless, projective techniques are considered useful by many clinicians, particularly as part of a test _____ .

What causes shyness? What can be done about it?

62. Shyness is a mixture of social _____ and social anxiety.

63. Shy persons tend to lack social _____ and they feel social anxiety (because they believe they are being evaluated by others).

64. Shy persons also have a _____ - _____ bias in their thinking (they tend to blame themselves for social failures).

65. Shyness is marked by heightened public self- _____ (awareness of oneself as a _____ object) and a tendency to regard shyness as a lasting _____ .

66. Shyness can be lessened by changing _____ - _____ beliefs and by improving social _____ .

Mastery Test

1. The hereditary aspects of a person's emotional nature define his or her
   a. character
   b. personality
   c. cardinal traits
   d. temperament

2. Two parts of the psyche that operate on all three levels of awareness are the
   a. id and ego
   b. ego and superego
   c. id and superego
   d. id and ego ideal

3. The four critical situations Miller and Dollard consider important in the development of personality are feeding, toilet training,
   a. sex, and aggression
   b. cleanliness, and language
   c. attachment, and imitation
   d. social learning

4. Scales that rate a person's tendencies for depression, hysteria, paranoia, and mania are found on the
   a. MMPI-2
   b. Rorschach
   c. TAT
   d. 16 PF

5. In the five-factor model, people who score high on openness to experience are
   a. intelligent
   b. extroverted
   c. choleric
   d. a personality type

6. Maslow used the term _____ to describe the tendency to make full use of personal potentials.
   a. full functionality
   b. self-potentiation
   c. ego-idealization
   d. self-actualization

7. Studies of reunited identical twins support the idea that
   a. personality traits are 70 percent hereditary
   b. fixations influence the expression of personality traits
   c. personality traits are altered by selective mating and placement in families of comparable status
   d. personality is shaped as much or more by environment as by heredity

8. A person's perception of his or her own personality is the core of
   a. temperament
   b. source traits
   c. self-concept
   d. trait-situation interactions

9. Which of the following concepts is NOT part of Dollard and Miller's behavioural model of personality?
   a. drive
   b. expectancy
   c. cue
   d. reward

10. The terms *structured* and *unstructured* refer to
    a. halo effects
    b. interviews
    c. questionnaires
    d. honesty tests

11. Behavioural theorists account for the existence of a conscience with the concept of
    a. traits of honesty and integrity
    b. the superego
    c. self-reinforcement
    d. conditions of worth

12. Feelings of pride come from the _____, a part of the _____.
    a. libido, conscience
    b. ego ideal, superego
    c. reality principle, superego
    d. superego, ego

13. Freud believed that boys identify with their fathers in order to resolve the _____ conflict.
    a. Animus
    b. Electra
    c. Oedipus
    d. Persona

14. Maslow regarded peak experiences as temporary moments of
    a. task-centring
    b. congruent selfhood
    c. self-actualization
    d. organismic valuing

15. Ambiguous stimuli are used primarily in the
    a. MMPI-2
    b. TAT
    c. Rorschach
    d. 16 PF

16. A person who is generally extroverted is more outgoing in some situations than in others. This observation supports the concept of
    a. trait-situation interactions
    b. behavioural genetic determinants
    c. situational fixations
    d. possible selves

17. Allport's concept of central traits is most closely related to Cattell's
    a. surface traits
    b. source traits
    c. secondary traits
    d. cardinal traits

18. According to Freud, tendencies to be orderly, obstinate, and stingy are formed during the _____ stage.
    a. genital
    b. anal
    c. oral
    d. phallic

19. Which of the following is NOT part of Carl Rogers's view of personality?
    a. possible selves
    b. organismic valuing
    c. conditions of worth
    d. congruence

20. Rating scales are primarily used in which approach to personality assessment?
    a. projective testing
    b. direct observation
    c. questionnaires
    d. the TAT technique

21. Which theory of personality places the greatest emphasis on the effects of the environment?
    a. trait
    b. psychodynamic
    c. behaviouristic
    d. humanistic

22. Freudian psychosexual stages occur in which order?
    a. oral, anal, genital, phallic
    b. oral, phallic, anal, genital
    c. genital, oral, anal, phallic
    d. oral, anal, phallic, genital

23. Rogers described mismatches between one's self-image and reality as a state of
    a. moral anxiety
    b. incongruence
    c. basic anxiety
    d. negative symbolization

24. All but one of the following are major elements of shyness except:
    a. private self-consciousness
    b. social anxiety
    c. *self-defeating thoughts*
    d. belief that shyness is a lasting trait

25. People who all grew up in the same culture would be most likely to have the same _____ traits.
    a. cardinal
    b. common
    c. secondary
    d. source

26. A trait profile is used to report the results of
    a. the 16 PF
    b. a structured interview
    c. the TAT
    d. the inkblot test

27. An emphasis on the situational determinants of actions is a key feature of _____ theories of personality.
    a. psychodynamic
    b. projective
    c. behaviourist
    d. humanist

28. Expectancies and the psychological situation are concepts important to
    a. the five-factor model
    b. development of the superego
    c. social learning theory
    d. Maslow

29. A male police officer who accepts emotional support from others, especially from women, would most likely be scored as _____ on the BSRI.
    a. masculine
    b. feminine
    c. androgynous
    d. expressive-nurturant

30. The subcategories of the Big Five dimensions are called
    a. common traits
    b. secondary traits
    c. sublevel traits
    d. facet traits

Solutions

Recite and Review

1. behaviour
2. evaluated
3. hereditary
4. behaviour
5. traits
6. types
7. personality
8. Personality
9. trait
10. theories
11. individual
12. secondary
13. surface; analysis
14. Personality; Factor
15. trait
16. universal
17. agreeableness; experience
18. Traits
19. traits
20. identical
21. unconscious
22. ego
23. principle; principle
24. superego
25. life; energy
26. anxiety; anxiety
27. conscious
28. unconscious
29. stages; oral
30. personality
31. personality
32. learning
33. situational
34. habits; Habits; reward
35. Social
36. psychological; value
37. activities
38. self
39. feeding; anger
40. imitation
41. masculine; feminine
42. Sex; Role
43. masculine; warmth
44. feminine
45. androgyny
46. good; free
47. peak; experiences
48. self; image
49. self; image; self; image
50. fully
51. self image
52. worth
53. positive; valuing
54. interviews; tests
55. interviews; interviewer; lower
56. rating; behaviour
57. Minnesota; Multiphasic; reliable
58. questionnaires
59. stimulus
60. inkblot; Thematic
61. low; test
62. social; social
63. evaluated
64. thinking; themselves
65. public; social
66. beliefs; social

Connections

1. C
2. J
3. A
4. I
5. B
6. G
7. D
8. E
9. F
10. H
11. E
12. G
13. I
14. J
15. B
16. A
17. H
18. C
19. F
20. D
21. J
22. H
23. G
24. F
25. I
26. A
27. D
28. E
29. B
30. C

Short-Answer Questions

1. In some cultures (ours, for instance), self-esteem is based on personal achievement, success, or competence. In cultures that emphasize mutual interdependence (Asian cultures, for example), self-esteem is related to group achievement or success.

2. Common traits are traits or characteristics that are shared by most members of a particular culture. For example, competitiveness is a fairly common trait in Western cultures.

3. Cardinal traits are such basic traits that everything a person does can be traced back to that trait.

4. Twin studies have shown that identical twins raised separately share much more than just physical appearance, voice quality, and gestures. Some studies have found that twins reared apart are far more similar than one would expect—including marrying spouses with the same name, taking the same kind of career training, and giving their firstborn children the same

name. However, other research has shown that unrelated individuals of the same age have also been found to share many characteristics.

5. Behavioural theories of personality suggest that personality is shaped through classical and operant conditioning, observational learning, patterns of reinforcement, extinction, discrimination, and generalization. Behavioural theories of personality focus on the external causes of behaviour.

6. In Freud's view, each stage of personality development has basic needs that must be met. If they are not, the person will, as an adult, still have to satisfy them. This is expressed in various personality styles. For example, in the oral stage, if as a child a person is fed too often, or prevented from sucking a thumb (frustrated), as an adult he may express oral needs by nail biting, overeating, and the use of sarcasm (oral aggression). The same holds true for toilet training.

7. Feeding and toilet training are critical situations for personality development. A basic active or passive view of the world is learned; if a child cries and gets fed, she learns that people are associated with pleasure. If she cries and is not fed, she associates people with frustration or discomfort. The same with toilet training; severe toilet training practices can leave an adult with negative attitudes about bodily functions.

8. Praise, attention, and approval from others (social reinforcement) shape personality. Girls are reinforced by parents and teachers for acting in appropriate ways, and not reinforced for behaving like boys. Boys are reinforced for acting in appropriate ways and not for acting like girls.

9. Children imitate the behaviour of those around them. Girls learn to be girls and boys learn to be boys by imitating their same-sexed parent, and by observing what happens when they, or others, imitate the opposite-sexed parent.

10. Identification is the child's attachment to those adults in the environment who provide love and caring. When children identify with certain adults, they will then imitate their behaviour.

11. Androgynous people are more adaptable since they do not feel bound by societal images of masculine or feminine behaviour. Masculine males have difficulty expressing caring and concern, and accepting emotional support from women. Feminine women may find it hard assert themselves.

12. Freud—personality consists of the id (inborn biological drives and urges), ego (involved with planning and deciding), and superego (conscience). A person feels anxiety when the ego is threatened by impulses from the id (neurotic anxiety) or fear of punishment from the ego (moral anxiety). Individuals develop their own way to calm these anxieties, often using defence mechanisms. Rogers—fully functioning individuals live in harmony with their deepest feelings and instincts. It is important for the self (flexible perception of a person's identity) and the ideal self (what you would most like to be) to be in harmony (congruent).

13. Shyness can be reduced by changing self-defeating attitudes and beliefs (that are really excuses for inaction) to more positive attitudes and beliefs. Social skills training (how to talk to people or start a conversation) can also help.

Final Survey and Review

1. Personality; patterns
2. Character
3. Temperament
4. traits
5. type
6. introvert; extrovert
7. self concept
8. theories
9. psychodynamic; humanistic
10. Trait
11. Allport; common
12. cardinal; central
13. Cattell; source; factor
14. Source; traits
15. profile
16. Five; factor
17. extroversion; neuroticism
18. interact; situations
19. 25; 30
20. heredity; environment
21. personality; conflicts
22. psychoanalytical; id; superego
23. pleasure; reality
24. conscience; ego
25. Libido; instincts
26. neurotic; moral
27. preconscious; unconscious
28. id; ego; superego
29. psychosexual; phallic
30. Fixations
31. feeding; toilet
32. Behavioural
33. determinants

34. drive; cue
35. cognitive
36. expectancies; reinforcement
37. Self; efficiency
38. reinforcement
39. toilet; training; aggression
40. Identification
41. third; androgynous
42. Bem; Inventory
43. warmth; concern
44. independent; assertive
45. adaptability
46. subjectivity; actualization
47. Maslow's; self; actualizers
48. symbolized; incongruent
49. incongruent; ideal
50. congruent
51. self evaluations
52. conditions
53. conditions; of; worth; organismic
54. observation; projective
55. unstructured; bias
56. situational; behavioural
57. Personality; Inventory; validity
58. Honesty
59. Projective
60. Rorschach; Apperception
61. validity; battery
62. inhibition
63. skills
64. self; defeating
65. consciousness; social; trait
66. self; defeating; skills

Mastery Test

1. D (p. 356)
2. B (p. 367)
3. A (p. 371)
4. A (p. 383)
5. A (p. 361)
6. D (p. 375)
7. D (p. 364)
8. C (p. 357)
9. B (p. 370)
10. B (p. 379)
11. C (p. 371)
12. B (p. 366)
13. C (p. 368)
14. C (p. 376)
15. C (p. 384)
16. A (p. 363)
17. B (p. 360)
18. B (p. 368)
19. A (p. 378)
20. B (p. 380)
21. C (p. 369)
22. D (p. 367)
23. B (p. 377)
24. A (p. 387)
25. B (p. 360)
26. A (p. 380)
27. C (p. 370)
28. C (p. 370)
29. C (p. 373)
30. D (p. 362)

Health, Stress, and Coping

Chapter Overview

Health psychologists study behavioural risk factors and health-promoting behaviours. Various "lifestyle" diseases are directly related to unhealthy personal habits. Sexually transmitted infections are a good example of how behavioural risk factors contribute to health risks. Stress is also a major risk factor. At work, prolonged stress can lead to burnout. Emotional appraisals greatly affect our stress reactions and coping attempts.

Frustration and conflict are common sources of stress. Major behavioural reactions to frustration include persistence, more vigorous responding, circumvention, direct aggression, displaced aggression, and escape or withdrawal. Five major types of conflict are approach-approach, avoidance-avoidance, approach-avoidance, double approach-avoidance, and multiple approach-avoidance.

Anxiety, threat, or feelings of inadequacy frequently lead to the use of defence mechanisms. Common defence mechanisms include compensation, denial, fantasy, intellectualization, isolation, projection, rationalization, reaction formation, regression, repression, and sublimation. Learned helplessness explains some depression and some failures to cope with threat. Mastery training acts as an antidote to helplessness.

A large number of life changes can increase susceptibility to illness. However, immediate health is more closely related to the severity of daily hassles or microstressors. Intense or prolonged stress may cause psychosomatic problems. Biofeedback may be used to combat stress and psychosomatic illnesses. People with Type A personalities run a heightened risk of suffering a heart attack. People with hardy personality traits are resistant to stress. The body reacts to stress in a pattern called the general adaptation syndrome (G.A.S.). In addition, stress may lower the body's immunity to disease.

A number of coping skills can be applied to manage stress. Most focus on bodily effects, ineffective behaviours, and upsetting thoughts.

Learning Objectives

After reading this chapter, students will be able to:

1. Describe the relationship between behaviour and health. Identify the major behavioural risk factors and health-promoting behaviours that contribute to lifestyle diseases.

2. Identify the behaviours that contribute to increasing and decreasing the risk for sexually transmitted infections.

3. Define stress. Identify the major factors that contribute to stress.

4. Define frustration. List the major causes of frustration and describe typical reactions to frustration.

5. Define conflict. Give an example of each of the five types of conflict and the most common response for each.

6. Identify the four steps that can be used to effectively manage conflicts.

7. Describe all the psychological defence mechanisms and show how they may help people cope with stress.

8. Describe the relationship between learned helplessness and depression.

9. Identify the major causes of depression in college and university students.

10. Describe the relationship between stress and health.

11. Explain the General Adaptation Syndrome.

12. Give examples of effective strategies for coping with stress.

Practice Quizzes

Recite and Review

What is health psychology? How does behaviour affect health?
Recite and Review: Pages 394–401

1. Health psychologists are interested in _____ that helps maintain and promote health. The related field of behavioural medicine applies psychology to _____ treatment and problems.

2. Most people today die from lifestyle diseases caused by unhealthy personal _____ .

3. Studies have identified a number of behavioural risk factors, which increase the chances of _____ (or _____) or injury.

4. A general disease-prone personality pattern also raises the risk of _____ (or _____).

5. Health-promoting _____ tend to maintain good health. They include practices such as getting regular exercise, controlling _____ and alcohol use, maintaining a balanced _____ , getting good medical care, avoiding _____ deprivation, and managing stress.

6. During the last 20 years there has been a steady _____ in the incidence of sexually transmitted infections (STIs).

7. Part of this increase is due to the emergence of _____ _____ deficiency syndrome (AIDS) caused by the human immunodeficiency _____ (HIV).

8. STIs have had a sizable impact on patterns of sexual behaviour, including increased awareness of high- _____ behaviours and some curtailment of _____ taking.

9. Health psychologists attempt to change _____ behaviours through community health _____ that educate people about risk factors and healthful behaviours.

What is stress? What factors determine its severity?

Recite and Review: Pages 401–403

10. Stress occurs when we are forced to _____ or adapt to external demands.

11. Stress is more damaging in situations involving pressure (responding at full capacity for long periods), a lack of _____ , unpredictability of the stressor, and _____ or repeated emotional shocks.

12. _____ is intensified when a situation is perceived as a threat and when a person does not feel competent to cope with it.

13. In _____ settings, prolonged stress can lead to burnout, marked by emotional _____ , depersonalization (detachment from others), and reduced personal accomplishment.

14. The _____ appraisal of a situation greatly affects our emotional response to it. Stress reactions, in particular, are related to an appraisal of _____ .

15. During a _____ appraisal some means of coping with a situation is selected. Coping may be either problem focused (managing the situation) or emotion focused (managing one's emotional reactions) or both.

What is frustration? What are the major causes of frustration? How do people react to it?

Recite and Review: Pages 403–405

16. Frustration is the negative emotional state that occurs when progress toward a _____ is _____ . Sources of frustration may be external or personal.

17. External frustrations are based on delay, failure, rejection, loss, and other direct blocking of motives. _____ frustration is related to personal characteristics over which one has little control.

18. Frustrations of all types become more _____ as the strength, urgency, or importance of the blocked motive increases.

19. Major behavioural reactions to frustration include persistence, more _____ responding, and circumvention of barriers.

20. Other reactions to frustration are _____ aggression, displaced aggression (including scapegoating), and escape, or _____ .

What is conflict? Are there different types of conflict? How do people react to conflict?

Recite and Review: Pages 405–408

21. _____ occurs when we must choose between contradictory alternatives.

22. Three basic types of conflict are approach-approach (choice between two _____ alternatives), avoidance-avoidance (both alternatives are _____), and approach-avoidance (a goal or activity has both positive and negative aspects).

23. More complex conflicts are double approach-avoidance (both alternatives have _____ and _____ qualities) and multiple approach-avoidance (several alternatives each have good and bad qualities).

24. Approach-approach conflicts are usually the _____ to resolve.

25. Avoidance conflicts are _____ to resolve and are characterized by inaction, indecision, freezing, and a desire to escape (called _____ the field).

26. People usually remain in approach-avoidance conflicts, but fail to fully resolve them. Approach-avoidance conflicts are associated with ambivalence (_____ feelings) and _____ approach.

27. Vacillation (wavering between choices) is the most common reaction to double _____ - _____ conflicts.

What are defence mechanisms? How do defence mechanisms helps us to cope with stress?

Recite and Review: Pages 408–411

28. Anxiety, threat, or feelings of _____ frequently lead to the use of psychological defence mechanisms. These are habitual strategies used to avoid or reduce anxiety.

29. A number of defence mechanisms have been identified, including denial, fantasy, intellectualization, isolation, projection, rationalization, _____ formation, regression, and _____ (motivated forgetting).

30. Two defence mechanisms that have some _____ qualities are compensation and sublimation.

How can we cope with feelings of helplessness and depression? Do some methods work better than others?

Recite and Review: Pages 411–414

31. Learned helplessness is a learned inability to overcome obstacles or to _____ punishment.

32. Learned helplessness explains the failure to cope with some threatening situations. The symptoms of learned helplessness and depression are nearly _____ .

33. Mastery _____ and hope act as antidotes to helplessness.

34. Depression (a state of deep sadness or despondency) is a serious emotional problem. Actions and thoughts that counter feelings of helplessness tend to _____ depression.

How is stress related to health and disease?

Recite and Review: Pages 414–420

35. Work with the Social Readjustment Rating Scale (SRRS) indicates that a large number of life _____ units (LCUs) can increase susceptibility to _____ or illness.

36. Immediate health is more closely related to the intensity and severity of daily annoyances, known as _____ or microstressors.

37. Intense or prolonged stress may damage the body in the form of psychosomatic disorders (illnesses in which _____ factors play a part).

38. Psychosomatic (mind-body) disorders have no connection to hypochondria, the tendency to imagine that one has a _____ .

39. During biofeedback training, bodily processes are _____ and converted to a signal that indicates what the body is doing.

40. Biofeedback allows alteration of many bodily activities. It shows promise for promoting _____ and self-regulation, and for treating some psychosomatic illnesses.

41. People with Type A (_____ -attack prone) personalities are competitive, striving, and frequently angry or hostile, and they have a chronic sense of _____ urgency.

42. _____ and hostility are especially likely to increase the chances of heart attack.

43. People who have traits of the hardy personality seem to be resistant to _____ , even if they also have Type A traits.

44. The body reacts to stress in a series of stages called the _____ adaptation syndrome (G.A.S.).

45. The stages of the G.A.S. are alarm, resistance, and exhaustion. The G.A.S. contributes to the development of _____ disorders.

46. Stress weakens the immune system and lowers the body's resistance to _____ (or _____).

What are the best strategies for managing stress?

Recite and Review: Psychology in Action

47. Most stress management skills focus on one of three areas: bodily effects, ineffective _____ , and upsetting _____ .

48. Bodily effects can be managed with exercise, meditation, progressive _____ , and guided _____ .

49. The impact of ineffective behaviour can be remedied by slowing down, getting organized, striking a balance between "good stress" and _____ , accepting your limits, and seeking social support.

50. A good way to control upsetting thoughts is to replace negative self-statements with _____ coping statements.

Connections

1. _____ risk factors
2. _____ tobacco
3. _____ refusal skills
4. _____ stress reaction
5. _____ burnout
6. _____ primary appraisal
7. _____ frustration
8. _____ displaced aggression
9. _____ apathy
10. _____ ambivalence

a. a leading cause of death
b. ANS arousal
c. blocked motive
d. health-damaging habits
e. psychological escape
f. scapegoat
g. approach-avoidance
h. "Am I in trouble?"
i. job stress
j. smoking prevention

11. _____ compensation
12. _____ denial
13. _____ fantasy
14. _____ intellectualization
15. _____ isolation
16. _____ projection
17. _____ rationalization
18. _____ reaction formation
19. _____ regression
20. _____ repression
21. _____ sublimation

a. Fulfilling unmet desires in imagined activities.
b. Separating contradictory thoughts into "logic-tight" mental compartments.
c. Preventing actions by exaggerating opposite behaviour.
d. Justifying your behaviour by giving reasonable but false reasons for it.
e. Unconsciously preventing painful thoughts from entering awareness.
f. Counteracting a real or imagined weakness by seeking to excel.
g. Retreating to an earlier level of development.
h. Attributing one's own shortcomings or unacceptable impulses to others.
i. Protecting oneself from an unpleasant reality by refusing to perceive it.
j. Working off unacceptable impulses in constructive activities.
k. Thinking about threatening situations in impersonal terms.

22. _____ learned helplessness
23. _____ mastery training
24. _____ Social Readjustment Rating Scale
25. _____ hassle
26. _____ STI
27. _____ psychosomatic
28. _____ biofeedback
29. _____ Type A
30. _____ general adaptation syndrome

a. life change units
b. risky sexual behaviour
c. mind-body
d. self-regulation
e. cardiac personality
f. alarm reaction
g. microstressor
h. hope
i. shuttle box

Short-Answer Questions

1. What is refusal skills training? How can refusal skills training be used in smoking prevention programs?
2. How is HIV transmitted from one person to another? How is it NOT spread?
3. Describe the similarities between emotions and the reaction to stress.
4. Briefly describe the emotional, physical, and behavioural signs of stress.
5. Explain how primary and secondary appraisal are used to cope with stress.
6. How does the perception of control over a stressor affect the amount of stress a person experiences?
7. Explain the difference between problem-focused coping and emotion-focused coping.
8. How does scapegoating help people deal with frustration?
9. What are some of the ways we can avoid needless frustration?
10. What are the advantages and disadvantages of using defence mechanisms to cope with stress?

11. How is helplessness learned? How might it be "unlearned"?
12. What are the five signs of depression?
13. How are hassles related to health?
14. What is the difference between a psychosomatic disorder and hypochondria?
15. What are the characteristics of a hardy personality?

Final Survey and Review

What is health psychology? How does behaviour affect health?

1. Health psychologists are interested in behaviour that helps maintain and promote health. The related field of _____ _____ applies psychology to medical treatment and problems.
2. Most people today die from _____ diseases caused by unhealthy personal habits.
3. Studies have identified a number of behavioural _____ _____ , which increase the chances of disease or injury.
4. A general _____ - _____ personality pattern also raises the risk of illness.
5. Health- _____ behaviours tend to maintain good health. They include practices such as getting regular exercise, controlling smoking and alcohol use, maintaining a balanced diet, getting good medical care, avoiding sleep _____ , and managing _____ .
6. During the last 20 years there has been a steady increase in the incidence of _____ _____ infections.
7. Part of this increase is due to the emergence of acquired immune _____ syndrome (AIDS) caused by the human _____ virus (HIV).
8. _____ have had a sizable impact on patterns of sexual behaviour, including increased awareness of high-risk behaviours and some curtailment of risk taking.
9. Health psychologists attempt to promote _____ through _____ _____ campaigns that educate people about risk factors and healthful behaviours.

What is stress? What factors determine its severity?

10. Stress occurs when we are forced to adjust or _____ to external _____ .
11. Stress is more damaging in situations involving _____ (responding at full capacity for long periods), a lack of control, unpredictability of the _____ , and intense or repeated emotional shocks.
12. Stress is intensified when a situation is perceived as a _____ and when a person does not feel _____ to cope with it.
13. In work settings, prolonged stress can lead to _____ , marked by emotional exhaustion, _____ (detachment from others), and reduced personal accomplishment.
14. The primary _____ of a situation greatly affects our emotional response to it. Stress reactions, in particular, are related to an _____ of threat.
15. During a secondary appraisal some means of coping with a situation is selected. Coping may be either _____ focused (managing the situation) or _____ focused (managing one's emotional reactions) or both.

What is frustration? What are the major causes of frustration? How do people react to it?

16. _____ is the negative emotional state that occurs when progress toward a goal is blocked. Sources of frustration may be external or _____ .

17. _____ frustrations are based on delay, failure, rejection, loss, and other direct blocking of motives. _____ frustration is related to personal characteristics over which one has little control.

18. Frustrations of all types become more intense as the strength, urgency, or importance of the _____ _____ increases.

19. Major behavioural reactions to frustration include _____ , more vigorous responding, and _____ of barriers.

20. Other reactions to frustration are direct aggression, _____ aggression (including _____), and escape, or withdrawal.

What is conflict? Are there different types of conflict? How do people react to conflict?

21. Conflict occurs when we must choose between _____ alternatives.

22. Three basic types of conflict are _____ - _____ (choice between two positive alternatives), avoidance-avoidance (both alternatives are negative), and _____ - _____ (a goal or activity has both positive and negative aspects).

23. More complex conflicts are _____ approach-avoidance (both alternatives have positive and negative qualities) and _____ approach-avoidance (several alternatives each have good and bad qualities).

24. _____ - _____ conflicts are usually the easiest to resolve.

25. _____ conflicts are difficult to resolve and are characterized by inaction, indecision, freezing, and a desire to escape (called leaving the field).

26. People usually remain in approach-avoidance conflicts, but fail to fully resolve them. Approach-avoidance conflicts are associated with _____ (mixed feelings) and partial approach.

27. _____ (wavering between choices) is the most common reaction to double approach-avoidance conflicts.

What are defence mechanisms? How do defence mechanisms help us to cope with stress?

28. Anxiety, threat, or feelings of inadequacy frequently lead to the use of psychological _____ _____ . These are habitual strategies used to avoid or reduce _____ .

29. A number of defence mechanisms have been identified, including _____ (refusing to perceive an unpleasant reality), fantasy, intellectualization, isolation, projection, _____ (justifying one's behaviour), reaction formation, regression, and repression.

30. Two defence mechanisms that have some positive qualities are _____ and _____ .

How can we cope with feelings of helplessness and depression? Do some methods work better than others?

31. Learned _____ is a learned inability to overcome obstacles or to avoid _____ .

32. The symptoms of learned helplessness and _____ are nearly identical.

33. _____ training and hope act as antidotes to helplessness.

34. _____ (a state of deep sadness or despondency) is a serious emotional problem. Actions and thoughts that counter feelings of _____ tend to reduce depression.

How is stress related to health and disease?

35. Work with the _____ _____ _____ Scale (SRRS) indicates that a large number of life change units (LCUs) can increase susceptibility to accident or illness.

36. Immediate health is more closely related to the intensity and severity of daily annoyances, known as hassles or _____ .

37. Intense or prolonged stress may damage the body in the form of _____ disorders (illnesses in which psychological factors play a part).

38. _____ (mind-body) disorders have no connection to _____ , the tendency to imagine that one has a disease.

39. During _____ training, bodily processes are monitored and converted to a _____ that indicates what the body is doing.

40. Biofeedback allows alteration of many bodily activities. It shows promise for promoting relaxation and self- _____ , and for treating some psychosomatic illnesses.

41. People with _____ _____ (heart attack prone) personalities are competitive, striving, and frequently _____ or hostile, and they have a chronic sense of time urgency.

42. Anger and hostility are especially likely to increase the chances of _____ _____ .

43. People who have traits of the _____ personality seem to be resistant to stress, even if they also have Type A traits.

44. The body reacts to stress in a series of stages called the general _____ _____ (G.A.S.).

45. The stages of the G.A.S. are _____ , resistance, and _____ . The G.A.S. contributes to the development of psychosomatic disorders.

46. Stress weakens the _____ system and lowers the body's resistance to illness.

What are the best strategies for managing stress?

47. Most stress management skills focus on one of three areas: bodily effects, _____ behaviour, and _____ thoughts.

48. Bodily effects can be managed with exercise, meditation, _____ relaxation, and _____ imagery.

49. The impact of ineffective behaviour can be remedied by slowing down, getting organized, striking a balance between "good stress" and relaxation, accepting your _____ , and seeking _____ support.

50. A good way to control upsetting thoughts is to replace _____ self-statements with positive _____ statements.

Mastery Test

1. When stressful events appear to be uncontrollable, two common reactions are
   a. apathy and double-approach conflict
   b. helplessness and depression
   c. assimilation and marginalization
   d. psychosomatic disorders and hypochondria

2. The *College Life Stress Inventory* is most closely related to the
   a. SRRS
   b. G.A.S.
   c. K.I.S.
   d. *Disease-Prone Personality Scale*

3. We answer the question "Am I okay or in trouble?" when making
   a. negative self-statements
   b. coping statements
   c. a primary appraisal
   d. a secondary appraisal

4. Janet has been working for a number of years as a teacher of children with special physical and emotional needs. Recently she has begun to feel overwhelmed by the demands of her job. Her doctor tells her she is experiencing burnout. She has all the following symptoms EXCEPT:
   a. emotional exhaustion
   b. depersonalization
   c. reduced accomplishment
   d. dependence on co-workers

5. Four-year-old Patrick displays childish speech and infantile play after his parents bring home a new baby. He shows signs of
   a. compensation
   b. reaction formation
   c. regression
   d. sublimation

6. Persistent but inflexible repsonses to frustration can become
   a. stereotyped behaviours
   b. imagined barriers
   c. negative self-statements
   d. sublimated and depersonalized

7. Which of the following behaviours is related to lifestyle diseases?
   a. drinking alcohol
   b. smoking tobacco
   c. illicit drug use
   d. all of the above are related to lifestyle diseases

8. Both mountain climbing and relationship problems
   a. are behavioural risk factors
   b. are appraised as secondary threats
   c. cause stress reactions
   d. produce the condition known as pressure

9. LCUs are used to assess
   a. burnout
   b. social readjustment
   c. microstressors
   d. what stage of the G.A.S. a person is in

10. Sujata is often ridiculed by her boss, who also frequently takes advantage of her. Deep inside, Sujata has come to hate her boss, yet on the surface she acts as if she likes him very much. It is likely that Sujata is using the defence mechanism called
    a. reaction formation
    b. Type B appraisal
    c. problem-focused coping
    d. sublimation

11. Lifestyle diseases are of special interest to _____ psychologists.
    a. health
    b. community
    c. wellness
    d. psychosomatic

12. Which of the following is NOT characteristic of the hardy personality?
    a. commitment
    b. a sense of control
    c. accepting challenge
    d. repression

13. Unhealthy lifestyles are marked by the presence of a number of
    a. health refusal factors
    b. behavioural risk factors
    c. cultural stressors
    d. Type B personality traits

14. The most effective response to a controllable stressor is
    a. problem-focused coping
    b. emotion-focused coping
    c. leaving the field
    d. depersonalization

15. Delay, rejection, failure, and loss are all major causes of
    a. pressure
    b. frustration
    c. conflict
    d. helplessness

16. There is evidence that the most important factor of Type A behaviour is
    a. time urgency
    b. anger and hostility
    c. competitiveness and ambition
    d. accepting too many responsibilities

17. A special danger in the transmission of STIs is that many people are _____ at first.
    a. non-infectious
    b. androgynous
    c. androgenital
    d. asymptomatic

18. A person is caught between "the frying pan and the fire" in an _____ conflict.
    a. approach-approach
    b. avoidance-avoidance
    c. approach-avoidance
    d. double appraisal

19. Which of the following is NOT one of the major health-promoting behaviours listed in the text?
    a. do not smoke
    b. get adequate help
    c. get regular exercise
    d. avoid eating between meals

20. Ambivalence and partial approach are very common reactions to what type of conflict?
    a. approach-approach
    b. avoidance-avoidance
    c. approach-avoidance
    d. multiple avoidance

21. Which of the following terms does not belong with the others?
    a. Type A personality
    b. stage of exhaustion
    c. displaced aggression
    d. psychosomatic disorder

22. Coping statements are a key element in
    a. stress inoculation
    b. the K.I.S. technique
    c. guided imagery
    d. refusal skills training

23. Which of the following typically minimizes the amount of stress experienced?
    a. predictable stressors
    b. repeated stressors
    c. uncontrollable stressors
    d. intense stressors

24. Scapegoating is closely related to which response to frustration?
    a. leaving the field
    b. displaced aggression
    c. circumvention
    d. reaction formation

25. The study of the ways in which stress and the immune system affect susceptibility to disease is called
    a. neuropsychosymptomology
    b. immunohypochondrology
    c. psychosomatoneurology
    d. psychoneuroimmunology

26. Refusal skills training is typically used to teach young people how to
    a. avoid drug use
    b. cope with burnout
    c. resist stressors at home and at school
    d. avoid forming habits that lead to heart disease

27. Which combination is most relevant to managing bodily reactions to stress?
    a. social support, self-pacing
    b. exercise, social support
    c. exercise, negative self-statements
    d. progressive relaxation, guided imagery

28. Stress reactions are most likely to occur when a stressor is viewed as a _____ during the _____.
    a. pressure, primary appraisal
    b. pressure, secondary appraisal
    c. threat, primary appraisal
    d. threat, secondary appraisal

29. External symptoms of the body's adjustment to stress are least visible in which stage of the general adaptation syndrome (G.A.S.)?
    a. alarm
    b. regulation
    c. resistance
    d. exhaustion

30. A perceived lack of control creates a stressful sense of threat when combined with a perceived
    a. sense of time urgency
    b. state of sublimation
    c. need to change secondary risk factors
    d. lack of competence

31. Which of the following risky behaviours increases from adolescence to adulthood for both males and females?
    a. binge drinking
    b. tobacco smoking
    c. sex without using a condom and multiple sex partners
    d. all of these risky behaviours increase

32. Mylene has missed most of her introductory psychology classes this semester. She didn't buy the book, so she hasn't been able to study for any of her exams. She hasn't turned in any assignments, either. However, when her friend asks her how she is doing in the course, she says, "Fine, I'm sure I'll get at least a B." Mylene is showing which of the following?
    a. regression
    b. rationalization
    c. denial
    d. projection

Solutions

Recite and Review

1. behaviour; medical
2. habits
3. disease; illness
4. illness; disease
5. behaviours; smoking; diet; sleep
6. increase
7. acquired immune; virus
8. risk; risk
9. risk; campaigns
10. adjust
11. control; intense
12. Stress
13. work; exhaustion
14. primary; threat
15. secondary
16. goal; blocked
17. Personal
18. intense
19. vigorous
20. direct; withdrawal
21. Conflict
22. positive; negative
23. positive; negative
24. easiest
25. difficult; leaving
26. mixed; partial
27. approach avoidance
28. inadequacy
29. reaction; repression
30. positive
31. avoid
32. identical
33. training
34. reduce
35. change; accident
36. hassles
37. psychological
38. disease
39. monitored
40. relaxation
41. heart; time
42. Anger
43. stress
44. general
45. psychosomatic
46. disease; illness
47. behaviour; thoughts
48. relaxation; imagery
49. relaxation
50. positive

Connections

1. D
2. A
3. J
4. B
5. I
6. H
7. C
8. F
9. E
10. G
11. F
12. I
13. A
14. K
15. B
16. H
17. D
18. C
19. G
20. E
21. J
22. I
23. H
24. A
25. G
26. B
27. C
28. D
29. E
30. F

Short-Answer Questions

1. Refusal skills training teaches people how to resist pressure to smoke or take drugs. It involves role playing.

2. HIV is transmitted through direct contact with infected body fluids, especially blood, semen, and vaginal secretions. It is not spread through casual contact, or through sweat, tears, or social kissing.

3. The ANS responds in a similar fashion to both stress and emotion. Responses include increases in heart rate, breathing, blood pressure, and muscle tension.

4. Emotional—anxiety, apathy, irritability and mental fatigue. Behavioural—self-destructive behaviour, avoiding responsibility, poor judgment, self-neglect. Physical—frequent illness, exhaustion, physical complaints.

5. Primary appraisal—deciding if a situation is a threat or not. Secondary appraisal—assess resources and decide how to meet the challenge.

6. It is easier to cope with a stressful situation if you feel you have some control over it.

7. Problem-focused coping—managing or altering the situation. Works best when the stressful situation is controllable. Emotion-focused coping—managing or altering the emotional reactions to the stress. Works better for dealing with situations that are not in the person's control.

8. Scapegoating—blaming another person or group for events that they really are not responsible for. The scapegoat becomes a target for displaced aggression.

9. 1. Identify the source—is it personal or external. 2. Is the source of frustration under your control at all? Can you change it? How hard would it be to change it? 3. If the source of frustration can be changed or removed, is it worth it? If the source of frustration is not under your control, or impossible to change, persistence is not likely to solve the problem. Separating real from imagined barriers is also helpful; don't waste energy on imaginary barriers.

10. Advantages—defence mechanisms reduce the anxiety associated with frustration and conflict. They keep people from being overwhelmed by immediate threats, and provide time for a person to learn to cope with the problem more effectively. Disadvantages—are not effective in the long term. The use of defence mechanisms takes large amounts of emotional energy and does not help people learn to deal effectively with problem situations.

11. Helplessness is learned when animals (and people) are placed in situations that they cannot control and from which they cannot escape. This could be a dog experiencing a painful and unavoidable electric shock or a student experiencing repeated failure in school. The dog will lie passively in his cage. The student may put off studying or doing assignments or give up easily. Helplessness could be unlearned by helping a person attribute failure to specific elements of the original situation (I need to allow more time to review math), rather than to general factors (I'm stupid).

12. 1. Consistent negative self-image. 2. Frequent self-criticism and self-blame. 3. Events that didn't used to be a problem now are. 4. Negative view of the future. 5. Feeling overwhelmed by responsibility.

13. Hassles are ongoing, daily stressors that do not involve major life changes. They are better predictors of day-to-day health and major life changes. Stress management skills are useful in dealing with hassles.

14. In a psychosomatic disorder, psychological factors contribute to damage to the body or to physical functioning. Examples of psychosomatic disorders are asthma, migraines, skin rashes or hives, colitis, and high blood pressure. People with hypochondria imagine that they are ill, but there are no physical signs, or damage.

15. People with a hardy personality are highly resistant to stress. They have a sense of commitment to their jobs and families. They feel that they have control over their lives and work, and they tend to see life as a series of challenges rather than a series of threats.

Final Survey and Review

1. behavioural; medicine
2. lifestyle
3. risk; factors
4. disease; prone
5. promoting; deprivation; stress
6. sexually transmitted
7. deficiency; immunodeficiency
8. STIs
9. health; community; health
10. adapt; demands
11. pressure; stressor
12. threat; competent
13. burnout; depersonalization
14. appraisal; appraisal
15. problem; emotion
16. Frustration; personal
17. External; Personal
18. blocked; motive
19. persistence; circumvention
20. displaced; scapegoating
21. contradictory
22. approach approach; approach avoidance
23. double; multiple
24. Approach; approach
25. Avoidance
26. ambivalence
27. Vacillation
28. defence; mechanisms; anxiety
29. denial; rationalization
30. compensation; sublimation
31. helplessness; punishment
32. depression
33. Mastery
34. Depression; helplessness
35. Social; Readjustment; Rating
36. microstressors
37. psychosomatic
38. Psychosomatic; hypochondria
39. biofeedback; signal
40. regulation
41. Type A; angry
42. heart attack
43. hardy
44. adaptation; syndrome
45. alarm; exhaustion
46. immune
47. ineffective; upsetting
48. progressive; guided
49. limits; social
50. negative; coping

Mastery Test

1. B (p. 411)
2. A (p. 421)
3. C (p. 402)
4. D (p. 403)
5. C (p. 409)

6. A (p. 426)
7. D (p. 395)
8. C (p. 401)
9. B (p. 414)
10. A (p. 409)
11. A (p. 304)
12. D (p. 418)
13. B (p. 395)
14. A (p. 403)

15. B (p. 403)
16. B (p. 417)
17. D (p. 399)
18. B (p. 406)
19. D (p. 398)
20. C (p. 406)
21. C (p. 404)
22. A (p. 425)
23. A (p. 401)

24. B (p. 404)
25. D (p. 420)
26. A (p. 398)
27. D (p. 423)
28. C (p. 402)
29. C (p. 420)
30. D (p. 402)
31. D (p. 395)
32. C (p. 409)

Psychological Disorders

Chapter Overview

Abnormal behaviour is defined by subjective discomfort, deviation from statistical norms, social non-conformity, and cultural or situational contexts. Disordered behaviour is also maladaptive. Major types of psychopathology are described by DSM-IV-TR. Insanity is a legal term, not a mental disorder.

Personality disorders are deeply ingrained maladaptive personality patterns, such as the antisocial personality. Anxiety disorders, dissociative disorders, and somatoform disorders are characterized by high levels of anxiety, rigid defence mechanisms, and self-defeating behaviour patterns.

Anxiety disorders include generalized anxiety disorder, panic disorder (with or without agoraphobia), agoraphobia, specific phobia, social phobia, obsessive-compulsive disorders, and post-traumatic or acute stress disorders. Dissociative disorders may take the form of amnesia, fugue, or identity disorder (multiple personality). Somatoform disorders centre on physical complaints that mimic disease or disability.

Psychodynamic explanations of anxiety disorders emphasize unconscious conflicts. The humanistic approach emphasizes faulty self-images. The behavioural approach emphasizes the effects of learning, particularly avoidance learning. The cognitive approach stresses maladaptive thinking patterns.

Schizophrenia is the most common psychosis. Four types of schizophrenia are disorganized, catatonic, paranoid, and undifferentiated. Explanations of schizophrenia emphasize environmental stress, inherited susceptibility, and biochemical abnormalities.

Mood disorders involve disturbances of emotion. Two moderate mood disorders are dysthymic disorder and cyclothymic disorder. Major mood disorders include bipolar disorders and major depressive disorder. Seasonal affective disorder is another common form of depression. Biological, psychoanalytic, cognitive, and behavioural theories of depression have been proposed. Heredity is clearly a factor in susceptibility to mood disorders.

Two basic approaches to treating major disorders are psychotherapy and medical therapies. Prolonged hospitalization has been discouraged by deinstitutionalization and by partial-hospitalization policies. Community mental health centres attempt to prevent mental health problems.

Suicide is statistically related to such factors as age, sex, marital status, ethnicity and place of residence. However, in individual cases the potential for suicide is best identified by a desire to escape, unbearable psychological pain, frustrated psychological needs, and a constriction of options. Suicide can sometimes be prevented by the efforts of family, friends, and mental health professionals.

Learning Objectives

After reading this chapter, students will be able to:

1. Define the terms *normal* and *abnormal*. Explain how subjective discomfort, statistical abnormality, social non-conformity, and cultural contexts all contribute to the definition of normal.

2. Explain how the DSM-IV-TR categorizes mental disorders.

3. Identify the personality disorders.

4. Describe the anxiety disorders, dissociative disorders, and somatoform disorders.

5. Outline the humanistic, behavoural, and cognitive approaches to the explanation of anxiety disorders.

6. Describe the different types of schizophrenia and identify the major causes.

7. Identify the mood disorders. Describe the biological, cognitive, and behavioural explanations for depression.

8. Show how suicide can be prevented.

Practice Quizzes

Recite and Review

How is normality defined, and what are the major psychological disorders?

Recite and Review: Pages 432–437

1. Psychopathology refers to mental _____ themselves or to psychologically _____ behaviour.

2. Formal definitions of abnormality usually take into account subjective _____ (private feelings of suffering or unhappiness).

3. Statistical definitions define abnormality as an extremely _____ or _____ score on some dimension or measure.

4. Social non-conformity is a failure to follow societal _____ for acceptable conduct.

5. Frequently, the _____ or situational context that a behaviour takes place in affects judgments of normality and abnormality.

6. _____ of the preceding definitions are relative standards.

7. A key element in judgments of disorder is that a person's _____ must be maladaptive (it makes it difficult for the person to _____ to the demands of daily life).

8. A _____ disorder is a significant impairment in psychological functioning.

9. Major disorders and categories of psychopathology are described in the Diagnostic and Statistical _____ of _____ Disorders (DSM-IV-TR).

10. In the past, the term *neurosis* was used to describe milder, _____ -related disorders. However, the term is fading from use.

11. *Insanity* is a _____ term defining whether a person may be held responsible for his or her actions. Sanity is determined in _____ on the basis of testimony by expert witnesses.

What is a personality disorder?
Recite and Review: Pages 438–439

12. Personality disorders are deeply ingrained _____ personality patterns.

13. Antisocial persons (sociopaths) seem to lack a _____ . They are _____ shallow and manipulative.

14. Individuals with an antisocial personality often had a _____ childhood (i.e., were neglected or suffered physical abuse). Evidence has also been found for neurological _____ in sociopaths.

What problems result when a person experiences high levels of anxiety?
Recite and Review: Pages 440–445

15. Anxiety disorders, dissociative disorders, and somatoform disorders involve high levels of _____ , rigid _____ mechanisms, and self-defeating behaviour patterns.

16. The term *nervous breakdown* has no formal meaning. However, "emotional breakdowns" do correspond somewhat to adjustment disorders, in which the person is overwhelmed by ongoing _____ _____ .

17. Anxiety disorders include generalized anxiety disorder (chronic _____ and worry) and panic disorder (anxiety attacks, panic, free- _____ anxiety).

18. Panic disorder may occur with or without agoraphobia (fear of _____ places, unfamiliar situations, or leaving the _____).

19. Other anxiety disorders are agoraphobia and specific phobia (irrational fears of _____ objects or situations).

20. In the anxiety disorder called social phobia, the person fears being _____ , evaluated, embarrassed, or humiliated by others in _____ situations.

21. Obsessive-compulsive disorders (obsessions and compulsions), and post-traumatic stress disorder or acute stress disorder (emotional disturbances triggered by severe _____) are also classified as _____ disorders.

22. Dissociative disorders may take the form of dissociative amnesia (loss of _____ and personal identity) or _____ fugue (flight from familiar surroundings).

23. A more dramatic problem is dissociative identity disorder, in which a person develops _____ personalities.

24. Somatoform disorders centre on physical complaints that mimic _____ or disability.

25. In hypochondriasis, individuals think that they have specific diseases, when they are, in fact _____ .

26. In a somatization disorder, the person has numerous _____ complaints. The person repeatedly seeks medical _____ for these complaints, but no organic problems can be found.

27. Pain disorder refers to discomfort for which there is no identifiable _____ cause.

28. In conversion disorders, actual symptoms of disease or disability develop but their causes are really _____ .

How do psychologists explain anxiety-based disorders?

Recite and Review: Pages 446–447

29. The psychodynamic approach emphasizes _____ conflicts within the personality as the cause of disabling anxiety.

30. The humanistic approach emphasizes the effects of a faulty _____ - _____ .

31. The behavioural approach emphasizes the effects of previous _____ , particularly avoidance _____ .

32. Some patterns in anxiety disorders can be explained by the _____ reduction hypothesis, which states that immediate _____ from anxiety rewards self-defeating behaviours.

33. According to the cognitive view, distorted _____ patterns cause anxiety disorders.

What are the major characteristics of schizophrenia? What causes it?

Recite and Review: Pages 448–454

34. Schizophrenia is marked by delusions, _____ (false sensations), and sensory changes.

35. Other symptoms of psychotic disorders are disturbed emotions, disturbed communication, and _____ disintegration.

36. Disorganized schizophrenia is marked by extreme _____ disintegration and silly, bizarre, or obscene behaviour. _____ impairment is usually extreme.

37. Catatonic schizophrenia is associated with stupor, _____ (inability to speak), _____ flexibility, and odd postures. Sometimes violent and agitated behaviour also occurs.

38. In paranoid schizophrenia (the most common type), outlandish delusions of grandeur and _____ are coupled with psychotic symptoms and personality breakdown.

39. *Undifferentiated schizophrenia* is the term used to indicate a _____ of clear-cut patterns of disturbance.

40. Current explanations of schizophrenia emphasize a combination of environmental _____ , inherited susceptibility, and biochemical _____ in the body or brain.

41. A number of environmental factors appear to increase the risk of developing schizophrenia. These include viral _____ during the mother's pregnancy and _____ complications.

42. Early psychological _____ (psychological injury or shock) and a disturbed _____ environment, especially one marked by deviant communication, also increase the risk of schizophrenia.

43. Studies of _____ and other close relatives strongly support heredity as a major factor in schizophrenia.

44. Recent biochemical studies have focused on abnormalities in brain _____ substances, especially dopamine and its receptor sites.

45. Additional abnormalities in brain structure or _____ have been detected in schizophrenic brains by the use of CT scans, MRI scans, and PET scans.

46. The dominant explanation of schizophrenia is the _____ -vulnerability model.

What are mood disorders? What causes depression?

Recite and Review: Pages 455–458

47. Mood disorders primarily involve disturbances of mood or _____ .

48. Long-lasting, though relatively moderate, _____ is called a dysthymic disorder.

49. Chronic, though moderate, swings in mood between _____ and _____ are called a cyclothymic disorder.

50. In a bipolar I disorder the person alternates between extreme mania and _____ .

51. In a bipolar II disorder the person is mostly _____ , but has had at least one episode of hypomania (mild _____).

52. The problem known as major depressive disorder involves extreme sadness and despondency, but no evidence of _____ .

53. Major mood disorders more often appear to be endogenous (produced from _____) rather than reactions to _____ events.

54. _____ affective disorder (SAD), which occurs during the _____ months is another common form of depression. SAD is typically treated with phototherapy.

55. Biological, psychoanalytic, cognitive, and _____ theories of depression have been proposed. Heredity is clearly a factor in susceptibility to mood disorders.

56. Psychotherapy is any psychological treatment for behavioural or emotional problems. _____ _____ disorders are more often treated medically, rather than with psychotherapy.

57. Hospitalization is often associated with the administration of _____ therapies, and it is also considered a form of treatment.

58. Prolonged hospitalization has been discouraged by _____ -hospitalization policies.

59. Halfway _____ within the community can help people make the transition from a hospital or institution to _____ living.

Why do people commit suicide? Can suicide be prevented?

Recite and Review: Psychology in Action

60. _____ is statistically related to such factors as age, sex, marital status, ethnicity, and place of residence.

61. Major risk factors for suicide include _____ or _____ abuse, a prior attempt, depression, hopelessness, antisocial behaviour, suicide by relatives, shame, failure, or rejection, and the availability of a _____ .

62. In individual cases the potential for suicide is best identified by a desire to _____ , unbearable psychological pain, frustrated psychological needs, and a constriction of _____ .

63. Suicidal _____ usually precede suicide threats, which progress to suicide attempts.

64. Suicide can often be prevented by the efforts of family, friends, and mental health professionals to establish _____ and rapport with the person, and by gaining day-by-day commitments from her or him.

Connections

1. _____ DSM
2. _____ drapetomania
3. _____ mood disorder
4. _____ somatoform disorder
5. _____ insanity
6. _____ organic disorder
7. _____ neurosis
8. _____ paraphilia
9. _____ pibloktoq

a. once considered a disorder
b. physical symptoms
c. legal problem
d. outdated term
e. sexual deviation
f. diagnostic manual
g. arctic hysteria
h. brain pathology
i. mania or depression

10. _____ dependent personality
11. _____ histrionic personality
12. _____ narcissistic personality
13. _____ antisocial personality
14. _____ obsessive-compulsive
15. _____ schizoid personality
16. _____ avoidant personality
17. _____ borderline personality
18. _____ paranoid personality
19. _____ schizotypal personality

a. self-importance
b. rigid routines
c. submissiveness
d. little emotion
e. attention seeking
f. unstable self-image
g. odd, disturbed thinking
h. suspiciousness
i. fear of social situations
j. no conscience

20. _____ adjustment disorder
21. _____ generalized anxiety
22. _____ panic disorder
23. _____ agoraphobia
24. _____ specific phobia
25. _____ social phobia
26. _____ PTSD
27. _____ acute stress disorder
28. _____ glove anesthesia
29. _____ dissociative fugue

a. afraid to leave the house
b. fears being observed
c. conversion disorder
d. one month after extreme stress
e. dissociation
f. less than a month after extreme stress
g. sudden attacks of fear
h. normal life stress
i. chronic worry
j. fears objects or activities

30. _____ schizotypal
31. _____ catatonic type
32. _____ paranoid type
33. _____ disorganized type
34. _____ psychological trauma
35. _____ twin studies
36. _____ dopamine
37. _____ delusion
38. _____ bipolar I
39. _____ bipolar II

a. incoherence, bizarre thinking
b. false belief
c. personality disorder
d. depression and hypomania
e. stuporous or agitated
f. severe mania and depression
g. genetics of schizophrenia
h. grandeur or persecution
i. chemical messenger
j. risk factor for schizophrenia

Short-Answer Questions

1. Is there a gender bias in judging abnormality? Explain.
2. Identify the four major risk categories for mental disorders.
3. What are the distinctive characteristics of the antisocial personality?
4. What is meant by the term *anxiety*?
5. What are the major features of anxiety-related problems?
6. What emotional changes occur in someone with a psychotic disorder such as schizophrenia?
7. Distinguish between delusions and hallucinations, using examples.
8. Explain the term *personality disintegration*.
9. What is a seasonal affective disorder? What causes it? How is it treated?
10. What is partial hospitalization? Why is it used to treat mental disorders?
11. What are the major factors that affect suicide rates?
12. What are the major risk factors for suicide?

Final Survey and Review

How is normality defined, and what are the major psychological disorders?

1. _____ refers to mental disorders themselves or to psychologically unhealthy behaviour.
2. Formal definitions of abnormality usually take into account _____ discomfort (private feelings of suffering or unhappiness).
3. _____ definitions define abnormality as an extremely high or low score on some dimension or measure.
4. _____ _____ - _____ is a failure to follow societal standards for acceptable conduct.
5. Frequently, the cultural or situational _____ that a behaviour takes place in affects judgments of normality and abnormality.
6. All of the preceding definitions are _____ standards.
7. A key element in judgments of disorder is that a person's behaviour must be _____ (it makes it difficult for the person to adapt to the environment).
8. A mental disorder is a significant impairment in _____ functioning.
9. Major disorders and categories of psychopathology are described in the _____ *and* _____ *Manual of Mental Disorders* (DSM-IV-TR).
10. In the past, the term _____ was used to describe milder, anxiety-related disorders. However, the term is fading from use.
11. _____ is a legal term defining whether a person may be held responsible for his or her actions. Sanity is determined in court on the basis of testimony by expert witnesses.

What is a personality disorder?

12. Personality disorders are deeply _____ maladaptive personality patterns.

13. _____ persons (sociopaths) seem to lack a conscience. They are emotionally shallow and _____ .

14. Antisocial personality is linked to traumatic _____ experiences and _____ problems.

What problems result when a person experiences high levels of anxiety?

15. Anxiety disorders, _____ disorders, and _____ disorders are characterized by high levels of anxiety, rigid defence mechanisms, and self-defeating behaviour patterns.

16. The term *nervous* _____ has no formal meaning. However, people do experience _____ disorders, in which the person is overwhelmed by ongoing life stresses.

17. Anxiety disorders include _____ anxiety disorder (chronic anxiety and worry) and _____ disorder (anxiety attacks, panic, free-floating anxiety).

18. Panic disorder may occur with or without _____ (fear of public places or leaving the home).

19. Other anxiety disorders are _____ (fear of public places, _____ situations, or leaving the home) and specific phobia (irrational fears of specific objects or situations).

20. In the anxiety disorder called _____ _____ , the person fears being observed, _____ , embarrassed, or humiliated by others in social situations.

21. _____ -compulsive disorders, and _____ - _____ stress disorder (PTSD) or _____ stress disorder (emotional disturbances triggered by severe stress) are also classified as anxiety disorders.

22. Dissociative disorders may take the form of dissociative _____ (loss of memory and personal identity) or dissociative _____ (confused identity and flight from familiar surroundings).

23. A more dramatic problem is dissociative _____ _____ , in which a person develops multiple personalities.

24. _____ disorders centre on physical complaints that mimic disease or disability.

25. In _____ , persons think that they have specific diseases, when they are, in fact, healthy.

26. In a _____ disorder, the person has numerous physical complaints. The person repeatedly seeks medical treatment for these complaints, but no organic problems can be found.

27. _____ _____ refers to discomfort for which there is no identifiable physical cause.

28. In _____ disorders, actual symptoms of disease or disability develop but their causes are psychological.

How do psychologists explain anxiety-based disorders?

29. The _____ approach emphasizes unconscious conflicts within the personality as the cause of disabling anxiety.

30. The _____ approach emphasizes the effects of a faulty self-image.

31. The _____ approach emphasizes the effects of previous learning, particularly _____ learning.

32. Some patterns in anxiety disorders can be explained by the anxiety _____ hypothesis, which states that immediate relief from anxiety rewards _____ - _____ behaviours.

33. According to the _____ view, distorted thinking patterns cause anxiety disorders.

What are the major characteristics of schizophrenia? What causes it?

34. Schizophrenia is marked by _____ (false beliefs), hallucinations, and _____ changes.

35. Other symptoms of psychotic disorders are disturbed emotions, disturbed _____ , and personality _____ .

36. Schizophrenia is distinguished by a split between thought and _____ , and by delusions, hallucinations, and _____ difficulties.

37. _____ schizophrenia is marked by extreme personality _____ and silly, bizarre, or obscene behaviour. Social impairment is usually extreme.

38. _____ schizophrenia is associated with stupor, mutism, waxy _____ , and odd postures. Sometimes violent and agitated behaviour also occurs.

39. In _____ schizophrenia (the most common type), outlandish delusions of _____ and persecution are coupled with psychotic symptoms and personality breakdown.

40. _____ schizophrenia is the term used to indicate a lack of clear-cut patterns of disturbance.

41. Current explanations of schizophrenia emphasize a combination of _____ stress, inherited susceptibility, and _____ abnormalities in the body or brain.

42. A number of _____ factors appear to increase the risk of developing schizophrenia. These include viral infection during the mother's pregnancy and birth complications.

43. Early _____ trauma and a disturbed family environment, especially one marked by _____ communication, also increase the risk of schizophrenia.

44. Studies of twins and other close relatives strongly support _____ as a major factor in schizophrenia.

45. Recent biochemical studies have focused on abnormalities in brain transmitter substances, especially _____ and its _____ sites.

46. Additional abnormalities in brain structure or function have been detected in schizophrenic brains by the use of _____ scans, _____ scans, and _____ scans.

47. The dominant explanation of schizophrenia is the stress- _____ model.

What are mood disorders? What causes depression?

48. Mood disorders primarily involve disturbances of _____ or emotion.

49. Long-lasting, though relatively moderate, depression is called a _____ disorder.

50. Chronic, though moderate, swings in mood between depression and elation are called a _____ disorder.

51. In a _____ _____ disorder the person alternates between extreme _____ and depression.

52. In a _____ _____ disorder the person is mostly depressed, but has had at least one episode of _____ (mild mania).

53. The problem known as _____ _____ disorder involves extreme sadness and despondency, but no evidence of mania.

54. Major mood disorders more often appear to be _____ (produced from within) rather than reactions to external events.

55. Seasonal _____ disorder (SAD), which occurs during the winter months is another common form of depression. SAD is typically treated with _____ (exposure to bright light).

56. _____ , psychoanalytic, _____ , and behavioural theories of depression have been proposed. Heredity is clearly a factor in susceptibility to mood disorders.

57. _____ is any psychological treatment for behavioural or emotional problems. Major mental disorders are more often treated medically.

58. Psychiatric _____ is often associated with the administration of medical therapies, and it is also considered a form of treatment.

59. Prolonged hospitalization has been discouraged by _____ - _____ policies.

60. _____ houses within the community can help people make the transition from a hospital or institution to independent living.

Why do people commit suicide? Can suicide be prevented?

61. Suicide is _____ related to such factors as age, sex, marital status, ethnicity, and place of _____ .

62. Major _____ _____ for suicide include drug or alcohol abuse, a prior attempt, depression, hopelessness, _____ behaviour, suicide by relatives, shame, failure, or rejection, and the availability of a firearm.

63. In individual cases the potential for suicide is best identified by a desire to escape, unbearable psychological _____ , _____ psychological needs, and a constriction of options.

64. Suicidal thoughts usually precede suicide _____ , which progress to suicide _____ .

65. Suicide can often be prevented by the efforts of family, friends, and mental health professionals to establish communication and _____ with the person, and by gaining day-by-day _____ from her or him.

Mastery Test

1. The difference between an acute stress disorder and PTSD is
   a. how long the disturbance lasts
   b. the severity of the stress
   c. whether the anxiety is free floating
   d. whether the dissociative behaviour is observed

2. A person is at greatest risk of becoming schizophrenic if he or she has
   a. schizophrenic parents
   b. a schizophrenic fraternal twin
   c. a schizophrenic mother
   d. a schizophrenic sibling

3. A core feature of all abnormal behaviour is that it is
   a. statistically extreme
   b. associated with subjective discomfort
   c. ultimately maladaptive
   d. marked by a loss of contact with reality

4. Excess amounts of dopamine in the brain, or high sensitivity to dopamine provides one major explanation for the problem known as
   a. PTSD
   b. schizophrenia
   c. major depression
   d. SAD

5. The descriptions "acro," "claustro," and "pyro" refer to
   a. common obsessions
   b. specific phobias
   c. free-floating anxieties
   d. hypochondriasis

6. Glove anesthesia implies the existence of a _____ disorder.
   a. organic
   b. depersonalization
   c. somatization
   d. conversion

7. In the stress-vulnerability model of psychotic disorders, vulnerability is primarily attributed to
   a. heredity
   b. exposure to influenza
   c. psychological trauma
   d. disturbed family life

8. A patient believes that she has a mysterious disease that is causing her body to fall apart. This is an example of
   a. SAD
   b. a delusion
   c. a neurosis
   d. a PTSD

9. Phototherapy is used primarily to treat
   a. postseasonal depression
   b. SAD
   c. catatonic depression
   d. affective psychoses

10. Psychopathology is defined as an inability to behave in ways that
    a. foster personal well-being
    b. match social norms
    c. lead to personal achievement
    d. do not cause anxiety

11. Which of the following is NOT characteristic of suicidal thinking?
    a. desires to escape
    b. psychological pain
    c. frustrated needs
    d. too many options

12. Fear of using a public washroom is
    a. a social phobia
    b. an acute stress disorder
    c. a panic disorder
    d. an adjustment disorder

13. A person who displays bizarre thinking, mutism, and delusions of persecution suffers from _____ schizophrenia.
    a. disorganized
    b. catatonic
    c. paranoid
    d. undifferentiated

14. There are major gaps in your memory of events; you feel like you are a stranger to yourself. It is likely that you are suffering from
    a. a somatization disorder
    b. a mood disorder
    c. a borderline personality disorder
    d. a dissociative disorder

15. A major problem with statistical definitions of abnormality is
    a. calculating the normal curve accurately
    b. choosing dividing lines between normal and abnormal
    c. that they do not apply to groups of people larger than 100
    d. that they do not take norms into account most of the time

16. DSM-IV-TR primarily describes and classifies _____ disorders.
    a. mental
    b. organic
    c. psychotic
    d. cognitive

17. A person who is a frequent "checker" may have which disorder?
    a. agoraphobic
    b. somatization
    c. free-floating fugue
    d. obsessive-compulsive

18. The most direct explanation for the anxiety-reducing properties of self-defeating behaviour is found in
    a. an overwhelmed ego
    b. avoidance learning
    c. the loss of meaning in one's life
    d. the concept of existential anxiety

19. People with a/an _____ personality disorder might be described as "charming" by people who don't know them well.
    a. avoidance
    b. schizoid
    c. antisocial
    d. dependent

20. One of the most powerful situational contexts for judging the normality of behaviour is
    a. culture
    b. gender
    c. statistical norms
    d. private discomfort

21. A person who is manic most likely suffers from a/an _____ disorder.
    a. anxiety
    b. somatoform
    c. organic
    d. mood

22. The principal problem in paranoid schizophrenia is
    a. delusions
    b. mutism
    c. disturbed emotions
    d. personality disintegration

23. A problem that may occur with or without agoraphobia is
    a. dissociative disorder
    b. somatoform disorder
    c. panic disorder
    d. obsessive-compulsive disorder

24. A conversion reaction is a type of _____ disorder.
    a. somatoform
    b. dissociative
    c. obsessive-compulsive
    d. post-traumatic

25. The existence, in the past, of "disorders" such as "drapetomania" and "nymphomania" suggests that judging normality is greatly affected by
    a. gender
    b. cultural disapproval
    c. levels of functioning
    d. subjective discomfort

26. Which of the following terms does NOT belong with the others?
    a. panic disorder
    b. somatoform disorder
    c. personality disorder
    d. dissociative disorder

27. Threats to one's self-image are a key element in the _____ approach to understanding anxiety and disordered functioning.
    a. Freudian
    b. humanistic
    c. existential
    d. behavioural

28. Cyclothymic disorder is most closely related to
    a. reactive depression
    b. major depressive disorder
    c. bipolar disorder
    d. SAD

29. Which of the following individuals has a higher risk of developing SAD?
    a. a student
    b. an individual born in the arctic
    c. an individual from the south who moved to the north
    d. a descendent of Icelandic settlers

Solutions

Recite and Review

1. disorders; unhealthy
2. discomfort
3. high; low
4. standards
5. cultural
6. All
7. behaviour; adapt
8. mental
9. Manual; Mental
10. anxiety
11. legal; court
12. maladaptive
13. conscience; emotionally
14. traumatic; problems
15. anxiety; defence
16. life; stresses
17. anxiety; floating
18. public; home
19. specific
20. observed; social
21. stress; anxiety
22. memory; dissociative
23. multiple
24. disease
25. healthy
26. physical; treatment
27. physical
28. psychological
29. unconscious
30. self image
31. learning; learning
32. anxiety; relief
33. thinking
34. hallucinations
35. personality
36. personality; Social
37. mutism; waxy
38. persecution
39. lack
40. stress; abnormalities
41. infection; birth
42. trauma; family
43. twins
44. transmitter
45. activity
46. stress
47. emotion
48. depression
49. depression; elation
50. depression
51. depressed; mania
52. mania
53. within; external
54. Seasonal; winter
55. behavioural
56. Major; mental
57. medical
58. partial
59. houses; independent
60. Suicide
61. alcohol; drug; firearm
62. escape; options
63. thoughts
64. communication

Connections

1. F
2. A
3. I
4. B
5. C
6. H
7. D
8. E
9. G
10. C
11. E
12. A
13. J
14. B
15. D
16. I
17. F
18. H
19. G
20. H
21. I
22. G
23. A
24. J

25. B
26. D
27. F
28. C
29. E
30. C
31. E
32. H
33. A
34. J
35. G
36. I
37. B
38. F
39. D

Short-Answer Questions

1. Yes. Women who conform to female stereotypes (emotional, irrational, dependent) and women who express more "masculine" characteristics (independent, aggressive, or unemotional) are more likely to be judged abnormal.

2. 1. Social conditions (poverty, overcrowding, homelessness). 2. Family factors (immature parents, parents with a history of mental disorders, parents who are criminals or abusive, lack of discipline, poor communication). 3. Psychological factors (stress, learning disorders, lack of control). 4. Biological factors (genetic disorders, poor prenatal care, low birth weight, chronic illnesses, physical disabilities, exposure to drugs or toxic chemicals, head injuries).

3. Lack of conscience, impulsivity, dishonesty, emotionally shallow, manipulative, poorly socialized;

incapable of feeling guilt, shame, fear, loyalty, and love.

4. Anxiety—feelings of dread, apprehension, and uneasiness based on a perceived sense of threat.

5. High levels of anxiety; self-defeating behaviour patterns; a tendency to use avoidance responses or use elaborate schemes to cope with daily life; overwhelming feelings of stress, insecurity, inferiority, unhappiness, and dissatisfaction with one's life.

6. Emotions may be severely disturbed. A person might be elated, depressed, over-emotional, or emotionally apathetic. Emotional expression may be exaggerated or out of proportion to the situation, or inappropriate.

7. Delusions are false beliefs (that a person is a famous historical figure, that their thoughts are being monitored or broadcast, etc.). Hallucinations are false perceptions or imaginary sensations (hearing voices, seeing things that are not there, or changes to the senses of taste or smell).

8. Personality disintegration occurs when thoughts, actions, and emotions are not coordinated. There may be delusions (false beliefs) and/or hallucinations (false perceptions). This can seriously interfere with a person's work and social interactions.

9. Seasonal Affective Disorder (SAD) is a type of depression that occurs during the fall and winter months. People with SAD have the following symptoms: difficulty staying awake or oversleeping, fatigue, cravings for carbohydrates and sweets (leading to overeating and weight gain), inability to cope, and social withdrawal. SAD is more common in northern latitudes (such as Canada) with short winter days. People who move from southern to northern latitudes are also susceptible. Cause—the body responds to shorter days by increasing the amount of melatonin released by the pineal gland. SAD is treated by exposure to bright light (phototherapy).

10. In partial hospitalization, patients spend only part of the time at a hospital. They may spend their days at the hospital and go home at night, or stay at home during the day and attend therapy sessions in the evening. Over time, the amount of time people spend at the hospital is gradually decreased. This allows people to use the tools that they are learning in therapy and helps them return to their regular lives.

11. Sex—men are more likely to complete suicide; women make more attempts. Age—suicide rates rise during adolescence, increase sharply in young adults, and continue increasing gradually. About half of all suicide cases are over age 44. Ethnicity—the suicide rate for Native peoples is about three times the natural average, although there is wide variation across Native groups. Province of residence—suicide rates in the territories are the highest in Canada, but statistics are difficult to interpret because of the extremely small populations. Suicide rates are highest in Quebec and Alberta, lowest in Newfoundland. Profession/income—suicide rates are higher for physicians and psychiatrists. Marital status—highest suicide rates are found among the divorced, followed by widowed, single, and married individuals.

12. Depression is a factor in 70 percent of all suicides. Other risk factors include drug or alcohol abuse, a prior suicide attempt, feelings of hopelessness or worthlessness, antisocial or impulsive behaviour, panic attacks or severe anxiety, a family history of suicide or attempted suicide, and the availability of a weapon. Times of divorce, separation, rejection, failure, bereavement, or loss are especially dangerous.

Final Survey and Review

1. Psychopathology
2. subjective
3. Statistical
4. Social; non conformity
5. context
6. relative
7. maladaptive
8. psychological
9. *Diagnostic*; *Statistical*
10. neurosis
11. Insanity
12. ingrained
13. Antisocial; manipulative
14. childhood; neurological
15. dissociative; somatoform
16. breakdown; adjustment
17. generalized; panic
18. agoraphobia
19. agoraphobia; unfamiliar
20. social; phobia; evaluated
21. Obsessive; post traumatic; acute
22. amnesia; fugue
23. identity disorder
24. Somatoform

25. hypochondriasis
26. somatization
27. Pain; disorder
28. conversion
29. psychodynamic
30. humanistic
31. behavioural; avoidance
32. reduction; self defeating
33. cognitive
34. delusions; sensory
35. communication; disintegration
36. emotion; communication
37. Disorganized; disintegration
38. Catatonic; flexibility
39. paranoid; grandeur
40. Undifferentiated
41. environmental; biochemical
42. environmental
43. psychological; deviant
44. heredity
45. dopamine; receptor
46. CT; MRI; PET
47. vulnerability
48. mood
49. dysthymic

50. cyclothymic
51. bipolar I; mania
52. bipolar II; hypomania
53. major; depressive
54. endogenous
55. affective; phototherapy
56. Biological; cognitive
57. Psychotherapy
58. hospitalization
59. partial hospitalization
60. Halfway
61. statistically; residence
62. risk; factors; antisocial
63. pain; frustrated
64. threats; attempts
65. rapport; commitments

Mastery Test

1. A (p. 443)
2. A (p. 451)
3. C (p. 434)
4. B (p. 452)
5. B (p. 442)
6. D (p. 445)

7. A (p. 454)
8. B (p. 448)
9. B (p. 457)
10. A (p. 433)
11. D (p. 461)
12. A (p. 442)
13. D (p. 449)
14. D (p. 444)
15. B (p. 433)
16. A (p. 434)
17. D (p. 443)
18. B (p. 446)
19. C (p. 438)
20. A (p. 433)
21. D (p. 455)
22. A (p. 449)
23. C (p. 441)
24. A (p. 445)
25. B (p. 434)
26. C (p. 440)
27. B (p. 446)
28. C (p. 455)
29. C (p. 457)

Therapies

Chapter Overview

Psychotherapies may be classified as individual, group, insight, action, directive, non-directive, or supportive, and combinations of these. Primitive and superstitious approaches to mental illness have included trepanning and demonology. More humane treatment began in 1793 with the work of Philippe Pinel in Paris.

Freudian psychoanalysis seeks to release repressed thoughts and emotions from the unconscious. Brief psychodynamic therapy has largely replaced traditional psychoanalysis.

Client-centred (or person-centred) therapy is a non-directive humanistic technique dedicated to creating an atmosphere of growth. Existential therapies focus on the meaning of life choices. Gestalt therapy attempts to rebuild thinking, feeling, and acting into connected wholes.

Behaviour therapists use behaviour modification techniques such as aversion therapy, systematic desensitization, operant shaping, extinction, and token economies.

Cognitive therapists attempt to change troublesome thought patterns. In rational-emotive behaviour therapy, clients learn to recognize and challenge their own irrational beliefs.

Group therapies, such as psychodrama and family therapy, may be based on individual therapy methods or special group techniques. Sensitivity groups, encounter groups, and large-group awareness trainings also try to promote constructive changes.

All psychotherapies offer a caring relationship, emotional rapport, a protected setting, catharsis, explanations for one's problems, a new perspective, and a chance to practise new behaviours. Many basic counselling skills underlie the success of therapies. Successful therapists may also need to overcome cultural barriers to be effective with people from diverse backgrounds.

Three medical approaches to the treatment of psychological disorders are pharmacotherapy, electroconvulsive therapy, and psychosurgery.

Cognitive and behavioural techniques such as covert sensitization, thought stopping, covert reinforcement, and desensitization can aid self-management. In most communities, competent therapists can be located through public sources or by referrals.

Learning Objectives

After reading this chapter, students will be able to:

1. Trace the history of psychotherapy from prehistoric to modern times.
2. Identify the major elements of psychoanalysis.
3. Describe client-centred therapy, existential therapy, and Gestalt therapy.
4. Critically evaluate psychological services available through the media, by telephone, and over the Internet.
5. Describe behaviour therapy. Show how aversion therapy and desensitization can be used to treat behavioural problems.
6. Explain the role of reinforcement in behaviour therapy.
7. Define cognitive therapy. Explain how cognitive therapy may be used to change thoughts and emotions.
8. Give examples of the different forms of group therapy.
9. Identify the core features of psychotherapy.
10. Describe the medical approaches to psychotherapy.
11. Show how behavioural principles may be applied to everyday problems.

Practice Quizzes

Recite and Review

What is psychotherapy and why is it undertaken? How did psychotherapy originate?
Recite and Review: Pages 468–469

1. Psychotherapy is any psychological techniques used to facilitate _____ changes in a person's personality, _____ , or adjustment.
2. Psychotherapy works fairly well for _____ , low self-esteem, some sexual problems, and marital conflicts.
3. For many people, the major benefit of therapy is that it provides comfort and _____ .
4. Psychotherapy can also promote personal _____ .
5. Approximately _____ percent of Canadians consulted a psychologist in the 1990s. Most of the clients seen by psychologists are women. Users tend to be middle-aged, single, _____ , or widowed, and have higher education and income.
6. Primitive approaches to mental illness were often based on _____ .
7. Trepanning involved boring a hole in the _____ .
8. Demonology attributed mental disturbance to supernatural forces and prescribed _____ as the cure.
9. More humane treatment began in 1793 with the work of Philippe Pinel who created the first _____ _____ in Paris.

How is Freudian psychoanalysis conducted?

Recite and Review: Pages 470–471

10. Sigmund Freud's psychoanalysis was the first formal _____ .

11. Psychoanalysis was designed to treat cases of hysteria (physical symptoms without known _____ causes).

12. Psychoanalysis seeks to release repressed thoughts, memories, and emotions from the _____ and resolve _____ conflicts.

13. The psychoanalyst uses _____ association, _____ analysis, and analysis of resistance and transference to reveal health-producing insights.

14. Some critics have argued that traditional psychoanalysis may frequently receive credit for _____ remissions of symptoms. However, psychoanalysis has been shown to be better than no treatment at all.

15. _____ psychodynamic therapy (which relies on psychoanalytic theory but is brief and focused) is as effective as other major therapies.

What are the major humanistic therapies?

Recite and Review: Pages 472–475

16. _____ therapies try to help people live up to their potentials and to give tendencies for mental health to emerge.

17. Carl Rogers's client-centred (or _____ -centred) therapy is non-directive and is dedicated to creating an atmosphere of growth.

18. In client-centred therapy, unconditional _____ regard, _____ (feeling what another is feeling), authenticity, and reflection are combined to give the client a chance to solve his or her own problems.

19. Existential therapies focus on the _____ one makes in life.

20. Clients in existential therapy are encouraged through confrontation and encounter to exercise free _____ , to take responsibility for their _____ , and to find _____ in their lives.

21. Frederick Perls's Gestalt therapy emphasizes immediate _____ of thoughts and feelings.

22. The goal of Gestalt therapy is to rebuild thinking, feeling, and acting into connected _____ and to help clients break through emotional blocks.

23. Media psychologists, such as those found on the radio, are supposed to restrict themselves to _____ listeners, rather than actually doing _____ .

24. Telephone therapists and cybertherapists working on the _____ may or may not be competent. Even if they are, their effectiveness may be severely limited.

25. In an emerging approach called telehealth, _____ is being done at a distance, through the use of videoconferencing (two-way _____ _____ links).

What is behaviour therapy?

Recite and Review: Pages 476–477

26. Behaviour therapists use various behaviour modification techniques that apply _____ principles to change human behaviour.

27. Classical conditioning is a basic form of _____ in which existing reflex responses are _____ with new conditioned stimuli.

28. In aversion therapy, classical conditioning is used to associate maladaptive behaviour with _____ or immediate discomfort in order to inhibit undesirable responses.

29. To be most effective, aversive _____ or event must be response contingent (closely connected with negative behaviour).

How is behaviour therapy used to treat phobias and anxieties?

Recite and Review: Pages 477–480

30. Classical conditioning also underlies _____ desensitization, a technique used to reduce fears, phobias, and anxieties.

31. In desensitization, gradual _____ and reciprocal inhibition (using one emotional state to block another) break the link between fear and particular situations.

32. Typical steps in desensitization are (1) construct a fear hierarchy; (2) learn to produce total _____ ; and (3) perform items on the hierarchy (from least to most disturbing).

33. Desensitization may be carried out in real settings or it may be done by vividly _____ scenes from the fear hierarchy.

34. Desensitization is also effective when it is administered vicariously; that is, when clients watch _____ perform the feared responses.

35. In a newly developed technique, virtual _____ exposure is used to present _____ stimuli to patients undergoing desensitization.

36. Another new technique called eye-movement desensitization shows promise as a treatment for traumatic _____ and _____ disorders.

What role does reinforcement play in behaviour therapy?

Recite and Review: Pages 480–482

37. Behaviour modification also makes use of operant principles, such as positive reinforcement, non-reinforcement, extinction, punishment, shaping, stimulus _____ , and _____ out.

38. Non-reward can extinguish troublesome behaviours. Often this is done by simply identifying and eliminating _____ .

39. Time out is an extinction technique in which attention and approval are withheld following undesirable _____ .

40. Time out can also be done by _____ a person from the setting in which misbehaviour occurs, so that it will not be reinforced.

41. To apply positive reinforcement and operant shaping, symbolic rewards known as tokens are often used. Tokens allow _____ reinforcement of selected target _____ .

42. Full-scale use of _____ in an institutional setting produces a token economy.

43. Toward the end of a token economy program, patients are shifted to social rewards such as recognition and _____ .

What is cognitive therapy? How does it change thoughts and emotions?
Recite and Review: Pages 483–485

44. Cognitive therapy emphasizes changing _____ patterns that underlie emotional or behavioural problems.

45. The goals of cognitive therapy are to correct distorted thinking and/or teach improved coping _____ .

46. Aron Beck's cognitive therapy for depression corrects major distortions in thinking, including _____ perception, overgeneralization, and all-or-nothing _____ .

47. In a variation of cognitive therapy called rational-emotive behaviour therapy (REBT), clients learn to recognize and challenge their own irrational _____ that lead to upsetting consequences.

How is psychotherapy done with groups of people?
Recite and Review: Pages 485–487

48. Group therapy may be a simple extension of _____ methods or it may be based on techniques developed specifically for groups.

49. In psychodrama, individuals use _____ playing, _____ reversals, and the mirror technique to gain insight into incidents resembling their real-life problems.

50. In family therapy, the family group is treated as a _____ so that the entire _____ system is changed for the better.

51. Although they are not literally _____ , sensitivity groups and encounter groups attempt to encourage positive personality change.

52. In recent years, commercially offered large-group awareness _____ have become popular.

53. The therapeutic benefits of large-group techniques are questionable and may reflect nothing more than a _____ placebo effect.

What do various therapies have in common?
Recite and Review: Pages 487–490

54. Psychotherapy does help people with certain psychological _____ and medical conditions such as _____ , hypertension, arthritis, diabetes and chronic low-back _____ .

55. To alleviate personal problems, all psychotherapies offer a caring relationship and _____ rapport in a protected _____ .

56. All therapies encourage catharsis and they provide explanations for the client's _____ .

57. In addition, psychotherapy provides a new perspective and a chance to practise new _____ .

58. Many basic _____ skills are used in therapy. These include listening actively and helping to clarify the problem.

59. Effective therapists also focus on feelings and avoid giving unwanted _____ .

60. It helps to accept the person's perspective, to reflect thoughts and feelings, and to be patient during _____ .

61. In counselling it is important to use _____ questions when possible and to maintain confidentiality.

62. Many _____ barriers to effective counselling and therapy exist.

63. Culturally skilled _____ have the knowledge and skills needed to intervene successfully in the lives of clients from diverse cultural backgrounds.

64. The culturally skilled counsellor must be able to establish rapport with a person from a _____ cultural background and adapt traditional theories and techniques to meet the needs of clients from non-European ethnic or racial groups, such as Native people.

How do psychiatrists treat psychological disorders?

Recite and Review: Pages 491–493

65. Three _____ (bodily) approaches to treatment of psychosis are pharmacotherapy (use of _____), electroconvulsive therapy (ECT) (brain shock for the treatment of depression), and psychosurgery (surgical alteration of the _____).

66. Pharmacotherapy is done with _____ tranquillizers (anti-anxiety drugs), antipsychotics (which reduce delusions and _____), and antidepressants (_____ elevators).

67. All psychiatric drugs involve a tradeoff between _____ and benefits.

68. Community mental health centres were created to help avoid or minimize _____ .

69. Community mental health centres also have as their goal the prevention of mental health problems through education, consultation, and _____ intervention.

How are behavioural principles applied to everyday problems?

Recite and Review: Psychology in Action

70. In covert sensitization, aversive _____ are used to discourage unwanted behaviour.

71. Thought stopping uses mild _____ to prevent upsetting thoughts.

72. Covert reinforcement is a way to encourage desired _____ by mental rehearsal.

73. Desensitization pairs _____ with a hierarchy of upsetting images in order to lessen fears.

How would a person go about finding professional help?

Recite and Review: Pages 497–499

74. In most communities, a competent and reputable therapist can usually be located through public sources of information or by a _____ .

75. Practical considerations such as _____ (or _____) and qualifications enter into choosing a therapist. However, the therapist's personal characteristics are of equal importance.

76. Self-help _____ , made up of people who share similar problems, can sometimes add valuable support to professional treatment.

Connections

1.	_____ trepanning	a.	old relationships
2.	_____ exorcism	b.	hysteria
3.	_____ Pinel	c.	total acceptance
4.	_____ Freud	d.	waiting list control
5.	_____ dream analysis	e.	client-centred
6.	_____ transference	f.	Bicêtre
7.	_____ spontaneous remission	g.	latent content
8.	_____ Rogers	h.	possession by the devil
9.	_____ unconditional postive regard	i.	release of evil spirits

10.	_____ authenticity	a.	telehealth
11.	_____ existentialist	b.	operant extinction
12.	_____ distance therapy	c.	no facades
13.	_____ Gestalt therapy	d.	thinking error
14.	_____ rapid smoking	e.	choice and responsibility
15.	_____ desensitization	f.	token economy
16.	_____ time out	g.	whole experiences
17.	_____ target behaviours	h.	aversion therapy
18.	_____ overgeneralization	i.	irrational beliefs
19.	_____ rational-emotive behaviour therapy	j.	fear hierarchy

20.	_____ psychodrama	a.	public education
21.	_____ family therapy	b.	enhanced self-awareness
22.	_____ sensitivity group	c.	emotional release
23.	_____ encounter group	d.	positive imagery
24.	_____ media psychologist	e.	shared problems
25.	_____ therapeutic alliance	f.	systems approach
26.	_____ catharsis	g.	aversive imagery
27.	_____ covert sensitization	h.	role reversals
28.	_____ covert reinforcement	i.	caring relationship
29.	_____ self-help group	j.	intense interactions

Short-Answer Questions

1. Why are psychological services underused in Canada?
2. Why are dreams important in psychoanalysis?
3. Why have many therapists switched from traditional psychoanalyis to other forms of therapy?
4. Explain the relationship of aversion therapy to classical conditioning.
5. How does desensitization work?
6. Why do the nannies on *Nanny 911* use time out so often?
7. What are the advantages of using tokens as reinforcement?
8. What role do community mental health centres or CLSCs play in the treatment of mental disorders?

9. When should a person seek professional help to deal with a psychological problem?

10. How might a person go about finding a therapist?

11. What are the danger signs that suggest a person should stop seeing a particular therapist?

Final Survey and Review

What is psychotherapy and why is it undertaken? How did psychotherapy originate?

1. _____ is any psychological technique used to facilitate positive changes in a person's _____ , behaviour, or adjustment.

2. Psychotherapy is most effective for phobias, low _____ - _____ , _____ _____ and _____ conflicts.

3. The major benefit of therapy is that it provides comfort, support, and a way to make _____ _____ in behaviour.

4. Psychotherapy is not always undertaken to _____ _____ or end a _____ .

5. Most Canadians who consulted a psychologist in the 1990s were women. Users also tend to be _____ - _____ ; single, separated, or widowed; and have a higher _____ and income.

6. _____ approaches to mental illness were often based on superstition.

7. _____ involved boring a hole in the skull.

8. _____ attributed mental disturbance to supernatural forces and prescribed exorcism as the cure.

9. More humane treatment began in 1793 with the work of Philippe _____ who created the first mental hospital in _____ .

How is Freudian psychoanalysis conducted?

10. Sigmund _____ _____ was the first formal psychotherapy.

11. Psychoanalysis was designed to treat cases of _____ (physical symptoms without known physical causes).

12. Psychoanalysis seeks to release _____ thoughts, memories, and emotions from the unconscious, and resolve unconscious conflicts.

13. The psychoanalyst uses free _____ , dream analysis, and analysis of _____ and transference to reveal health-producing insights.

14. Some critics have argued that traditional psychoanalysis may frequently receive credit for spontaneous _____ of symptoms. However, psychoanalysis has been shown to be better than no treatment at all.

15. Brief _____ therapy (which relies on _____ theory but is brief and focused) is as effective as other major therapies.

What are the major humanistic therapies?

16. Humanistic therapies try to help people live up to their _____ and to give tendencies for mental health to emerge.

17. Carl _____ client-centred (or person-centred) therapy is non- _____ and is dedicated to creating an atmosphere of growth.

18. In client-centred therapy, _____ positive regard, empathy, authenticity, and _____ (restating thoughts and feelings) are combined to give the client a chance to solve his or her own problems.

19. _____ therapies focus on the choices one makes in life.

20. Clients in existential therapy are encouraged through _____ and _____ to exercise free will, to take responsibility for their choices, and to find meaning in their lives.

21. Frederick Perls's _____ therapy emphasizes immediate awareness of thoughts and feelings.

22. The goal of Perls's approach is to rebuild thinking, feeling, and acting into connected wholes and to help clients break through _____ _____ .

23. _____ psychologists, such as those found on the radio, are supposed to restrict themselves to educating listeners, rather than actually doing therapy.

24. Telephone therapists and _____ working on the Internet may or may not be competent. Even if they are, their effectiveness may be severely limited.

25. In an emerging approach called _____ , therapy is being done at a distance, through the use of _____ (two-way audio-video links).

What is behaviour therapy?

26. _____ therapists use various behaviour _____ techniques that apply learning principles to change human behaviour.

27. _____ conditioning is a basic form of learning in which existing _____ responses are associated with new conditioned stimuli.

28. In _____ therapy, classical conditioning is used to associate maladaptive behaviour with pain in order to inhibit undesirable responses.

29. To be most effective, an aversive stimuli or event must be _____ _____ (closely connected with negative behaviour).

How is behaviour therapy used to treat phobias and anxieties?

30. Classical conditioning also underlies systematic _____ , a technique used to reduce fears, phobias, and anxieties.

31. In this approach, gradual exposure and reciprocal _____ (e.g., relaxation blocking _____) break the link between fear and particular situations.

32. Typical steps are (1) construct a fear _____ ; (2) learn to produce total relaxation; and (3) perform items on the _____ (from least to most disturbing).

33. Desensitization may be carried out in real settings or it may be done by vividly imagining scenes from the _____ _____ .

34. Desensitization is also effective when it is administered _____ ; that is, when clients watch models perform the feared responses.

35. In a newly developed technique, _____ reality _____ is used to present fear stimuli to patients undergoing desensitization.

36. Another new technique called _____ - _____ desensitization shows promise as a treatment for traumatic memories and stress disorders.

What role does reinforcement play in behaviour therapy?

37. Behaviour modification also makes use of _____ principles, such as positive reinforcement, non-reinforcement, _____ (eliminating responses), punishment, _____ (moulding responses), stimulus control, and time out.

38. _____ - _____ (or _____ - _____) can extinguish troublesome behaviours. Often this is done by simply identifying and eliminating reinforcers.

39. Time out is an _____ technique in which attention and approval are withheld following undesirable responses.

40. Time out can also be done by removing a person from the _____ in which misbehaviour occurs, so that it will not be _____ .

41. To apply positive reinforcement and operant shaping, symbolic rewards known as _____ are often used. These allow immediate reinforcement of selected _____ behaviours.

42. Full-scale use of symbolic rewards in an institutional setting produces a _____ _____ .

43. Toward the end of such programs, patients are shifted to _____ rewards such as recognition and approval.

What is cognitive therapy? How does it change thoughts and emotions?

44. _____ therapy emphasizes changing thinking patterns that underlie emotional or behavioural problems.

45. Its goals are to correct distorted thinking and/or teach improved _____ skills.

46. Aron _____ therapy for depression corrects major distortions in thinking, including selective perception, _____ , and all-or-nothing thinking.

47. In a variation called _____ - _____ _____ therapy (REBT), clients learn to recognize and challenge their own irrational beliefs that lead to upsetting consequences.

How is psychotherapy done with groups of people?

48. _____ therapy may be a simple extension of individual methods or it may be based on techniques developed specifically for _____ .

49. In _____ , individuals use role playing, role _____ , and the mirror technique to gain insight into incidents resembling real-life problems.

50. In _____ therapy, the _____ group is treated as a unit so that the entire family system is changed for the better.

51. Although they are not literally psychotherapies, sensitivity groups and _____ groups attempt to encourage positive personality change.

52. In recent years, commercially offered large-group _____ trainings have become popular.

53. The therapeutic benefits of large-group techniques are questionable and may reflect nothing more than a therapy _____ effect.

What do various therapies have in common?

54. _____ does help people with certain psychological disorders and _____ conditions such as headaches, _____ , arthritis, diabetes, and chronic low-back pain.

55. To alleviate personal problems, all psychotherapies offer a caring relationship and emotional _____ in a _____ setting.

56. All therapies encourage _____ (emotional release) and they provide explanations for the client's problems.

57. In addition, psychotherapy provides a new _____ and a chance to practise new behaviours.

58. Many basic counselling skills are used in therapy. These include listening _____ and helping to _____ the problem.

59. Effective therapists also focus on _____ and avoid giving unwanted advice.

60. It helps to accept the person's _____ , to _____ thoughts and feelings, and to be patient during silences.

61. In counselling it is important to use open questions when possible and to maintain _____ .

62. Many cultural _____ to effective counselling and therapy exist.

63. _____ _____ counsellors have the knowledge and skills needed to intervene successfully in the lives of clients from diverse cultural backgrounds.

64. The aware counsellor must be able to establish _____ with a person from a different cultural background and _____ traditional theories and techniques to meet the needs of clients from non-European ethnic or racial groups such as Native people.

How do psychiatrists treat psychological disorders?

65. Three somatic approaches to treatment of psychosis are _____ (use of drugs), _____ therapy (ECT), and psychosurgery.

66. Pharmacotherapy is done with minor tranquillizers (anti-anxiety drugs), _____ (which control delusions and hallucinations), and _____ (mood elevators).

67. All psychiatric drugs involve a tradeoff between risks and _____ .

68. _____ _____ health centres were created to help avoid or minimize hospitalization.

69. These centres also have as their goal the _____ of mental health problems through education, consultation, and crisis _____ .

How are behavioural principles applied to everyday problems?

70. In _____ sensitization, aversive images are used to discourage unwanted behaviour.

71. _____ _____ uses mild punishment to prevent upsetting thoughts.

72. Covert _____ is a way to encourage desired responses by mental rehearsal.

73. _____ pairs relaxation with a hierarchy of upsetting images in order to lessen fears.

How could a person go about finding professional help?

74. In most communities, a _____ and reputable therapist can usually be located through public sources of information or by a referral.

75. Practical considerations such as cost and qualifications enter into choosing a therapist. However, the therapist's _____ _____ are of equal importance.

76. _____ - _____ groups made up of people who share similar _____ can sometimes add valuable support to professional treatment.

Mastery Test

1. To demonstrate that spontaneous remissions are occurring, you could use a
   a. patient-defined hierarchy
   b. waiting-list control group
   c. target behaviour group
   d. short-term dynamic correlation

2. In desensitization, relaxation is induced to block fear. This is known as
   a. systematic adaptation
   b. vicarious opposition
   c. stimulus control
   d. reciprocal inhibition

3. Role reversals and the mirror technique are methods of
   a. psychodrama
   b. person-centred therapy
   c. family therapy
   d. brief psychodynamic therapy

4. One thing that both trepanning and exorcism have in common is that both were used
   a. to treat schizophrenia
   b. by Pinel in the Bicêtre Aslyum
   c. to remove evil spirits
   d. to treat cases of hysteria

5. Unconditional positive regard is a concept particularly associated with
   a. Beck
   b. Frankl
   c. Perls
   d. Rogers

6. Many of the claimed benefits of large-group awareness training appear to represent a _____ effect.
   a. remission
   b. education
   c. placebo
   d. transference

7. Inducing seizures is a part of
   a. Gestalt therapy
   b. antidepressant therapy
   c. ECT
   d. cybertherapy

8. Which counselling behaviour does not belong with the others?
   a. paraphrasing
   b. judging
   c. reflecting
   d. active listening

9. In psychoanalysis, the process most directly opposite to free association is
   a. resistance
   b. transference
   c. symbolization
   d. remission

10. Identification of target behaviours is an important step in designing
    a. a desensitization hierarchy
    b. activating stimuli
    c. token economies
    d. encounter groups

11. A person who wants to lose weight looks at a dessert and visualizes bugs crawling all over it. The person is using
    a. systematic adaptation
    b. covert sensitization
    c. stress inoculation
    d. systematic desensitization

12. Which of the following is NOT a humanistic therapy?
    a. client-centred
    b. Gestalt
    c. existential
    d. cognitive

13. Not many emergency room doctors drive without using their seatbelts. This is most likely due to
    a. systematic desensitization
    b. aversion therapy
    c. covert reinforcement
    d. the mirror technique

14. Telephone counsellors have little chance of using which element of effective psychotherapy?
    a. empathy
    b. non-directive reflection
    c. the therapeutic alliance
    d. accepting the person's frame of reference

15. Which of the following is a self-management technique?
    a. thought stopping
    b. vicarious reality exposure
    c. REBT
    d. EMDR

16. Which statement about psychotherapy is true?
    a. Most therapists are equally successful.
    b. Most techniques are equally successful.
    c. Therapists and clients need not agree about the goals of therapy.
    d. Effective therapists instruct their clients not to discuss their therapy with anyone else.

17. Analysis of resistances and transferences is a standard feature of
    a. client-centred therapy
    b. Gestalt therapy
    c. REBT
    d. psychoanalysis

18. Both classical and operant conditioning are the basis for
    a. desensitization
    b. token economies
    c. behaviour therapy
    d. aversion therapy

19. Each of the following statements is an example of an irrational belief EXCEPT
    a. If every important person in my life does not love me, I am worthless.
    b. There is always a perfect solution to any problem, and it is awful if this solution is not found.
    c. It is awful when things are not the way I would like them to be.
    d. There are some things in my life that I have control over.

20. Deep lesioning is a form of
    a. ECT
    b. psychosurgery
    c. pharmacotherapy
    d. PET

21. Identifying and removing rewards is a behavioural technique designed to bring about
    a. operant shaping
    b. extinction
    c. respondent aversion
    d. token inhibition

22. Culturally skilled counsellors must be aware of their own cultural backgrounds, as well as
    a. the percentage of ethnic populations in the community
    b. that of their clients
    c. the importance of maintaining confidentiality
    d. the life goals of minorities

23. A behavioural therapist would treat Helene's acrophobia with
    a. desensitization
    b. aversion therapy
    c. covert sensitization
    d. cybertherapy

24. Which technqiue most closely relates to the idea of non-directive therapy?
    a. confrontation
    b. dream analysis
    c. role reversal
    d. reflection

25. About half of psychotherapy patients say they feel better after the first _____ sessions.
    a. 4
    b. 8
    c. 12
    d. 20

26. Overgeneralization is a thinking error that contributes to
    a. depression
    b. somatization
    c. phobias
    d. emotional reprocessing

27. Death, freedom, and meaning are special concerns of
    a. REBT
    b. cognitive therapy
    c. existential therapy
    d. psychodrama

28. An intense awareness of present experience and breaking through emotional impasses is the heart of
    a. action therapy
    b. Gestalt therapy
    c. time-limited therapy
    d. REBT

29. The ABCs of REBT stand for
    a. anticipation, behaviour, conduct
    b. action, behaviour, conflict
    c. activating experience, belief, consequence
    d. anticipation, belief, congruent experience

30. Which of the following is NOT a "distance therapy"?
    a. REBT
    b. telephone therapy
    c. cybertherapy
    d. telehealth

31. Virtual reality exposure is a type of
    a. psychodrama
    b. ECT therapy
    c. cognitive therapy
    d. desensitization

32. ECT is most often used to treat
    a. psychosis
    b. anxiety
    c. hysteria
    d. depression

33. Which of the following is most often associated with community mental health programs?
    a. pharmacotherapy
    b. covert reinforcement
    c. crisis intervention
    d. REBT

Solutions

Recite and Review

1. positive; behaviour
2. phobias
3. support
4. growth
5. 2.15; separated
6. superstition
7. skull
8. exorcism
9. mental; hospital
10. psychotherapy
11. physical
12. unconscious; unconscious
13. free; dream
14. spontaneous
15. Brief
16. Humanistic
17. person
18. positive; empathy
19. choices
20. will; choices; meaning
21. awareness
22. wholes
23. educating; therapy
24. Internet
25. therapy; audio video
26. learning
27. learning; associated
28. pain
29. stimuli
30. systematic
31. exposure
32. relaxation
33. imagining
34. models
35. reality; fear
36. memories; stress
37. control; time
38. reinforcers
39. responses
40. removing
41. immediate; behaviours
42. tokens
43. approval
44. thinking
45. skills
46. selective; thinking
47. beliefs
48. individual
49. role; role
50. unit; family
51. psychotherapies
52. trainings
53. therapy
54. disorders; headaches; pain
55. emotional; setting
56. problems
57. behaviours
58. counselling
59. advice
60. silences
61. open
62. cultural
63. counsellors
64. different
65. somatic; drugs; brain
66. minor; hallucinations; mood
67. risks
68. hospitalization
69. crisis
70. images
71. punishment
72. responses
73. relaxation
74. referral
75. cost; fees
76. groups

Connections

1. I
2. H
3. F
4. B
5. G
6. A
7. D
8. E
9. C
10. C
11. E
12. A
13. G
14. H
15. J
16. B
17. F
18. D
19. I
20. H
21. F
22. B
23. J
24. A
25. I
26. C
27. G
28. D
29. E

Short-Answer Questions

1. People are unaware of what psychologists actually do, potential clients do not know how to go about finding a psychologist, people lack the financial resources to pay for psychological services, government cuts to publicly funded services have reduced accessibility, and many people believe that they should be able to solve their own problems without outside help.

2. The major elements of psychoanalysis are free association (saying whatever comes into one's head without concern that it is embarrassing, illogical, painful, or socially unacceptable), dream analysis (looking for hidden or latent content by the use of dream symbols), analysis of resistance (discovering unconscious

conflicts), and analysis of transference (the patient acting as if the therapist is a parent or other significant figure).

3. Traditional psychoanalysis is costly in time (can go on for years) and money. Many psychotherapists have switched to brief psychodynamic therapy, using direct questions to reveal unconscious conflicts, or actively provoking emotional reactions.

4. Aversion therapy uses the process of classical conditioning to associate strong negative responses or aversions to unwanted behaviours, including smoking, drinking, and gambling. Techniques such as rapid smoking or giving a painful electric shock to someone while drinking are used. The goal is to associate the unwanted behaviour with the negative or aversive response, rather than to a pleasurable one.

5. Desensitization is based on reciprocal inhibition (using one emotional state to counteract the effects of another). For example, it is impossible to be both tense and relaxed at the same time. If a person has a fear of snakes, desensitization could be used to replace the tension usually associated with the fear with relaxation. This will usually eliminate the fear.

6. Time out involves removing the child from a situation in which behaviour is reinforced. Putting a child in a time out prevents any rewards (including attention from parents) after misbehaviour. Eventually, the unwanted behaviour will be extinguished since it is not being reinforced.

7. The advantage of using tokens as reinforcements is that they can be given immediately. They can then be exchanged for candy, food, access to recreation facilities, television, or other privileges.

8. Community mental health programs (or CLSCs) can play an important role in the delivery of mental health services. They can offer a wide variety of services, including prevention, counselling, consultation, education, and crisis intervention.

9. People should seek professional help when the level of psychological discomfort or distress is similar to that which would send them to a doctor or dentist if it were physical. Another signal is significant changes in behaviour, including changes in the quality of work (or schoolwork), increased absenteeism, increase in the use of drugs and/or alcohol, and changes in relationships with others. Persistent, disturbing suicidal thoughts or impulses suggest that a person seek help immediately.

10. Therapists can be found through the Yellow Pages, community mental health centres or CLSCs, the Canadian Mental Health Association, provincial professional organizations, crisis hotlines or centres, and newspaper and/or radio advertising. In addition, many colleges and universities across Canada offer psychological counseling.

11. Run, do not walk, away if the therapist makes sexual advances; is physically and/or verbally aggressive; is hostile, controlling, or belittling; talks more about his own problems than about yours; encourages excessive dependence; or demands that clients keep everything that goes on in therapy a secret. All unprofessional behaviour should be reported.

Final Survey and Review

1. Psychotherapy; personality
2. self esteem; sexual; problems; marital
3. constructive; changes
4. solve; problems; crisis
5. middle aged; education
6. Primitive
7. Trepanning
8. Demonology
9. Pinel; Paris
10. Freud's; psychoanalysis
11. hysteria
12. repressed
13. association; resistance
14. remission
15. psychodynamic; psychoanalytic
16. potentials
17. Roger's; directive
18. unconditional; reflection
19. Existential
20. confrontation; encounter
21. Gestalt
22. emotional; blocks
23. Media
24. cybertherapists
25. telehealth; videoconferencing
26. Behaviour; modification
27. Classical; reflex
28. aversion
29. response; contingent
30. desensitization
31. inhibition; fear
32. hierarchy; hierarchy
33. fear; hierarchy
34. vicariously

35. virtual; exposure
36. eye movement
37. operant; extinction; shaping
38. Non reward; non reinforcement
39. extinction
40. setting; reinforced
41. tokens; target
42. token economy
43. social
44. Cognitive
45. coping
46. Beck's; overgeneralization
47. rational emotive; behaviour
48. Group; groups
49. psychodrama; reversals
50. family; family
51. encounter
52. awareness
53. placebo
54. Psychotherapy; medical; hypertension
55. rapport; protected
56. catharsis
57. perspective
58. actively; clarify
59. feelings
60. perspective; reflect

61. confidentiality
62. barriers
63. Culturally; skilled
64. rapport; adapt
65. pharmacotherapy; electroconvulsive
66. antipsychotics; antidepressants
67. benefits
68. Community; mental
69. prevention; intervention
70. covert
71. Thought; stopping
72. reinforcement
73. Desensitization
74. competent
75. personal; characteristics
76. Self help; problems

Mastery Test

1. B (p. 471)
2. D (p. 477)
3. A (p. 486)
4. C (p. 469)
5. D (p. 472)
6. C (p. 487)
7. C (p. 492)

8. B (p. 489)
9. A (p. 470)
10. C (p. 482)
11. B (p. 494)
12. D (p. 472)
13. B (p. 476)
14. C (p. 488)
15. A (p. 495)
16. B (p. 487)
17. D (p. 470)
18. C (pp. 476, 480)
19. D (p. 484)
20. B (p. 492)
21. B (p. 481)
22. B (p. 490)
23. A (p. 478)
24. D (p. 472)
25. B (p. 487)
26. A (p. 483)
27. C (p. 472)
28. B (p. 473)
29. C (p. 484)
30. A (p. 473)
31. D (p. 479)
32. D (p. 492)
33. C (p. 493)

Social Behaviour

Chapter Overview

Social psychology is the study of behaviour in social situations. Affiliating with others is related to needs for approval, support, friendship, information, and reassurance. Social comparison theory holds that we affiliate to evaluate our actions, feelings, and abilities.

Interpersonal attraction is increased by frequent contact, physical attractiveness, competence, similarity, and self-disclosure. Romantic love is marked by mutual absorption between lovers who also like one another. Evolutionary psychology attributes human mating patterns to the reproductive challenges faced by men and women since the dawn of time.

Attribution theory summarizes how we make inferences about behaviour. The fundamental attributional error is to think that the actions of others are the result of internal causes. Because of an actor-observer bias, we tend to attribute our own behaviour to external causes.

Social influence refers to how our behaviour is changed by the behaviour of others. Examples are conformity, groupthink, obedience, and complying with direct requests. Self-assertion involves clearly stating your wants and needs to others. Learning to be assertive can be aided by role playing.

Attitudes have belief, emotional, and action components. Attitudes are formed through direct contact, interacting with others, child-rearing, group pressures, peer-group influences, the mass media, and chance conditioning. Attitude change is related to reference group membership, deliberate persuasion, and personal experiences. Effective persuasion occurs when characteristics of the communicator, the message, and the audience are well matched. Cognitive dissonance theory explains how attitudes are maintained and changed.

Prejudice is a negative attitude held toward out-group members. Prejudice can be attributed to scapegoating, personal prejudice, group norms, and authoritarian personality traits. Intergroup conflict leads to hostility and stereotyping. Status inequalities tend to build prejudices. Equal-status contact and superordinate goals tend to reduce these problems.

Ethologists blame aggression on instincts. Biological explanations emphasize brain mechanisms and physical factors. Aggression tends to follow frustration, especially when aggression cues are present. Social learning theory relates aggressive behaviour to the influence of aggressive models.

Four decision points that must be passed before we give help to others are noticing, defining an emergency, taking responsibility, and selecting a course of action. Helping is less likely at each point when other potential helpers are present. Giving help tends to encourage others to help, too.

Multiculturalism is an attempt to give equal status to different ethnic, racial, and cultural groups. Cultural awareness is a key element in promoting greater social harmony.

Learning Objectives

After reading this chapter, students will be able to:

1. Define affiliation. Identify the reasons people affiliate.
2. Describe the factors that contribute to interpersonal attraction.
3. Compare interpersonal attraction and romantic attraction.
4. Describe the influence of evolution on mate selection.
5. Explain group structure, group cohesiveness, and norms.
6. Explain attribution and explain the fundamental attribution error.
7. Explain conformity, obedience, compliance, and self-assertion.
8. Identify the basic components of attitudes. Explain how attitudes are acquired and how they may be changed.
9. Describe the theory of cognitive dissonance.
10. Discuss the causes of prejudice and intergroup conflict.
11. Define aggression. Explain aggression from a biological perspective.
12. Explain the frustration-aggression hypothesis.
13. Explain aggression from the standpoint of social learning theory.
14. Discuss the factors that contribute to bystander apathy and bystander intervention.

Practice Quizzes

Recite and Review

Why do people affiliate? What factors influence interpersonal attraction?

Recite and Review: Pages 507–512

1. Social psychology studies how individuals behave, think, and feel in _____ situations.
2. The need to affiliate is tied to needs for _____ , support, friendship, and _____ .
3. Additionally, research indicates that we sometimes affiliate to _____ anxiety and uncertainty.
4. Social comparison theory holds that we affiliate to _____ our actions, feelings, and abilities.
5. Children are attracted to those who are similar in _____ , age, race, and _____ activity. Older children (those starting high school) are more attracted to those who _____ out and who are aggressive.
6. Initial acquaintance and _____ are influenced by physical attractiveness (beauty), competence (high ability), and _____ (being alike).
7. A large degree of _____ on many dimensions is characteristic of _____ selection, a pattern called homogamy.
8. Self-disclosure (_____ oneself to others) occurs to a greater degree if two people like one another.

9. Self-disclosure follows a reciprocity _____ : Low levels of self-disclosure are met with low levels in return, whereas moderate self-disclosure elicits more personal replies.

10. Overdisclosure tends to inhibit _____ - _____ by others. What is considered overdisclosure will vary from culture to culture.

11. Self-disclosure between friends will typically increase in _____ school.

12. Romantic love can be distinguished from liking by the use of attitude scales. Dating couples _____ and _____ their partners but only _____ their friends.

13. Romantic love is also associated with greater _____ absorption between people.

14. Evolutionary psychology attributes human _____ patterns to the differing reproductive challenges faced by men and women since the dawn of time.

How does group membership affect individual behaviour?

Recite and Review: Pages 513–515

15. One's position in _____ defines a variety of roles to be played.

16. _____ _____ , which may be achieved or ascribed, are particular behaviour patterns associated with social positions.

17. When two or more _____ roles are held, role conflict may occur.

18. Positions within _____ typically carry higher or lower levels of status. High status is associated with special privileges and respect.

19. Group structure refers to the organization of _____ , communication pathways, and power within a group.

20. Group cohesiveness is basically the degree of _____ among group members.

21. Norms are _____ of conduct enforced (formally or informally) by _____ . Group membership helps avoid _____ .

22. Attribution theory is concerned with how we make inferences about the _____ of behaviour.

23. Behaviour can be attributed to internal _____ or external _____ .

24. The fundamental attributional _____ is to ascribe the actions of others to _____ causes. This is part of the actor-observer bias, in which we ascribe the behaviour of others to _____ causes, and our own behaviour to _____ causes.

25. As early as _____ , boys start to take credit for success.

What have social psychologists learned about conformity, obedience, compliance, and self-assertion?

Recite and Review: Pages 516–523

26. Social influence refers to alterations in _____ brought about by the behaviour of _____ .

27. Conformity to group pressure is a familiar example of social influence. Virtually everyone _____ to a variety of broad social and cultural _____ .

28. Conformity pressures also exist within small _____ . The famous Asch experiments demonstrated that various _____ pressures encourage conformity.

29. Groupthink refers to compulsive conformity in group _____ _____ . Victims of groupthink seek to maintain each other's approval, even at the cost of critical thinking.

30. Obedience to _____ has been investigated in a variety of experiments, particularly those by Stanley Milgram.

31. _____ in Milgram's studies decreased when the victim was in the same room, when the victim and subject were face to face, when the authority figure was absent, and when others refused to obey.

32. Compliance with direct _____ by a person who has little or no social _____ is another means by which behaviour is influenced.

33. Three strategies for inducing compliance are the _____ -in-the-door technique, the door-in-the- _____ approach, and the low-ball technique.

34. Recent research suggests that in addition to excessive obedience to _____ , many people show a surprising passive compliance to unreasonable _____ .

35. Self-assertion involves clearly stating one's _____ and _____ to others.

36. Aggression expresses one's feelings and desires, but it _____ others.

37. Learning to be _____ is accomplished by role playing and rehearsing assertive actions.

How are attitudes acquired and changed?

Recite and Review: Pages 523–528

38. Attitudes are learned tendencies to respond in a _____ or _____ way.

39. Attitudes are made up of a belief component, an emotional component, and an _____ component.

40. Attitudes may be formed by _____ contact, interaction with others, the effects of _____ -rearing practices, and social pressures from group membership.

41. Peer group influences, the mass _____ , and _____ conditioning (accidental learning) also appear to be important in attitude formation.

42. The _____ consequences of actions, how we think others will _____ our actions, and habits all influence whether attitudes are converted to actions.

43. Attitudes held with conviction are most likely to be _____ in behaviour.

44. People tend to change their attitudes to match those of their reference group (a group the person _____ with and refers to for guidance).

45. Effective persuasion occurs when characteristics of the communicator, the _____ , and the audience are well matched.

46. In general, a likable and believable communicator who repeats a credible message that arouses _____ in the audience and states clear-cut _____ will be persuasive.

47. Maintaining and changing attitudes is closely related to needs for _____ in thoughts and actions. Cognitive dissonance theory explains the dynamics of such needs.

48. Cognitive dissonance occurs when there is a _____ between thoughts or between thoughts and actions.

49. The amount of reward or justification (reasons) for one's actions influences whether _____ occurs.

50. We are motivated to _____ dissonance when it occurs, often by changing beliefs or attitudes.

What causes prejudice and intergroup conflict?

Recite and Review: Pages 528–533

51. Prejudice is a _____ attitude held toward members of various out-groups.

52. Racism, ageism, and sexism are specific types of prejudice based on race, age, and _____ (or _____).

53. One theory attributes prejudice to scapegoating, which is a type of displaced _____ .

54. A second account says that prejudices may be held for personal reasons such as direct threats to a person's well-being (personal prejudice) or simply through adherence to group _____ (group prejudice).

55. Prejudiced individuals tend to have an authoritarian _____ , characterized by rigidity, inhibition, intolerance, and _____ -simplification.

56. Authoritarians tend to be very ethnocentric (they use their own _____ as a basis for judging all others).

57. Intergroup _____ gives rise to hostility and the formation of social stereotypes (oversimplified images of members of various groups).

58. Symbolic prejudice, or prejudice expressed in _____ ways, is common today.

59. _____ inequalities (differences in power, prestige, or privileges) tend to build prejudices.

60. Equal-status contact (social interaction on an equal footing) tends to _____ prejudice.

61. Superordinate _____ (those that rise above all others) usually reduce intergroup conflict.

62. On a small scale, jigsaw _____ (which encourage cooperation through _____ interdependence) have been shown to be an effective way of combating prejudice.

How do psychologists explain human aggression?

Recite and Review: Pages 534–538

63. Ethologists explain aggression as a natural expression of inherited _____ .

64. Biological explanations emphasize brain mechanisms and physical factors that _____ the threshold (trigger point) for aggression.

65. According to the frustration- _____ hypothesis, frustration and aggression are closely linked.

66. Aggression has been divided into _____ types: _____ aggression and reactive aggression.

67. Frustration is only one of many aversive _____ that can arouse a person and make aggression more likely. Aggression is especially likely to occur when _____ cues (stimuli associated with aggression) are present.

68. Social learning theory has focused attention on the role of aggressive _____ in the development of aggressive behaviour .

69. Aggressive _____ on television encourage aggression because they desensitize (lower the sensitivity of) _____ to violence and disinhibit (remove restraints against) aggressive impulses.

Why are bystanders so often unwilling to help in an emergency?

Recite and Review: Pages 539–542

70. Prosocial behaviour is _____ , constructive, or altruistic toward others.

71. Bystander apathy is the unwillingness of bystanders to offer _____ to others during emergencies.

72. Four decision points that must be passed before a person gives help are _____ , defining an emergency, taking responsibility, and selecting a course of action.

73. Helping is _____ likely at each point when other potential helpers are present.

74. Helping is encouraged by general arousal, empathic _____ , being in a good mood, low effort or _____ , and perceived similarity between the victim and the helper.

What can be done to lower prejudice and promote social harmony?

Recite and Review: Psychology in Action

75. Multiculturalism is an attempt to give _____ status to different ethnic, racial, and cultural groups.

76. Greater tolerance can be encouraged by neutralizing stereotypes with individuating information (which helps see others as _____).

77. Tolerance comes from looking for commonalties with others and by avoiding the effects of just-world _____ , self-fulfilling prophecies, and _____ competition.

78. _____ awareness is a key element in promoting greater social harmony.

Connections

1.	_____ superordinate	a.	privilege and importance
2.	_____ ascribed role	b.	rule or standard
3.	_____ achieved role	c.	aggression target
4.	_____ status	d.	above all others
5.	_____ cohesiveness	e.	over-simplified image
6.	_____ norm	f.	uncomfortable clash
7.	_____ stereotype	g.	group centered
8.	_____ ethnocentric	h.	unequal treatment
9.	_____ scapegoat	i.	assigned role
10.	_____ discrimination	j.	degree of attraction
11.	_____ dissonance	k.	voluntary role

12. _____ attribution		a.	relating self to others
13. _____ authoritarianism		b.	honest expression of needs
14. _____ need to affiliate		c.	following authority
15. _____ social comparison		d.	aggression cue
16. _____ symbolic prejudice		e.	yielding to requests
17. _____ weapons effect		f.	rewards and punishments
18. _____ conformity		g.	altruistic behaviour
19. _____ group sanctions		h.	desire to associate
20. _____ obedience		i.	matching behaviour
21. _____ compliance		j.	F Scale
22. _____ assertiveness		k.	modern bias
23. _____ prosocial		l.	cause of one's behaviour

Short-Answer Questions

1. Briefly describe social comparison theory.
2. What are the effects of self-disclosure on relationships?
3. What did Milgram's studies of obedience demonstrate?
4. What is meant by the foot-in-the-door technique?
5. What is meant by the door-in-the-face technique?
6. What is meant by the low-ball technique?
7. What is assertiveness training?
8. What strategies can be used to reduce dissonance?
9. What is the difference between prejudice and discrimination?
10. What are the warning signs for school violence?
11. How can parents reduce the impact of TV watching on their children's behaviour?
12. How can a person become more tolerant?

Final Survey and Review

Why do people affiliate? What factors influence interpersonal attraction?

1. _____ _____ studies how individuals behave, think, and feel in social situations.
2. The _____ to _____ is tied to additional needs for approval, support, friendship, and information.
3. Additionally, research indicates that we sometimes affiliate to reduce _____ and uncertainty.
4. Social _____ theory holds that we affiliate to evaluate our actions, feelings, and abilities.
5. Children are attracted to those who are _____ in sex, age, race and preferred activity. Older children (those starting high school) are more likely to be attracted to those who stand out and who are _____ .

6. Initial acquaintance and attraction are influenced by _____ attractiveness (beauty), _____ (high ability), and similarity.

7. A large degree of similarity on many dimensions is characteristic of mate selection, a pattern called _____ .

8. _____ - _____ (revealing oneself to others) occurs to a greater degree if two people like one another.

9. Self-disclosure follows a _____ norm: Low levels of self-disclosure are met with low levels in return, whereas moderate self-disclosure elicits more personal replies.

10. _____ (excessive) tends to inhibit self-disclosure by others. What is considered overdisclosure will _____ from culture to culture.

11. Self-disclosure between friends will typically _____ in high school.

12. Romantic love can be distinguished from liking by the use of _____ _____ . Dating couples love and like their partners but only like their friends.

13. Romantic love is also associated with greater mutual _____ between people.

14. _____ psychology attributes human mating patterns to the differing _____ challenges faced by men and women since the dawn of time.

How does group membership affect individual behaviour?

15. One's position in groups defines a variety of _____ to be played.

16. Social roles, which may be _____ or _____ , are particular behaviour patterns associated with social positions.

17. When two or more contradictory roles are held, role _____ may occur.

18. Positions within groups typically carry higher or lower levels of _____ . _____ _____ is associated with special privileges and respect.

19. Group _____ refers to the organization of roles, _____ pathways, and power within a group.

20. Group _____ is basically the degree of attraction among group members.

21. _____ are standards of conduct enforced (formally or informally) by groups. Group _____ helps people deal with loneliness.

22. _____ theory is concerned with how we make inferences about the causes of behaviour.

23. Behaviour can be attributed to _____ causes or _____ causes.

24. The _____ _____ error is to ascribe the actions of others to internal causes. This is part of an actor- _____ bias, in which we ascribe the behaviour of others to internal causes, and our own behaviour to external causes.

25. Girls are more likely to _____ their own performance than boys. He's _____ , she's _____ .

What have social psychologists learned about conformity, obedience, compliance, and self-assertion?

26. _____ _____ refers to alterations in behaviour brought about by the behaviour of others.

27. _____ to group pressure is a familiar example of social influence. Virtually everyone conforms to a variety of broad social and _____ norms.

28. Conformity pressures also exist within small groups. The famous _____ experiments demonstrated that various group _____ encourage conformity.

29. _____ refers to compulsive conformity in group decision making. Its victims seek to maintain each other's _____ , even at the cost of critical thinking.

30. _____ to authority has been investigated in a variety of experiments, particularly those by Stanley _____ .

31. Obedience in his studies _____ when the victim was in the same room, when the victim and subject were face to face, when the _____ figure was absent, and when others refused to obey.

32. _____ with direct requests by a person who has little or no social power is another means by which behaviour is influenced.

33. Three strategies for getting people to comply are the foot-in-the- _____ technique, the _____ -in-the-face approach, and the _____ - _____ technique.

34. Recent research suggests that in addition to excessive obedience to authority, many people show a surprising _____ compliance to unreasonable requests.

35. _____ - _____ involves clearly stating one's wants and needs to others.

36. _____ expresses one's feelings and desires, but it hurts others.

37. Learning to be assertive is accomplished by _____ _____ and rehearsing assertive actions.

How are attitudes acquired and changed?

38. Attitudes are _____ _____ to respond in a positive or negative way.

39. Attitudes are made up of a _____ component, an _____ component, and an action component.

40. Attitudes may be formed by direct _____ , interaction with others, the effects of child-rearing practices, and social pressures from _____ _____ .

41. _____ group influences, the mass media, and chance _____ (accidental learning) also appear to be important in attitude formation.

42. The immediate _____ of actions, how we think others will evaluate our actions, and _____ all influence whether attitudes are converted to actions.

43. Attitudes held with _____ are most likely to be expressed in behaviour.

44. People tend to change their attitudes to match those of their _____ group (a group the person identifies with and refers to for guidance).

45. Effective persuasion occurs when characteristics of the _____ , the message, and the _____ are well matched.

46. In general, a likable and believable _____ who repeats a credible message that arouses emotion in the _____ and states clear-cut conclusions will be persuasive.

47. Maintaining and changing attitudes is closely related to needs for consistency in thoughts and actions. Cognitive _____ theory explains the dynamics of such needs.

48. Cognitive _____ occurs when there is a clash between _____ or between thoughts and actions.

49. The amount of _____ or _____ (reasons) for one's actions influences whether dissonance occurs.

50. We are motivated to reduce dissonance when it occurs, often by changing _____ or _____ , rather than behaviour.

What causes prejudice and intergroup conflict?

51. Prejudice is a negative attitude held toward members of various _____ - _____ .

52. _____ , _____ , and _____ are specific types of prejudice based on race, age, and gender.

53. One theory attributes prejudice to _____ , which is a type of _____ aggression.

54. A second account says that prejudices may be held for personal reasons such as direct threats to a person's well-being (_____ prejudice) or simply through adherence to group norms (_____ prejudice).

55. Prejudiced individuals tend to have an _____ personality, characterized by rigidity, inhibition, intolerance, and oversimplification.

56. Authoritarians tend to be very _____ (they use their own group as a basis for judging all others).

57. Intergroup conflict gives rise to hostility and the formation of _____ _____ (oversimplified images of members of various groups).

58. _____ prejudice, or prejudice expressed in disguised ways, is common today.

59. Status _____ (differences in power, prestige, or privileges) tend to build prejudices.

60. _____ - _____ contact (social interaction on an equal footing) tends to reduce prejudice.

61. _____ goals (those that rise above all others) usually reduce intergroup conflict.

62. On a small scale, _____ classrooms (which encourage cooperation through mutual _____) have been shown to be an effective way of combating prejudice.

How do psychologists explain human aggression?

63. _____ explain aggression as a natural expression of inherited instincts.

64. Biological explanations emphasize brain mechanisms and physical factors that lower the _____ (trigger point) for aggression.

65. According to the _____ -aggression hypothesis, _____ and aggression are closely linked.

66. Aggression has been divided into two types: _____ aggression and _____ aggression.

67. Frustration is only one of many _____ stimuli that can arouse a person and make aggression more likely. Aggression is especially likely to occur when aggression _____ (stimuli associated with aggression) are present.

68. _____ _____ theory has focused attention on the role of aggressive models in the development of aggressive behaviour.

69. Aggressive models on television encourage aggression because they _____ (lower the sensitivity of) viewers to violence and _____ (remove restraints against) aggressive impulses.

Why are bystanders so often unwilling to help in an emergency?

70. Prosocial behaviour is helpful, constructive, or _____ toward others.

71. Bystander _____ is the unwillingness of bystanders to offer help to others during emergencies.

72. Four decision points that must be passed before a person gives help are noticing, defining an _____ , taking _____ , and selecting a course of action.

73. Helping is less likely at each point when other _____ _____ are present.

74. Helping is encouraged by general arousal, _____ arousal, being in a good mood, low effort or risk, and perceived _____ between the victim and the helper.

What can be done to lower prejudice and promote social harmony?

75. _____ is an attempt to give equal status to different ethnic, racial, and cultural groups.

76. Greater tolerance can be encouraged by neutralizing stereotypes with _____ information (which helps see others as individuals).

77. Tolerance comes from looking for commonalties with others and by avoiding the effects of _____ - _____ beliefs, _____ - _____ prophecies, and social competition.

78. Cultural _____ is a key element in promoting greater social harmony.

Mastery Test

1. Homogamy is directly related to
   a. competence
   b. similarity
   c. beauty
   d. proximity

2. The weapons effect refers to the fact that weapons can serve as aggression
   a. thresholds
   b. cues
   c. models
   d. inhibitors

3. Suspicion and reduced attraction are associated with
   a. reciprocity
   b. self-disclosure
   c. competence and proximity
   d. overdisclosure

4. During his four years at a Canadian military college, Chris's attitudes toward his fellow Francophone students has become less positive, while his identification with Anglophone students has increased. This is an example of
   a. personal prejudice
   b. group prejudice
   c. the prejudiced personality
   d. symbolic prejudice

5. One thing that *reduces* the chances that a bystander will give help in an emergency is
   a. heightened arousal
   b. empathic arousal
   c. others who could help
   d. similarity to the victim

6. One consequence of seeing aggression portrayed on TV is a loss of emotional response, called
   a. disinhibition
   b. disassociation
   c. deconditioning
   d. desensitization

7. If you are speaking to a well-informed audience, it is important to _____ if you want to persuade them.
   a. repeat your message
   b. give both sides of the argument
   c. be likable
   d. appeal to their emotions

8. "Prime Minister of Canada" is
   a. an ascribed role
   b. an achieved role
   c. a structural norm
   d. a cohesive role

9. Where attribution is concerned, wants, needs, motives, or personal characteristics are perceived as
   a. external causes
   b. situational attributions
   c. discounted causes
   d. internal causes

10. Asch is to _____ experiments as Milgram is to _____ experiments.
    a. compliance, assert
    b. conformity, obedience
    c. autokinetic, social power
    d. groupthink, authority

11. Social psychology is the scientific study of how people
    a. behave in the presence of others
    b. form into groups and organizations
    c. form and maintain interpersonal relationships
    d. make inferences about the behaviour of others

12. A person who first agrees with a small request is later more likely to comply with a larger demand. This is an example of the
    a. low-ball technique
    b. set-the-hook technique
    c. door-in-the-face effect
    d. foot-in-the-door effect

13. Which view of human aggression is most directly opposed to that of the ethologists?
    a. social learning
    b. brain mechanisms
    c. attributional
    d. innate releaser

14. Creating superordinate goals is an important way to
    a. reduce group conflict
    b. break the frustration-aggression link
    c. promote bystander intervention
    d. reverse self-fulfilling prophecies

15. A key element in the effectiveness of jigsaw classrooms is
    a. deindividuation
    b. the promotion of self-fulfilling prophecies
    c. mutual interdependence
    d. selecting competent student leaders

16. Group structure involves all but one of which of the following elements?
    a. roles
    b. communication pathways
    c. allocation of power
    d. social comparisons

17. Research has shown that teenagers are more likely to engage in risky behaviours because
    a. they want to annoy their parents
    b. their high level of hormones promotes such risky behaviours
    c. they want to conform to the norms of their group
    d. they are trapped by the foot-in-the-door phenomenon

18. Groupthink is a type of _____ that applies to decision making in groups.
    a. conformity
    b. social comparison
    c. social power
    d. obedience

19. A good antidote for social stereotyping is
    a. adopting just-world beliefs
    b. creating self-fulfilling prophecies
    c. accepting status inequalities
    d. seeking individuating information

20. In Milgram's studies, the smallest percentage of subjects followed orders when
    a. the teacher and learner were in the same room
    b. the teacher received orders by phone
    c. the teacher and learner were face to face
    d. the experiment was conducted off campus

21. The most basic attributional error is to attribute the behaviour of others to _____ causes, even when they are caused by _____ causes.
    a. inconsistent, consistent
    b. internal, external
    c. random, distinctive
    d. situational, personal

22. In an experiment, most women waiting to receive a shock preferred to wait with others who
    a. were about to be shocked
    b. did not share their fears
    c. were trained to calm them
    d. had been shocked the day before

23. Evolutionary theories attribute mate selection, in part, to the _____ faced by men and women of past generations.
    a. food-gathering habits
    b. tribal customs
    c. maternal instincts
    d. differing reproductive needs

24. Which of the following gives special privileges to a member of a group?
    a. convergent norms
    b. high cohesiveness
    c. actor-observer bias
    d. high status

25. Your actions are most likely to agree with your attitudes when
    a. the actions reverse an old habit
    b. the attitudes are held with conviction
    c. you know that others disagree with your position
    d. you score high on an attitude scale

26. When we are subjected to conformity pressures, the _____ of a majority is more important than the number of people in it.
    a. unanimity
    b. cohesion
    c. proximity
    d. comparison level

27. If it is easier for Caucasian Canadians to get automobile insurance than it is for African Canadians, then African Canadians have experienced
    a. discrimination
    b. scapegoating
    c. ethnocentrism
    d. personal prejudice

28. Research shows study that attitudes may be affected by
    a. membership groups
    b. child-rearing
    c. reference groups
    d. chance conditioning

29. If you respond aggressively to someone's insults you are displaying what type of aggression?
    a. symbolic
    b. proactive
    c. aversive
    d. reactive

Solutions

Recite and Review

1. social
2. approval; information
3. reduce
4. evaluate
5. sex; preferred; stand
6. attraction; similarity
7. similarity; mate
8. revealing
9. norm
10. self disclosure
11. high
12. like; love; like
13. mutual
14. mating
15. groups
16. Social; roles
17. contradictory
18. groups
19. roles
20. attraction
21. standards; groups; loneliness
22. causes
23. causes; causes
24. error; internal; internal; external
25. kindergarten
26. behaviour; others
27. conforms; norms
28. groups; group
29. decision making
30. authority
31. Obedience
32. requests; power
33. foot; face
34. authority; requests
35. wants; needs
36. hurts
37. assertive
38. positive; negative
39. action
40. direct; child
41. media; chance
42. immediate; evaluate
43. expressed
44. identifies
45. message
46. emotion; conclusions
47. consistency
48. clash
49. dissonance
50. reduce
51. negative
52. gender; sex
53. aggression
54. norms
55. personality; over
56. group
57. conflict
58. disguised
59. Status
60. reduce
61. goals
62. classrooms; mutual
63. instincts
64. lower
65. aggression
66. two; proactive
67. stimuli; aggression
68. models
69. models; viewers
70. helpful
71. help
72. noticing
73. less
74. arousal; risk
75. equal
76. individuals
77. beliefs; social
78. Cultural

Connections

1. D
2. I
3. K
4. A
5. J
6. B
7. E
8. G
9. C
10. H
11. F
12. L
13. J
14. H
15. A
16. K
17. D
18. I
19. F
20. C
21. E
22. B
23. G

Short-Answer Questions

1. Social comparison theory suggests that we judge ourselves by comparing our actions, feelings, opinions, and abilities to those of other people, usually of similar background or characteristics to ourselves.

2. Moderate amounts of self-disclosure lead to increases in trust and intimacy. Overdisclosure, or disclosure that is too rapid or intimate, results in suspicion and reduces attraction. There are cultural differences in what is considered inappropriate disclosure.

3. Milgram's studies of obedience demonstrated that people will comply with orders from someone in authority even when compliance is presumed to cause pain to another person. The prestige of the authority figure increased compliance. The closer the subject was to the person he was supposed to hurt, the less the compliance.

4. Foot-in-the-door—a person who first complies with a small request is more likely to comply with a larger one later.
5. Door-in-the-face—a person who does not agree to a larger request first is more likely to agree to a smaller one later.
6. Low-ball technique—getting someone to agree to a request and then changing the terms to less-desirable ones (you ask your friend for a ride to the airport; after he agrees you tell him the flight is at 5 a.m.).
7. Assertiveness training is designed to help people become better at speaking up for their own needs and desires. It involves group exercises, videotaping, staged conflicts, and mirrors to teach people to speak up honestly and confidently for their own needs.
8. Changing attitudes, adding supporting thoughts, changing the importance of dissonant thoughts, reducing the amount of perceived choice, and changing behaviour all can be used to reduce dissonance.
9. Prejudice—negative emotional attitudes toward members of a specific group. Discrimination—unequal treatment of people just because they are members of a specific group.
10. Students prone to violence reject authority, have trouble paying attention and listening, do poorly in school, are disruptive and skip class, frequently get in fights, are easily frustrated and react with extreme anger to disappointment or criticism, blame others for their problems and seek revenge, watch violent movies and TV programs and play violent video or computer games, have few friends and are often rejected or teased by peers, are cruel to pets or other animals, and use alcohol and/or drugs or inhalants.
11. Parents can limit total viewing time, avoid using the television as a babysitter, monitor what a child is watching and change channels as needed, actively seek appropriate programs, watch television with the child and talk about what they see, discuss social conflicts and violent situations with the child, and show by their disapproval that violent TV characters are not the ones to look up to.
12. To increase tolerance, people need to be aware of stereotyping and break down barriers by getting to know individuals from different racial or ethnic groups, think of people as individuals rather than members of a group, watch for "just-world" beliefs (people get what they deserve), be aware of self-fulfilling prophecies, and keep in mind that different does not mean inferior.

Final Survey and Review

1. Social; psychology
2. need; affiliate
3. anxiety
4. comparison
5. similar; aggressive
6. physical; competence
7. homogamy
8. Self disclosure
9. reciprocity
10. Overdisclosure; vary
11. increase
12. attitude; scales
13. absorption
14. Evolutionary; reproductive
15. roles
16. achieved; ascribed
17. conflict
18. status; High; status
19. structure; communication
20. cohesiveness
21. Norms; membership
22. Attribution
23. internal; external
24. fundamental; attributional; observer
25. discount; skilled; lucky
26. Social; influence
27. Conformity; cultural
28. Asch; sanctions
29. Groupthink; approval
30. Obedience; Milgram
31. decreased; authority
32. Compliance
33. door; door; low; ball
34. passive
35. Self assertion
36. Aggression
37. role; playing
38. learned; tendencies
39. belief; emotional
40. contact; group; membership
41. Peer; conditioning
42. consequences; habits
43. conviction
44. reference
45. communicator; audience
46. communicator; audience
47. dissonance
48. dissonance; thoughts
49. reward; justification
50. beliefs; attitudes
51. out groups
52. Racism; ageism; sexism
53. scapegoating; displaced
54. personal; group
55. authoritarian
56. ethnocentric
57. social; stereotypes
58. Symbolic
59. inequalities
60. Equal status
61. Superordinate
62. jigsaw; interdependence

63. Ethologists
64. threshold
65. frustration; frustration
66. proactive; reactive
67. aversive; cues
68. Social; learning
69. desensitize; disinhibit
70. altruistic
71. apathy
72. emergency; responsibility
73. potential; helpers
74. empathic; similarity
75. Multiculturalism
76. individuating
77. just world; self fulfilling
78. awareness

Mastery Test

1. B (p. 509)
2. B (p. 536)
3. D (p. 510)
4. B (p. 529)
5. C (p. 539)
6. D (p. 537)
7. B (p. 526)
8. B (p. 513)
9. D (p. 514)
10. B (pp. 516, 519)
11. A (p. 507)
12. D (p. 520)
13. A (p. 534)
14. A (p. 532)
15. C (p. 532)
16. D (p. 513)
17. C (p. 517)
18. A (p. 517)
19. D (p. 543)
20. B (p. 520)
21. B (p. 515)
22. A (p. 507)
23. D (p. 512)
24. D (p. 513)
25. B (p. 525)
26. A (p. 518)
27. A (p. 528)
28. C (p. 525)
29. D (p. 536)